McCulloch v. Maryland at 200

Debating John Marshall's Jurisprudence

Edited by
Gary J. Schmitt and Rebecca Burgess

AEI

AMERICAN ENTERPRISE INSTITUTE

ISBN-13: 978-0-8447-5027-9 (hardback)
ISBN-13: 978-0-8447-5028-6 (paperback)

The American Enterprise Institute (AEI) is a nonpartisan, nonprofit, 501(c)(3) educational organization and does not take institutional positions on any issues. The views expressed here are those of the author(s).

American Enterprise Institute
1789 Massachusetts Avenue, NW
Washington, DC 20036
www.aei.org

Contents

Introduction: John Marshall and the Politics of *McCulloch v. Maryland*

GARY J. SCHMITT

In recognition of the 200th anniversary of the Supreme Court's landmark decision in *McCulloch v. Maryland*, AEI's Program on American Citizenship commissioned five distinguished scholars to author essays keyed to that decision. The program hosted a panel discussion with the authors to present their initial drafts in late February 2019. The chapters that follow are the finalized versions of those essays. In addition, following the panel presentation and generated by that panel's discussion, Nelson Lund, university professor at George Mason University's Antonin Scalia Law School, published a short essay in Law & Liberty on *McCulloch* that we asked him to expand and that is now included in our volume.

The decision in *McCulloch* found that the US Congress had the constitutional power to charter a national bank and, further, that Maryland's effort to tax the bank violated the federal government's sovereign authority in this matter. As important as the actual decision was, it is Chief Justice John Marshall's opinion in the case that has gone down in American history as a landmark for its guidance in assessing the constitutional scope of the nation's legislative authority. Famously, the chief justice wrote:

> We think the sound construction of the Constitution must allow to the national legislature that discretion with respect to the means by which the powers it confers are to be carried into execution which will enable that body to perform the high duties assigned to it in the manner most beneficial to the people. Let the end be legitimate, let it be within the scope of the Constitution, and all means which are appropriate, which are plainly adapted to that end, which are not prohibited, but consist with the letter and spirit of the Constitution, are Constitutional.[1]

Maryland's lawyers had argued that the necessary and proper clause concluding Article I, Section 8 of the Constitution should be read as limiting Congress' implied powers to those that could be said to be "strictly necessary." On the heels of critiquing this reading, the chief justice declared, in what has become one of the most famous sentences in American constitutional history, "We must never forget that it is *a Constitution* we are expounding."[2]

Arguably, Marshall's opinion in *McCulloch*, along with his opinion in *Marbury v. Madison*, cementing the Court's authority to engage in judicial review of enacted statutes' constitutionality, is the most significant of the chief justice's many far-reaching opinions. As his first biographer summarily put it, this was the "greatest of Marshall's treatises on government."[3] Given the potential importance of this case's decision for how the nation was to be governed, Marshall's opinion generated significant criticism both public and private. And, as the following chapters show, Marshall's opinion still generates debate today.

Chapter 1, authored by Nelson Lund, jumps straight into this fray. As its title indicates ("The Destructive Legacy of *McCulloch v. Maryland*"), the chapter sees the 200th anniversary of the case as an apt time to reevaluate Marshall's argument and its contribution to American constitutional jurisprudence. Troubled by the use of *McCulloch* to justify expansive federal power, Lund zeroes in on why he believes the opinion has lent itself to such abuse.

Michael Zuckert, professor emeritus at the University of Notre Dame, continues this critique in Chapter 2, "The Sound of the Third Hand Clapping: James Madison's Reading of the Necessary and Proper Clause." He argues that, in the congressional debate over the establishment of the First National Bank, James Madison offers a distinct and coherent middle ground between Thomas Jefferson's and Alexander Hamilton's reading of the clause. Less expansive than Hamilton's interpretation but not as limiting as Jefferson's, Madison argues that the clause cannot be read in such a way as to give Congress the implied authority to pass legislation creating the bank. As such, Zuckert argues, Madison offers a prospective rebuttal to Marshall's argument and decision in *McCulloch*.

Christopher Wolfe, professor of politics at the University of Dallas, contributes Chapter 3, "*McCulloch v. Maryland* and John Marshall's

Constitutional Interpretation." In contrast with the two preceding chapters, Wolfe argues for the soundness of Marshall's opinion. He offers that, when read closely, it actually provides a model of constitutional jurisprudence that is distinctly different from that put forward by many, if not most, modern Supreme Court justices.

The author of Chapter 4 is Robert Webking, professor of political science at the University of Texas at El Paso. In "'A Friend of the Constitution': John Marshall's Defense of *McCulloch v. Maryland*," Webking unpacks the chief justice's anonymously written defense of his opinion and his rebuttal to the broader charge that the decision rested on a false reading of the constitutional order as ratified in 1787. Diving into these essays, Webking also discovers Marshall's claim that the decision in *McCulloch* does not—as is widely assumed—rest on a reading of the necessary and proper clause; even if the clause had been "entirely omitted," Webking argues, the law establishing the bank would have been constitutional.

Abram N. Shulsky, senior fellow at the Hudson Institute, broadens the debate over the Court's decision and the bank's establishment with Chapter 5: "How an Economist Might View *McCulloch v. Maryland*." Shulsky examines the financial and economic reasons for the bank's creation, not the least of which was stimulating the commercial character of the young republic and, over time, enhancing the nation's geopolitical power, in the model of the Bank of England.

The sixth and final chapter, "*McCulloch v. Maryland* and John Marshall's Judicial Statesmanship," is authored by AEI Resident Scholar Adam J. White. White wrestles with whether a justice should ever be thought of as engaging in statesmanship given statesmanship's inherent political character. Turning to Edmund Burke's views regarding statesmanship, White develops a theory of judicial restraint that, he argues, is reflected in Marshall's opinion in *McCulloch*. Instead of an assertion of judicial power, White argues that a more exacting reading of Marshall's opinion reveals this landmark decision is not as far-reaching as it is often understood to be. It is couched in terms that respect both precedent and the judgment of the other branches of government about the nation's needs.

—〜—

Certainly, John Marshall's history before becoming chief justice reveals a man quite capable of handling the complexities and practicalities of political life. Despite coming from a modest background—hardscrabble, frontier Virginia and limited formal education[4]—Marshall would have been seen as a significant member of the founding generation even if he had never served as chief justice.

As a young lieutenant in a Virginia regiment, Marshall fought in Virginia and served at Valley Forge and, by dint of character and abilities, quickly rose in the estimation of Gen. George Washington and his aide-de-camp, Alexander Hamilton. With the war ending, Marshall began a law practice in Richmond, Virginia, and, in fairly short order, was elected to the Virginia House of Delegates. Despite his relative youth, he was subsequently selected to serve on the Council of State—a body elected by the two houses of the Virginia legislature to assist the governor in exercising his duties. Along with James Madison, Marshall was a key successful defender of the new constitution at the Virginia Ratifying Convention and assisted Madison in drafting a proposed "bill of rights" that convention members argued should be added to the document in exchange for their approval.

With the rise of party politics in the 1790s, Marshall became a leading figure among Virginia Federalists. In that role, he rallied public opinion there in favor of President George Washington's controversial Proclamation of Neutrality in 1793 and the even more controversial Jay Treaty with Great Britain in 1794.

Not long after succeeding Washington as president, John Adams asked Marshall to join the team of Elbridge Gerry and Charles Cotesworth Pinckney in negotiating a new accord with postrevolutionary France. The diplomatic effort came to naught, as the French side demanded in exchange for a new peace treaty that the United States provide France with a substantial low-interest loan and a significant bribe to the French foreign minister, Charles Maurice de Talleyrand. When the French demand was eventually exposed ("the XYZ Affair"), along with the American commissioners' refusal to pay, Marshall was hailed as a diplomatic hero and became forever associated with the phrase: "millions for defense but not one cent for tribute."

More prominent now than ever, Virginia Federalists solicited Marshall to run for a seat in the US Congress, which he successfully did in the spring of 1799. Scarcely a year later, Marshall was confirmed as Adams' secretary of state, despite being unaware of the president's nomination and the Senate's consent to his nomination. In the nine-month period he served in that role, Marshall oversaw the federal government's move to the new capital city, negotiations with the Barbary States and Spain, and the completion of a treaty ending the Quasi-War with France.

It would be surprising if Marshall's success as a lawyer, state and national legislator, diplomat and cabinet official, and author of a multivolume biography of Washington did not affect in some fashion his greatest role: chief justice of the US Supreme Court. Of course, Marshall was not the first chief justice. In little over a decade, three others had held the post before him. Undoubtedly, Marshall saw an opportunity others did not. His 34-year tenure as chief justice is still a record.

As a key proponent of the Constitution's ratification, an expositor of that document in Virginia and elsewhere, a lawyer participating in cases involving its interpretation, and a student of William Blackstone's *Commentaries on the Laws of England*, Marshall was fully aware of the distinct duties that sitting on the nation's highest court would entail. Yet, if the principles undergirding the governing order were to be thought clear and not constantly open to debate and, in turn, if the broader public were to gain deeper respect for the Constitution, then the more unanimity the Court showed in interpreting the document, the better.

To that end, Marshall ended the Court's practice whereby each justice issued a separate opinion in every decision taken by the Court. While dissents were still allowed, the chief justice strove for a unified voice from the bench. Of the 1,129 Supreme Court decisions during Marshall's time as chief justice, fewer than 90 were not unanimous. Of the nearly 550 opinions that Marshall penned, only three dozen decisions failed to gain full concurrence from the other justices. As remarkable as those figures are, they are even more noteworthy when one recalls that Marshall was the last justice nominated by a Federalist president. For three decades his new colleagues were all appointed by presidents whose parties (Republican, Republican-Democrat, and Democrat) were not necessarily in sync with the Federalist understanding of the constitutional order and its underlying principles.

The idea that Marshall, as chief justice, might, within the limits of his judicial duties, exercise a principled prudence should not surprise. In

Marbury v. Madison (1803), for example, Marshall affirmed that it was "the province and duty of the judicial department to say what the law is" and, since the Constitution was law, the Court could and should strike down an act of Congress when it conflicted with the Constitution.[5] Yet, as Robert Faulkner points out, the straightforward logic Marshall lays out here to legitimate judicial review stays clear of the earlier argument found in *Federalist* 78 that the underlying purpose of judicial review is to forestall the "ill humours" that popular government and majority rule might impose on a minority or government itself. Issuing his opinion in the wake of the "Revolution of 1800" and the ascendency of the Jefferson-led government, "Marshall's caution," Faulkner suggests, was likely generated by his recognition that the American public was now "considerably more democratically inclined"; it would not do to shove in their face the Court's potential role in frustrating their will.[6] Hence, the more prosaic justification for judicial review.

Similarly, the chief justice avoided a confrontation with President Thomas Jefferson by arguing that, under Article III of the Constitution, the Court had no authority to issue a writ of mandamus ordering the delivery of William Marbury's commission as a justice of peace by Secretary of State Madison. Marshall's reading of the law here was far from obvious. However, the near certainty that Jefferson, acting under his own views about the chief executive's constitutional authority to interpret his powers, would refuse to obey the Court's order was obvious. Issuing the writ and having the president ignore it would leave the "least dangerous branch" looking even more powerless. From this perspective, Marshall's jurisprudence sacrificed the immediate paper victory for the longer-term, more substantial victory of cementing the Court's role as constitutional arbiter.[7]

While understanding Marshall's opinion in the bank case should always start with a careful reading of his legal analysis, one should never lose sight of Marshall's broader hope to craft arguments for the Court's decisions that might have lasting significance and acceptance. As Marshall probably understood, this would be no easy task with the matter at hand in *McCulloch v. Maryland*.

—꩜—

Marshall issued his opinion in *McCulloch* in a period designated by American history books as the Era of Good Feelings (1815–25), so called because the partisan divide between Republicans and Federalists had ended due to the decisive electoral victories of the former and the demise of the latter. However, the era was hardly without heated policy and constitutional debate. Indeed, as some of the chapters that follow note, *McCulloch* itself was the object of such debate and was seen as having a potentially pivotal say in resolving those disputes to the loss of one partisan faction or another.

Beyond the narrow legal issues pertaining to the bank's constitutionality, its ability to increase the amount of currency in circulation nationally and provide greater monetary stability was understood by advocates as supporting the idea that the United States should be a republic of a certain kind: a large commercial republic. Not only would such a republic increase wealth and, in turn, national power, but it would, as commerce expanded, also increase ties between regions of the country and reinforce citizen interest in protecting the essential right to property. As much as the system of separated powers, a modern liberal economy was thought to be essential for sustaining the larger goals of a new political order.

Others, however, read the bank's monopoly position—and the fact that considerable discretion over the country's economic life was being delegated to a relatively few private individuals—as running contrary to the new government's republican spirit and design. Madison in particular wondered whether the bank was, as he put it sometime later, part of Treasury Secretary Alexander Hamilton's larger plan "to administer the government . . . into what he thought it ought to be" by expanding executive branch authority and thereby moving policy decisions further away from Congress, the more republican branch of government.[8]

Marshall's argument against a restricted view of the necessary and proper clause was thus understandably seen as having significant implications. The first issue was whether a more expansive understanding of Congress' implied authorities—which may or may not have exactly reflected Marshall's own views in the matter—included the power to support internal improvements (roads, canals, and such) that went beyond those arguably necessary for carrying out discrete constitutional requirements, such as delivering the mail or moving military forces where needed. In time,

Congress and the executive branch accepted such broad authority that it became the underlying legitimating authority for the "American system"—a system of tariffs to promote American manufacturing (mostly found in the North) and generate revenues to support infrastructure improvements (mostly benefiting the agricultural West).

On its face, the system appeared to tie together the expanding nation and increase its overall industrial power. However, from the viewpoint of the exporting South, which now faced protectionist tariffs abroad, it was far from an equitable system. Indeed, it appeared to result in the "majority faction" that Madison had promised in *Federalist* 10 would be *less* likely to appear because of "the greater variety of parties and interests" resulting from America's "greater number of citizens and extent of territory."[9]

Further fueling the South's anxiety about accepting a liberal reading of congressional powers—and the parallel resurrection of Anti-Federalist-inspired theories about the federal union as a compact of states—was of course the question of slavery. In 1787, the Articles of Confederation Congress passed the Northwest Ordinance, which established the rules for governing the territories north of the Ohio River and east of the Mississippi. It outlined the path for those territories to enter the union as states and, as part of that process, banned slavery in the territories. Congress, operating under the new Constitution, reaffirmed each provision in 1789.

By 1819, however, when *McCulloch* was decided, the economic "necessity" of slavery's expansion into the West and the possibility of slavery's expansion into new states carved from the Louisiana Purchase territories were running headlong into the question of whether Congress has the power to effectively ban slavery in new states. In the weeks just before Marshall issued his opinion, Rep. James Tallmadge of New York introduced and the House passed a measure amending the statute granting Missouri accession into the Union; the amendment banned further import of slaves into the territory and freed any children of slaves born thereafter. The Senate rejected the measure, with slave states' senators arguing that the matter was for the people of the new states to decide, not Congress.

The Missouri Compromise the following year "settled" the issue of slavery's expansion by dividing the Western territories into two halves:

one allowing slavery in new states, the other not. However, at the time of *McCulloch*, the debate over Congress' authority was very much alive. Marshall made no mention of slavery, but, surely, it was on everyone's mind.

—⚶—

A fundamental feature of the new republic was its written constitution. Along with a system of separated powers, proponents thought that spelling out the powers and duties of each branch would functionally guarantee the new government would be limited in its ends and means. However, as even Madison admits in *Federalist* 44, it would be foolish to think that one could possibly draft a document involving a "complete digest of laws on every subject to which the Constitution relates."[10] Inevitably, the need would arise to infer what other authorities were thought to be "necessary and proper" to conduct the government's business. And, just as inevitable, disputes would arise as to what unstated powers might be constitutional (or not) and what the grounds would be for making that judgment.

This does not mean that the Constitution is a blank slate on which any interpretation can be pasted. More often than is appreciated, the document's central features and text guide the government's day-to-day operations. In the case of the necessary and proper clause, its original meaning is limned to a degree by comparing it with the similar phrasing ("expressly delegated") found in the earlier Articles of Confederation. It is also instructive that the clause concludes a section that lists the authorities to be *given* to the new Congress—as opposed to Article I, Section 9's list of things Congress cannot do. Taken together, it is reasonable to interpret the clause as giving Congress additional powers beyond the strictly necessary.

But this gets one only so far: "Necessary and proper" may be read as confined to carrying out the specific, enumerated powers laid out elsewhere in the Constitution, or it may read as empowering Congress to carry out those enumerated powers in light of the objects, the broader constitutional ends, for which the specific authorities are intended. For Madison and others, the latter interpretation provides too much latitude for a republican government of limited ends. For Hamilton and friends, the former provides too little latitude for the republican government to be as effective as it was envisioned to be.

Determining the intent behind a particular provision is no less problematic than determining what the text, in this instance necessary and proper, is meant to convey. When the law establishing the First National Bank was passed by the First Congress, 18 of the 55 delegates to the Constitutional Convention were members of either the Senate or the House of Representatives.[11] In the Senate, the committee preparing the measure for consideration included five members from the Philadelphia convention. Only one of these, Pierce Butler from South Carolina, voted against the bill but did so largely on sectional grounds and from worries about delegating such power to such few hands; Butler actually admitted he was in favor of a bank but believed the already existing Bank of North America could handle the government's needs.

After passage in the Senate in January 1791, the House took up the bill on February 1. The next day, Madison, "father of the Constitution," gave extended remarks against the bank on grounds of policy and the Constitution. When he turned to the necessary and proper clause, he argued that it should be read as giving Congress implied powers but only those necessary in a "natural and obvious" way "to effectuate" the enumerated authorities—which, to his mind, the establishment of a bank was not.[12] To bolster his argument, Madison turned to the Constitutional Convention, where, he noted, the delegates had voted down the general power of incorporation. If the Constitution's drafters had intended Congress to have such an "independent and substantive prerogative," then, Madison argued, they would have listed it in the document.[13]

Putting aside whether the convention's decision not to give Congress a general power of incorporation prohibits Congress from incorporating a specific entity (a bank) as a means to execute particular enumerated powers, Madison's turn to the Philadelphia meeting was not taken as definitive. Elbridge Gerry suggested that the memories and intentions of the delegates would invariably vary and, as such, they were "not a sufficient authority for Congress . . . to construe the Constitution."[14] None of the nine House members who had also been in the convention objected to Gerry's response to Madison, and the bill passed by a vote of 39 to 20.

After Washington signed the bank bill, nascent Republicans continued to think that Congress had overreached. Even so, there was some uncertainty among their ranks. James Monroe, then a senator from Virginia and an ally of Jefferson, argued that the measure had "exceed[ed] the power of Congress" and that it did not "appear . . . to flow from" any constitutional power. "But," even he admitted, "in this I may be wrong."[15]

In time, the Republican-dominated Congress allowed the 20-year charter of the First National Bank to lapse. However, the decision to let the charter lapse was a close-run thing. By 1811 President Madison's Treasury Secretary Albert Gallatin was in favor of rechartering the bank, and Congress' decision not to do so was by a margin of a single vote in each chamber.[16] Following the War of 1812 and acknowledging the difficulties the federal government had in raising sufficient funds to fight the war, Madison inched toward favoring the establishment of a second national bank, diffidently telling Congress in late 1815: "The probable operation of a national bank will merit consideration."[17] Four months later, Congress passed and Madison signed the bill chartering a second national bank for a 20-year period.

With this Republican vote and Madison's signature, Congress' power to establish a bank would seem to have been settled as a constitutional matter. As Marshall noted in the opening of his opinion in *McCulloch*:

> It has been truly said that this can scarcely be considered as an open question entirely unprejudiced by the former proceedings of the Nation respecting it. The principle now contested was introduced at a very early period of our history, has been recognised by many successive legislatures, and has been acted upon by the Judicial Department, in cases of peculiar delicacy, as a law of undoubted obligation.[18]

As Caleb Nelson has written, "James Madison and other prominent founders did not consider the Constitution's meaning to be fully settled at the moment it was written. . . . [But they believed] subsequent interpreters would help 'fix' its meaning on disputed points." Eventually, "once practice had settled upon one of the possible interpretations of a disputed provision, they expected that interpretation to persist."[19] As Madison himself would write some years later, such fixing was "reasonable" because society needs settled law, and the "exposition of the law publicly made, and repeatedly confirmed by the constitutional authority, carries with it, by fair inference, the sanction" of people's representatives and the courts.[20]

Yet, as Madison knew when he wrote this in 1831, the matter was not fixed. President Andrew Jackson would veto the bank's rechartering the following year on policy and constitutional grounds, arguing that, as the nation's chief executive, he also had an obligation to interpret a law's constitutionality and that he found "nothing in [the bank's] legitimate functions which makes it necessary or proper."[21] As Justice Joseph Story noted in his *Commentaries on the Constitution*, published the following year, the question of the bank and Congress' authority to establish a bank was "up to this very hour, still debated." And while Story believed the issue should no longer be an "open question," he admitted that, to the extent it still was, then one might regretfully conclude that the Constitution is "forever to remain an unsettled text."[22]

—⚭—

We should not take Story's last comment as signaling his doubt that the meaning of the Constitution's text is always open to new interpretations. Presumably, in writing *Commentaries*, he thought some interpretations are sounder than others. However, the very fact that Story thought it necessary to write *Commentaries* indicates that he did not take for granted that, under the pressure of political life, new and different views would not arise that challenge earlier opinions and precedents.

As the history of Marshall's opinion in *McCulloch v. Maryland* and the debate over the national banks suggest, important policy issues cannot help but generate great interest. And, with great interest, attempts to legitimate or contest that policy decision by reference to the Constitution almost always arise. This does not mean abandoning questions of constitutionality to prevailing politics. To the contrary, it substantiates the need to revisit the most important cases, such as we do here, to keep alive the dialogue about the Constitution's first principles as a necessary and proper component of maintaining an effective but still limited form of republican government. The debate never ends, and, as such, the obligation to return again and again to the opinions of the greatest cases never ceases as well.

Notes

1. *McCulloch v. Maryland*, 17 US 316, 421 (1819).
2. *McCulloch v. Maryland*, 17 US 316, 407 (1819).
3. Alfred J. Beveridge, *The Life of John Marshall: The Building of the Nation 1815–1835* (Washington, DC: Beard Books, 2000), 308.
4. Although John Marshall's formal education was limited, he was relatively well schooled in key classics by his mother and, for a short time, by a tutor who lived with the family. For background on Marshall's life, his tenure as chief justice, and the underlying principles guiding his jurisprudence, see Joel Richard Paul, *Without Precedent: Chief Justice John Marshall and His Times* (New York: Riverhead Books, 2018); and Robert K. Faulkner, *The Jurisprudence of John Marshall* (Princeton, NJ: Princeton University Press, 1968).
5. *Marbury v. Madison*, 5 US 137, 177 (1803).
6. Faulkner, *The Jurisprudence of John Marshall*, 210–13.
7. Paul, *Without Precedent*, 254–59.
8. James Madison's point here is that, by interpreting Congress' constitutional powers broadly, allowing Congress (in turn) to pass laws with systemic policy implications (such as creating the bank and supporting domestic manufacturing with high tariffs and subsidies), and reading the president's Article II authorities expansively, Madison's *Federalist* coauthor had attempted, under the color of the law, to establish a system of government that was neither what the Constitutional Convention nor the state ratifying conventions thought they had approved. Max Farrand, ed., *The Records of the Federal Convention of 1787, Volume 3* (New Haven, CT: Yale University Press, 1911), 533–34.
9. James Madison, *Federalist No. 10: The Same Subject Continued: The Union as a Safeguard Against Domestic Faction and Insurrection*, Congress.gov, November 23, 1787, https://www.congress.gov/resources/display/content/The+Federalist+Papers#TheFederalistPapers-10.
10. James Madison, *Federalist No. 44: Restrictions on the Authority of the Several States*, Congress.gov, January 25, 1788, https://www.congress.gov/resources/display/content/The+Federalist+Papers#TheFederalistPapers-44. "No language is so copious as to supply words and phrases for every complex idea, or so correct as not to include many equivocally denoting different ideas." See James Madison, *Federalist No. 37: Concerning the Difficulties of the Convention in Devising a Proper Form of Government*, Congress.gov, January 11, 1788, https://www.congress.gov/resources/display/content/The+Federalist+-Papers#TheFederalistPapers-37. Compounding the interpretative problem, according to Madison, was that the Constitution was employing "known ideas" and "old words" for a new kind of government. James Madison, Letter to Edward Livingston, April 17, 1824, https://founders.archives.gov/documents/Madison/04-03-02-0291.
11. See Benjamin B. Klubes, "The First Federal Congress and the First National Bank: A Case Study in Constitutional Interpretation," *Journal of the Early Republic* 10, no. 1 (Spring 1990): 19–41, https://www.jstor.org/stable/3123277?seq=1#page_scan_tab_contents.
12. *Annals of Congress*, House of Representatives, 1st Congress, 3rd Session, 1947

(February 2, 1791), http://rs6.loc.gov:8081/cgi-bin/ampage?collId=llac&fileName=002/llac002.db&recNum=335.

13. *Annals of Congress,* House of Representatives, 1st Congress, 3rd Session, 1950 (February 2, 1791), http://rs6.loc.gov:8081/cgi-bin/ampage?collId=llac&fileName=002/llac002.db&recNum=336.

14. *Annals of Congress,* House of Representatives, 1st Congress, 3rd Session, 2004 (February 7, 1791), http://rs6.loc.gov:8081/cgi-bin/ampage?collId=llac&fileName=002/llac002.db&recNum=363.

15. James Monroe, Letter to Nicholas Lewis, February 7, 1791, http://monroepapers.com/items/show/481.

16. Federal Reserve Bank of the Philadelphia, *The First Bank of the United States: A Chapter in the History of Central Banking,* June 2009, 10, https://www.philadelphiafed.org/-/media/publications/economic-education/first-bank.pdf.

17. James Madison, "Seventh Annual Message" (speech, US Congress, Washington, DC, December 5, 1815), https://millercenter.org/the-presidency/presidential-speeches/december-5-1815-seventh-annual-message.

18. *McCulloch v. Maryland,* 17 US 316, 401 (1819).

19. Caleb Nelson, "Originalism and Interpretive Conventions," *University of Chicago Law Review* 70, no. 2 (2003): 521, https://chicagounbound.uchicago.edu/cgi/viewcontent.cgi?article=5210&context=uclrev.

20. James Madison, Letter to Charles J. Ingersoll, June 25, 1831, https://founders.archives.gov/documents/Madison/99-02-02-2374.

21. Andrew Jackson, "Bank Veto" (speech, US Senate, Washington, DC, July 10, 1832), https://millercenter.org/the-presidency/presidential-speeches/july-10-1832-bank-veto.

22. Joseph Story, *Commentaries on the Constitution of the United States, Volume 3* (Boston, MA: Hilliard, Gray, and Company, 1833), Chapter XXV, Sec. 1254.

1

The Destructive Legacy of
McCulloch v. Maryland

NELSON LUND

McCulloch v. Maryland is arguably the Supreme Court's single most influential opinion and certainly one of its most celebrated.[1] In a 1919 biography of its author, Albert Beveridge wrote:

> In effect John Marshall [in *McCulloch*] rewrote the fundamental law of the Nation; or perhaps it may be more accurate to say that he made a written instrument a living thing, capable of growth, capable of keeping pace with the advancement of the American people and ministering to their changing necessities. This greatest of Marshall's treatises on government may well be entitled the "Vitality of the Constitution."[2]

Later, Justice Felix Frankfurter concurred with James Bradley Thayer's assessment that "the conception of the nation that Marshall derived from the Constitution and set forth in *M'Culloch v. Maryland* is his greatest single judicial performance."[3] More recently, an academic discussion of "canonical cases" began "with a legal document that generates no contention at all: John Marshall's opinion in *McCulloch v. Maryland*, which established an expansive view of national power under the U.S. Constitution."[4]

As these and countless other commentators have recognized, *McCulloch*'s importance arises from its doctrine of implied congressional powers, which has been applied even to constitutional amendments adopted decades after the *McCulloch* decision.[5] Revered though it may now be, Chief Justice Marshall's opinion provoked a hostile commotion when it was issued, so much so that he was moved to defend it in a series of anonymous newspaper essays.[6] The opinion remained controversial for many years, and it deserves to become controversial once again.

The issue in *McCulloch* was whether the Second Bank of the United States could legally refuse to pay a tax that the state of Maryland imposed on its Baltimore branch. After deciding that Congress had an implied constitutional power to incorporate a bank, the Court held that Maryland's tax was unconstitutional. Both conclusions were debatable, but the opinion was unanimous. Marshall articulated an elegant and defensible legal standard for assessing congressional exercises of implied powers, but his application of that standard was extremely lax.

Subsequently, *McCulloch* was used to justify expanding federal power far beyond its proper constitutional bounds. Although Marshall's opinion lends itself to this use, the decision need not and should not be relied on as a precedent for such expansion. *McCulloch*'s bicentennial is an apt occasion for reevaluating its indisputably significant contribution to American jurisprudence.

The Bank Controversy Begins

The constitutionality of a national bank was thoroughly debated during the founding period. When President George Washington appointed Alexander Hamilton secretary of the treasury, one of his first projects was to stabilize the government's fiscal affairs. As part of that initiative, Hamilton offered Congress a detailed proposal for the incorporation of a predominantly private bank in which the federal government would be a minority shareholder. This government-sponsored enterprise would provide banking services to the government, but it would operate like other banks for its owners' profit.

The Senate passed the bill, apparently without much discussion. The House of Representatives also approved it by a large margin, but Rep. James Madison led a vigorous opposition. His constitutional objections began with the principle that Congress has only the powers given to it in Article I of the Constitution. Implied powers certainly exist, as the necessary and proper clause confirms,[7] but every one must be closely tied to the end and nature of an enumerated power. He argued that once one accepts devices, such as the proposed bank, that are merely conducive or indirectly related to the exercise of an enumerated power, "a chain may be formed that will reach every object of legislation, every object within the whole compass of political economy."[8] That would violate the principle that the federal government is one of limited powers, and it would subvert the states' reserved powers.

Madison also mentioned in passing that the Constitutional Convention had rejected a proposal to give Congress an enumerated power to grant charters of incorporation. As it happens, Madison himself made that proposal. Apart from any relevance the convention's decision might have to the constitutional issue (which is open to considerable doubt), Madison's proposal suggests that his argument for a narrow reading of implied powers was not based on policy objections to this particular power or on political or policy objections to Hamilton's bank proposal.[9] Although his own administration had proposed the bill, President Washington sought opinions about its constitutionality from members of his cabinet.

Edmund Randolph's Opinion

The attorney general was the first to respond.[10] Randolph went into some detail about the specific functions of the proposed corporation and about how those functions might be tied to specific powers conferred on Congress by the Constitution. His conclusion was the same as Madison's:

> If the laying and collecting of taxes brings with it every thing which, in the opinion of Congress, may facilitate the payment of taxes; if to borrow money sets political speculation loose, to conceive what may create an ability to lend; if to regulate commerce is to range in the boundless mazes of projects for the apparently best scheme to invite from abroad, or to diffuse at home, the precious metals; if to dispose of or to regulate property of the United States, is to incorporate a bank, that stock may be subscribed to it by them, it may without exaggeration be affirmed that a similar construction on every specified federal power, will stretch the arm of Congress into the whole circle of state legislation.[11]

Randolph's opinion is notably careful to reject some arguments that would have supported his conclusion that the proposed bank was unconstitutional. He contended, for example, that the Constitution's use of the word "proper" in the necessary and proper clause does not add to the limits on implied powers that would otherwise exist.

Similarly, Randolph rejected an argument according to which the Constitution's enumeration of some powers that might have been inferred implies that similar un-enumerated powers (such as a power to establish corporations) should not be inferred. And he refused to rely on statements supposedly made at Philadelphia and in the ratifying conventions: "Ought not the Constitution to be decided on by the import of its own expressions? What may not be the consequence if an almost unknown history should govern the construction?"[12]

Thomas Jefferson's Opinion

The secretary of state also believed the bank bill was unconstitutional, in part for reasons similar to those on which Madison and Randolph primarily relied.[13] In significant respects, however, he went further.

Jefferson, for example, began with a long list of ways in which he believed that particular aspects of the bank bill were inconsistent with various state laws. Why that was relevant to the bill's constitutionality he did not explain. Nor would it have been easy to do so. Congress is authorized to override state laws when acting within the scope of the powers granted by the Constitution, and Congress is not authorized to exceed those powers whether or not doing so would conflict with state law.

Unlike Randolph, Jefferson relied on reports that the Constitutional Convention had rejected a proposal to give Congress power to establish corporations. One objection to the proposal, he apparently had heard, was that Congress "would have a power to erect a bank, which would render the great cities, where there were prejudices and jealousies on the subject, adverse to the reception of the Constitution." Here again, he seems to have thought this was self-evidently relevant. But it certainly was not. Indeed, Jefferson was apparently the only participant in the bank debates who believed that such reports should affect the interpretation of the Constitution.[14]

Perhaps most important, Jefferson argued that the word "necessary" in the necessary and proper clause means *absolutely* necessary. The Constitution, he maintained, was "intended to lace [Congress] up straitly within the enumerated powers, and those without which, as means, those powers could not be carried into effect . . . that is to say, to those means without which the grant of power would be nugatory."[15] Jefferson seemed to think that unless one took this extremely narrow view of implied powers, there would be no limits at all on Congress.

Did he really believe this? Oddly, Jefferson's opinion ends with an implicit concession that the bill's constitutionality may have been a much closer question than his whole preceding string of arguments and assertions had suggested:

> It must be added, however, that unless the President's mind on a view of everything which is urged for and against this bill, is tolerably clear that it is unauthorized by the Constitution; if the pro and the con hang so even as to balance his judgment, a just respect for the wisdom of the legislature would naturally decide the balance in favor of their opinion. It is chiefly for cases where they are clearly misled by error, ambition, or interest, that the Constitution has placed a check in the negative of the President.[16]

The opinion leaves us to wonder what Jefferson thought could reasonably be said against his position and why he was not sure he had refuted those arguments. It also leaves us to wonder why he later told Madison that anyone who attempted to establish or operate a branch of the bank in Virginia would be guilty of treason against the state and should be sentenced to death by the state courts.[17]

Alexander Hamilton's Opinion

Writing under extreme pressure created by the constitutional deadline for the president's decision, the secretary of the treasury produced a powerfully detailed defense of the constitutionality of his bank proposal.[18] He attempted to refute every argument advanced by the other two cabinet members, and he offered his own alternative legal analysis.

In several passages, especially those refuting the arguments that were peculiar to Jefferson's shoddy opinion, Hamilton was, in my view, completely successful. For example, not only was Jefferson's interpretation of the word "necessary" contrary to ordinary usage but it would also absurdly cripple the government and thus make the necessary and proper clause into what Hamilton called "a rule to justify the overleaping of the bounds of constitutional authority, [rather] than to govern the ordinary exercise of it."[19]

Hamilton's principal response to Randolph met the attorney general's argument head-on. Randolph had canvased several enumerated congressional powers and set out additional powers that he thought could be inferred from them. Hamilton argued that these implied powers were incomplete and that the power of incorporation was as easy to infer as many others that would not be controversial. A lot can be said for Hamilton's objection to Randolph's opinion on this point.

It is much less clear that Hamilton's own criterion for assessing the scope of the legislature's implied powers is sound. He argued that every government has the inherent power to employ those means that have a natural relation to any lawful end. Accordingly, the federal government may use "all means" that relate to pursuing such ends "to the best and greatest advantage." But the Constitution does not, he said, authorize Congress to supervise the health, safety, or morals of Philadelphia residents, so a federal corporation may not be established for that purpose. Similarly, said Hamilton, "the constitutional test of a right application [of money] must always be, whether it be for a purpose of general or local nature."[20]

Skeptics such as Madison and Randolph could justifiably have wondered whether a distinction between general and local purposes is capable of providing any real security against the danger that so concerned them. But Hamilton made a stronger argument in defense of the bank bill itself. He analyzed in considerable detail the relation between the establishment of a bank and the enumerated congressional powers dealing with trade, government finances, and national defense. The ability to exercise those powers would, in many circumstances, be extremely constrained without access to banking services, and a law ensuring those services' availability would not necessarily be a step toward occupying what Madison called "the whole compass of political economy."[21]

Notwithstanding Hamilton's thorough defense of the bill, President Washington apparently remained uneasy. He discussed the issue several times with Rep. Madison, who drafted a veto message at his request.[22] In the end, Washington approved the legislation without comment.

Establishment of the Second Bank of the United States

The charter that Washington signed expired by its terms in 1811, and Congress did not pass a bill reestablishing a bank until 1815. By then, Madison was president. He disapproved the bill, saying in his veto message that he did not think it offered the government sufficient "security for attaining the public objects of the institution."[23] But he added that constitutional objections were "precluded in my judgment by repeated recognitions under varied circumstances of the validity of such an institution in acts of the legislative, executive, and judicial branches of the Government, accompanied by indications in different modes, of a concurrence of the general will of the nation."[24]

The next year, Congress passed a bill that satisfied President Madison's policy concerns, and he signed it. Like its predecessor, the Second Bank of the United States was a federally chartered private corporation in which the federal government owned a 20 percent interest. The First Bank, created at a time when there were only three or four state-chartered banks in the whole country, served a pretty obvious and pressing government purpose.[25] By 1816, some 246 banks had been established.[26]

Competition from the Second Bank could threaten state banks' profits and even their viability, which had obvious political implications. Less obviously, the proliferation of state banks might have affected the constitutional issue because it lessened the need for a national bank and increased the opportunity for federal interference with state policies. It is at least arguable that what was necessary and proper in 1791 might not have met that criterion in 1816.

John Marshall and Congress' Implied Powers

McCulloch was not the first case to consider the extent of Congress' implied powers. In *United States v. Fisher*, the Court upheld a statutory provision requiring that debts to the United States be given priority when distributing the assets of an insolvent or bankrupt debtor.[27] Although Marshall asked what the source of congressional authority for the regulation was, he rather strangely ignored the bankruptcy clause.[28] After alluding instead to the necessary and proper clause, he offered this analysis:

> Congress must possess the choice of means, and must be empowered to use any means which are in fact conducive to the exercise of a power granted by the constitution.
>
> The government is to pay the debt of the union, and must be authorised to use the means which appear to itself most eligible to effect that object.[29]

Any means at all, no matter how unnecessary or improper they may be? *Fisher*'s holding looks like a free pass that exempts Congress from any meaningful judicial scrutiny. And if there was a good reason to rule so broadly, instead of relying on the bankruptcy clause, Marshall did not say what it was.

Fisher is not mentioned in *McCulloch*, which proceeds more judiciously.[30] The opinion includes an acknowledgment that the principle of limited and enumerated powers "is now universally admitted," along with two distinct arguments for upholding the bank.[31] First, the constitutionality of a national bank, "if not put at rest by the [long] practice of the Government, ought to receive a considerable impression from that practice."[32] Only a "bold and plain usurpation," Marshall suggested, would justify the Court in repudiating an established exercise of congressional power.[33] Second, even without such an established practice, both the dictates of reason and the necessary and proper clause authorize Congress to choose appropriate means of executing the powers given to it.[34]

Marshall set forth this second conclusion in what became a celebrated legal test.

> Let the end be legitimate, let it be within the scope of the Constitution, and all means which are appropriate, which are plainly adapted to that end, which are not prohibited, but consist with the letter and spirit of the Constitution, are Constitutional.[35]

Although *McCulloch* contains other language that resembles the parallel passage in *Fisher*,[36] this formulation is carefully calibrated to respect both the federal government's legitimate needs and the limited scope of federal power. Marshall, moreover, promises that the Court will stop Congress from invoking its lawful powers as a pretext for accomplishing objects not entrusted to it.[37]

As an abstract matter, even Madison and Randolph might have acquiesced to this general rule from *McCulloch*. But how does one determine which means are appropriate and which are inconsistent with the spirit of the Constitution? How plainly must a means be adapted to a legitimate end? And how should a court investigate the possibility that the exercise of a granted power is a pretext for usurpation? Depending on how such questions are answered in specific cases, the apparent difference between *Fisher* and *McCulloch* could easily disappear.

Unfortunately, *McCulloch* does little more than gesture vaguely at the contribution a bank can make to the exercise of Congress' enumerated powers.[38] This contrasts with the detailed exposition in Hamilton's opinion, with which Marshall was quite familiar. When you add that the economy's banking sector was far more developed in 1816 than it had been in 1791, Marshall could be seen as suggesting, in the spirit of *Fisher*, that the Court should rubber-stamp congressional exercises of power whenever there has not been "a bold and plain usurpation."

It would no doubt be unreasonable to expect judges to demand the kind of detailed argument about the need for a bank that Hamilton offered to President Washington. But there were some obvious reasons for doubting that this particular bank law was consistent with the spirit of the Constitution. The *McCulloch* opinion never mentions that Congress had not established a government agency but instead had incorporated an essentially private bank controlled by private shareholders who sought profits for themselves. That institution, moreover, was given competitive advantages over state banks.

Shouldn't the Second Bank's lawyers at least have been required to justify these features of the law, perhaps with evidence that the government's ability to carry out its legitimate functions was threatened by deficiencies in the existing banks? And how did the Court know that the Second Bank was structured to serve the government's interests rather than as a pretext to enrich the private shareholders? For example, did the bank's practice of establishing branches anywhere it chose serve any real purpose other than increasing private profits?

Such questions were raised by Maryland's lawyers. Marshall ignored those questions while expatiating without any clear necessity on the political theory of the union. He plausibly rejected conclusions that could have crippled the federal government, but he did not address serious issues raised by the specific statute before the Court. He presumably could have provided a reasoned justification for the statute's problematic aspects, and such a justification might have persuaded reasonable and disinterested observers.[39] If Marshall had taken this path, it would be harder to interpret *McCulloch* as a slightly disguised reaffirmation of *Fisher*'s blatant invitation to congressional overreach. Unfortunately, the opinion's airy silence in the face of these problems has made it all too easy to treat *McCulloch* as just such an invitation.

How could this silence have been justified? David S. Schwartz maintains that Marshall was writing in the shadow of controversies about the federal government's power over internal improvements, control of the money supply, and the scope of the commerce clause.[40] For that reason, Schwartz believes, "The most logical inference from *McCulloch*'s failure to [construe one or more specific enumerated powers] is that Marshall wanted to avoid interpreting any enumerated powers, and thereby embroiling the Court in further controversy."[41] Perhaps. But a jurist with half of John Marshall's legal skills could easily have upheld the statute, after addressing its problematic aspects, without effectively resolving other cases not before the Court.

In any event, there was an even easier way to avoid further controversy, and Marshall himself showed what it was. As President Madison had already pointed out, the constitutionality of the Second Bank was not politically controversial. Like Madison, Marshall attributed great significance to this fact:

It has been truly said that this can scarcely be considered as an open question entirely unprejudiced by the former proceedings of the Nation respecting it. The principle now contested was introduced at a very early period of our history, has been recognised by many successive legislatures, and has been acted upon by the Judicial Department, in cases of peculiar delicacy, as a law of undoubted obligation. . . .

. . . It would require no ordinary share of intrepidity to assert that a measure adopted under these circumstances was a bold and plain usurpation to which the Constitution gave no countenance.[42]

He could have stopped there, as President Madison did in his 1815 veto message, and held (rightly or wrongly) that the issue had been settled by concrete expressions of the nation's general will. Instead, Marshall went on to discuss the *hypothetical* case that would have been presented "were the question entirely new."[43] Thus, he unnecessarily opened up questions that he then declined to address. This made for a much *broader* ruling than the case required according to Marshall's own analysis.[44]

In a private letter written a few months after *McCulloch* was decided, Madison denounced the opinion because of "the high sanction given to a latitude in expounding the Constitution, which seems to break down the landmarks intended by a specification of the powers of Congress; and to substitute for a definite connection between means and ends, a legislative discretion as to the former, to which no practical limit can be assigned."[45] Consistent with the venerable traditions of the common law, he believed, judicial interpretation of the laws (including the Constitution) should result from a course of particular decisions, rather than having those decisions proceed "from a previous and abstract comment on the subject."

Implicitly rebuking those who framed the constitutional controversy over the bank as a choice between a license for a potentially all-powerful federal leviathan and a return to the pathetic weakness of the confederation, Madison maintained:

There is certainly a reasonable medium between expounding the Constitution with the strictness of a penal or other ordinary Statute, and expounding it with a laxity, which may vary its essential character, and encroach on the local sovereignties with which it was meant to be reconcilable.

And if experience were to show that the federal government's powers are deficient, Madison added, the Constitution itself spells out the proper mode of drawing new powers from their legitimate source.[46]

The Constitutionality of Maryland's Tax

McCulloch's analysis of Maryland's tax is even weaker than its insouciant discussion of the constitutional issues the federal statute raised. Much of the analysis is devoted to refuting an extreme claim advanced by Maryland's lawyers, according to which the states have an absolute and unfettered constitutional right to tax the federal government. Marshall ably refuted this theory and rightly refused to adopt a doctrine whose logic would leave the nation's fisc at the mercy of hostile or irresponsible state governments. It does not follow, however, that Maryland's tax on the Baltimore branch was prohibited.

Some passages in *McCulloch* suggest that any state tax on a federal instrumentality is inherently unconstitutional,[47] presumably even if authorized by Congress.[48] But no constitutional provision says or implies that such a general ban exists, and it would border on absurdity to say that Congress is powerless to authorize a state tax on a federal instrumentality.[49] Perhaps Marshall only meant to advance the more modest and plausible claim that the statute establishing the bank forbade the states to tax it.[50]

The supremacy clause provides that the Constitution and federal statutes are the supreme law of the land, by which judges are bound, "any Thing in the Constitution or Laws of any State to the Contrary notwithstanding."[51] That means a state law may not override any provision of the federal Constitution or a valid federal statute. If asked, Congress might have banned a tax like Maryland's, or it might have expressly acquiesced to such a tax. But Congress was not asked and did not answer.

Marshall seemed to think it was obvious that Maryland's tax violated the statute establishing the bank. That conclusion was not even close to being evident. The statute did not address the permissibility of state taxes one way or the other, and Marshall offered no argument for inferring that this tax was forbidden.

Nor would it have been easy to do so. Maryland taxed its own banks separately from out-of-state banks, using somewhat different tax structures.[52] The default tax on Maryland banks applied to their capital stock, while the default tax on other banks applied to certain transactions. As an alternative to the default tax, all banks could satisfy their obligations with a specified lump-sum payment.

For out-of-state banks, the rate was $15,000 per year. State banks were permitted to make a joint payment of $200,000 that would cover their obligations for the next 20 years. Precise comparisons would require additional information, but there is no apparent reason to suppose that the tax on the national bank would have been especially burdensome. In May 1819, the Baltimore branch was capitalized at $5,646,000 and had recently recorded loans of $9,289,000.[53] In light of those figures, $15,000 per year seems a modest annual assessment.

Unlike the state-chartered banks, moreover, the Second Bank had the flexibility to choose each year between the default tax or the lump sum, depending on which was most advantageous at that time. The tax on the national bank could have had an even less adverse effect than the tax Maryland imposed on its own banks.

The more important point, of course, involves the absolute rather than the comparative effect of Maryland's tax on the national bank, and there is some evidence on this question. At least one director of the national bank apparently thought that sound policy would dictate yielding to the tax.[54] When the bank did challenge Maryland's statute, the lawsuit was apparently an "amicable controversy."[55]

If the tax actually posed a real threat, one would expect that the bank or the Treasury Department would have planned, in the event it was upheld in court, to ask Congress to expressly preempt it, as Congress certainly could have done. On the contrary, Secretary of the Treasury William Crawford believed that a bill to exempt the Baltimore branch from the state tax would have been *defeated* in Congress.[56] The assumption that Maryland's tax was a threat to the national bank, a proposition for which Marshall offered no evidence, was likely false.

The practical effect of *McCulloch* was to create, through judicial fiat, a law that Congress had not enacted and possibly would have refused to enact. This form of judicial governance is now conducted under the rubric of "obstacle preemption." This is an interpretive device through which the Supreme Court enforces policies that the justices like to imagine the legislature would enact if asked, but which it has not enacted. Obstacle preemption has since become a standard routine in the activist repertoire of the modern Court, which in no way excuses the *McCulloch* Court for exercising a power that did not belong to it.[57] The Supreme Court, not Maryland, violated the Constitution.

Apart from the unconstitutionality of the ruling in *McCulloch*, its scope is thrown into doubt by some confusing concluding dicta. The opinion's last paragraph draws an unexplained distinction between a forbidden tax on the bank's operations, on the one hand, and permissible taxes on certain bank property, on the other.

> [This declaration of unconstitutionality] does not extend to a tax paid by the real property of the bank, in common with the other real property within the State, nor to a tax imposed on the interest which the citizens of Maryland may hold in this institution, in common with other property of the same description throughout the State. But this is a tax on the operations of the bank, and is, consequently, a tax on the operation of an instrument employed by the Government of the Union to carry its powers into execution. Such a tax must be unconstitutional.[58]

Does "in common with" mean that a state can tax federal entities so long as it also taxes other similar entities? If so, Maryland's tax should have been upheld because it did tax other banks as well (a fact that Marshall did not mention). If not, is it because the bank's "operations" were constitutionally different from its real property and the proprietary interest of Marylanders? Why would that be? And are these the *only* objects a state may tax? What about the bank's movable property and its employees' salaries?

Or does "in common with" mean "uniformly with"? Uniform tax rates can affect different objects of taxation differently, even when they are objects of the same kind, and it may often be impossible to tell in advance what those effects will be. And what would happen if a state imposed a uniform tax rate on the operations of all banks or on their real estate while separately subsidizing the state-chartered banks but not the national bank? Would that violate whatever principle of uniformity Marshall had in mind? He did not explain how one should go about answering these and many other questions.

Marshall avoided hard questions about the bank statute's constitutionality by deferring to Congress' judgment about the scope of its own powers. But he refused to leave hard questions about the desirability of banning all state taxes on the bank or tolerating some of them, when the Constitution clearly left those questions squarely in Congress' hands. Judging from the fulsome encomiums that have swelled *McCulloch*'s reputation over the past two centuries, the irony is apparently easy to overlook.[59]

President Jackson on the Authority of *McCulloch*

In 1832, Andrew Jackson issued an elaborate veto message when presented with a bill to recharter the Second Bank before its term expired.[60] Like Madison, he acknowledged that a sufficiently clear and durable national consensus could settle debatable constitutional questions. But the bank precedents established by past practice were mixed, and controversies over the issue had persisted.

Nor did *McCulloch* settle the matter. In Jackson's view, the Supreme Court has no authority to control the president in exercising his legislative powers. In any event, Jackson maintained that *McCulloch* had merely decided in general terms that incorporating a bank is permissible, leaving the political branches to exercise their own constitutional judgment on particular legislative proposals.

Jackson provided a detailed analysis of many unconstitutional features he perceived, rightly or wrongly, in this particular bank's structure. He agreed that a bank could constitutionally be established, and he offered to propose a way to do it. But he rightly refused to conflate a judicial decision or majority sentiment in Congress with what Madison called "the general will of the nation."

In *McCulloch*, Marshall predicted that "the question respecting the extent of the powers actually granted [by the Constitution] is perpetually arising, and will probably continue to arise so long as our system shall exist."[61] Quite right. And Jackson understood that a mere Supreme Court opinion is not a good reason to treat that question as closed. Unfortunately, his sense of responsibility to the Constitution went out of fashion. Too many presidents and legislators came to believe that the Constitution allows Congress to do anything that an incurious and indulgent Supreme Court will countenance.

McCulloch's Destructive Legacy

The Court rarely rules that Congress has exceeded its powers except when it violates an individual right that the justices have selected for enforcement from the Constitution[62] or have exuberantly imputed to it.[63] From the New Deal through the mid-1990s, the justices signaled that the commerce clause gives Congress authority to regulate virtually everything in human life that is not protected by one of these judicially favored individual rights.[64]

Thus, if a small business buys and sells products across state lines, that is all it takes to justify congressional regulation of labor relations in the company.[65] The federal government can decide how much workers must be paid and how long they may work, so long as their employer produces goods destined for another state.[66] The commerce power can be used to ban racial discrimination at any small business that uses products from another state or serves customers from other states.[67]

Limits can be put on the crops a farmer may grow, even for his or her own use at home, if such use by enough farmers could affect the price of farm products in other states.[68] A local loan shark can be prosecuted under federal law because some other loan sharks belong to gangs that have interstate operations.[69] Good luck finding anyone who does much of anything that is not also done by some interstate enterprise or could not affect interstate commerce if enough people did it.

In 1995, the Supreme Court's decision in *United States v. Lopez* shocked the legal world by finding that Congress had exceeded its commerce clause authority when it criminalized the possession of a firearm in or near a school.[70] The Court concluded that the law had nothing to do with commerce or any economic activity and that the conduct it regulated could not substantially affect interstate commerce through repetition elsewhere. Five years later, the Court reviewed a statute that created a civil cause of action for victims of "gender-motivated violence" and held that Congress may not regulate violent criminal conduct solely because of the aggregate effect of such conduct on interstate commerce.[71]

Lopez did not purport to overrule any prior decisions, and the opinion raised more questions about the scope of the commerce power than it answered. But because the Court had finally identified *something* that is beyond Congress' reach, many observers hoped or feared that the decision signaled a coming restoration of the principle of limited and enumerated federal powers. Soon enough, such expectations proved to have been misplaced.

Congress reenacted the gun-free school zone law, along with a new provision requiring prosecutors to prove that the firearm had at some time traveled in interstate commerce. *Lopez* had signaled that this was one way for the legislature to convert a local activity into one that Congress could regulate, and the new statute has been upheld.[72] If an object acquires a magical power to subject anyone who possesses it to Congress' regulatory jurisdiction, merely because the object (or even some component of it) crossed state lines at some time in the past, the Constitution's principle of enumerated powers is not much more than a guideline for drafting statutes.[73]

Congress has not yet reenacted the "gender-motivated violence" statute, but it apparently need only require that a plaintiff prove some interstate nexus. Perhaps the defendant had moved across a state line to attend college.[74] Or perhaps the tort was allegedly committed while he or she wore clothing manufactured in another state. Or perhaps he or she drove to the scene of the incident in an automobile containing parts manufactured out of state.

In addition to the interstate-nexus maneuver, *Lopez* also alluded to regulations forming an essential part of a larger regulation of economic activity, in which the regulatory scheme could be undercut unless intrastate activity is regulated.[75] This was the basis on which a federal regulation controlling agricultural products grown for home consumption was upheld, and the Court extended the doctrine by applying it to marijuana grown and consumed in a state where the government specifically authorized use of the plant for medical purposes.[76]

So far, the Court has recognized only trivial or symbolic limits on the commerce clause's reach. In *National Federation of Independent Business v. Sebelius*,[77] for example, five justices, including Chief Justice John Roberts, concluded that the commerce clause does not authorize Congress to force consumers to participate in commerce by purchasing specified health insurance policies that they do not want. But Roberts then joined the four who dissented from this conclusion in upholding the program anyway. The legal mandate to purchase specified insurance policies was characterized as a mere suggestion, and the statutory penalty for noncompliance was interpreted as a tax that consumers were free to avoid by complying with the suggestion. Thus, the limitation on Congress' power under the commerce clause turned out to be purely symbolic.[78]

Conclusion

It was neither necessary nor proper for *McCulloch* to assume without analysis that all the features of the Second Bank were necessary and proper. Nor was it necessary and proper for later Courts to adopt a *Fisher*-esque level of deference as the standard for judging the boundaries of congressional power. Like Marshall, all the current justices can say that the abstract principle of limited and enumerated powers is "now universally admitted."[79] But the legacy of his opinion has been the effective destruction of that principle.

McCulloch famously proclaimed that "we must never forget that it is *a Constitution* we are expounding."[80] This sonorous aphorism is frequently, if unnecessarily and improperly, taken to mean that it is *merely* a constitution, which judges are free (or obligated) to amend under the guise of interpretation. That attitude has triumphed historically and perhaps irrevocably. Constitutional law is widely regarded now as a branch of political philosophy or as a field on which to play junior varsity statesmanship or, not infrequently, as an arena for flamboyant moral posturing or a weapon of partisan warfare.

Rather than submissively celebrate these developments, we could choose to stop forgetting that the Constitution was originally meant to be a law and that it was meant to be more authoritative than what the Supreme Court says about it. If we did, *McCulloch* and its rank progeny would become controversial once again.

Acknowledgments

This chapter builds on a post that appeared on March 1, 2019, in the "Liberty Forum" on the Liberty Fund's Law & Liberty website. For helpful comments on an early draft, I am grateful to Stephen G. Gilles, Jack Lund, Mara Lund, and John O. McGinnis.

Notes

1. *McCulloch v. Maryland*, 17 US 316 (1819).
2. Albert J. Beveridge, *The Life of John Marshall, Vol. 4* (Boston, MA: Houghton Mifflin, 1919), 308. I am indebted to Kevin Walsh for calling my attention to this passage.
3. Felix Frankfurter, "John Marshall and the Judicial Function," *Harvard Law Review* 69, no. 2 (December 1955): 219, https://www.jstor.org/stable/pdf/1337866.pdf.
4. Jack M. Balkin and Sanford Levinson, "The Canons of Constitutional Law," *Harvard Law Review* 111, no. 1 (February 1998): 973, https://digitalcommons.law.yale.edu/cgi/viewcontent.cgi?article=1259&context=fss_papers.
5. "The *McCulloch v. Maryland* standard is the measure of what constitutes 'appropriate legislation' under § 5 of the Fourteenth Amendment. Correctly viewed, § 5 is a positive grant of legislative power authorizing Congress to exercise its discretion in determining whether and what legislation is needed to secure the guarantees of the Fourteenth Amendment." *Katzenbach v. Morgan*, 384 US 641, 651 (1966).
6. The essays are collected in Gerald Gunther, ed., *John Marshall's Defense of McCulloch v. Maryland* (Palo Alto, CA: Stanford University Press, 1969).
7. US Const. art. I, § 8, cl. 18. "The Congress shall have Power . . . To make all Laws which shall be necessary and proper for carrying into Execution the foregoing Powers, and all other Powers vested by this Constitution in the Government of the United States, or in any Department or Officer thereof."
8. James Madison, "Speech on the Bank Bill 2 February 1791," Online Library of Liberty, Liberty Fund, https://oll.libertyfund.org/pages/1791-madison-speech-on-the-bank-bill.
9. In context, Madison was not claiming that events at the Constitutional Convention are relevant to the Constitution's interpretation. See John O. McGinnis and Michael B. Rappaport, "Unifying Original Intent and Original Public Meaning," *Northwestern*

University Law Review 113, no. 6 (2019): 1410–11, https://scholarlycommons.law.northwestern.edu/cgi/viewcontent.cgi?article=1379&context=nulr.

10. Edmund Randolph, Letter to President George Washington, February 12, 1791.

11. Edmund Randolph, "Enclosure: Opinion on the Constitutionality of the Bank, 12 February 1791," National Archives, Founders Online, https://founders.archives.gov/documents/Washington/05-07-02-0200-0002.

12. Randolph, "Enclosure: Opinion on the Constitutionality of the Bank, 12 February 1791."

13. Thomas Jefferson, "Opinion on the Constitutionality of the Bill for Establishing a National Bank, 15 February 1791," National Archives, Founders Online, https://founders.archives.gov/documents/Jefferson/01-19-02-0051.

14. See McGinnis and Rappaport, "Unifying Original Intent and Original Public Meaning," 1409–12.

15. Jefferson, "Opinion on the Constitutionality of the Bill for Establishing a National Bank, 15 February 1791."

16. Jefferson, "Opinion on the Constitutionality of the Bill for Establishing a National Bank, 15 February 1791."

17. See Mark R. Killenbeck, *M'Culloch v. Maryland: Securing a Nation* (Lawrence, KS: University Press of Kansas, 2006).

18. Alexander Hamilton, "Opinion as to the Constitutionality of the Bank of the United States: 1791," Yale Law School, Avalon Project, https://avalon.law.yale.edu/18th_century/bank-ah.asp.

19. Hamilton, "Opinion as to the Constitutionality of the Bank of the United States: 1791."

20. Hamilton, "Opinion as to the Constitutionality of the Bank of the United States: 1791."

21. Madison, "Speech on the Bank Bill 2 February 1791."

22. See Killenbeck, *M'Culloch v. Maryland*, 28.

23. James Madison, "Veto Message on the National Bank," University of Virginia, Miller Center, January 30, 1815, https://millercenter.org/the-presidency/presidential-speeches/january-30-1815-veto-message-national-bank.

24. Madison, "Veto Message on the National Bank."

25. See Richard E. Ellis, *Aggressive Nationalism: McCulloch v. Maryland and the Foundation of Federal Authority in the Young Republic* (Oxford, UK: Oxford University Press, 2007), 42; and Bray Hammond, *Banks and Politics in America: From the Revolution to the Civil War* (Princeton, NJ: Princeton University Press, 1957), 128.

26. See Ellis, *Aggressive Nationalism*, 42.

27. *United States v. Fisher*, 6 US 358 (1805).

28. US Const. art. I, § 8, cl. 4. "The Congress shall have Power . . . To establish . . . uniform Laws on the subject of Bankruptcies throughout the United States."

29. *United States v. Fisher*, 6 US 396 (1805).

30. In Chapter 3 of this volume, Christopher Wolfe endorses the *Fisher* formulation on the ground that "the judge has no legitimate power to evaluate how necessary or proper a means is." Marshall himself took a different view in his anonymous defense of *McCulloch*: "The court may be mistaken in the 'propriety and necessity' of [the Bank].

I do not think so; but others may honestly entertain this opinion." Gunther, *John Marshall's Defense of McCulloch v. Maryland*, 190.

31. Marshall's use of the word "now" indicates that the Constitution had previously been interpreted differently by at least some people. Recent scholarship suggests that there was significant early support for the view that Congress possesses inherent legislative powers that are independent of those enumerated in the Constitution. See John Mikhail, "The Necessary and Proper Clauses," *Georgetown Law Journal* 102, no. 1 (April 2014): 1045–132, https://georgetownlawjournal.org/articles/89/necessary-proper-clauses/pdf; and Richard Primus, "'The Essential Characteristic': Enumerated Powers and the Bank of the United States," *Michigan Law Review* 117, no. 1 (December 2018): 415–97, https://papers.ssrn.com/sol3/papers.cfm?abstract_id=3197330. I disagree with that interpretation of the Constitution, and *McCulloch* unequivocally rejects it as well: "This Government is acknowledged by all to be one of enumerated powers. The principle that it can exercise only the powers granted to it would seem too apparent to have required to be enforced by all those arguments which its enlightened friends, while it was depending before the people, found it necessary to urge; that principle is now universally admitted." *McCulloch v. Maryland*, 17 US 316, 405 (1819).

32. *McCulloch v. Maryland*, 17 US 316, 401 (1819).

33. *McCulloch v. Maryland*, 17 US 316, 402 (1819).

34. *McCulloch v. Maryland*, 17 US 316, 409–19 (1819).

35. *McCulloch v. Maryland*, 17 US 316, 421 (1819).

36. *McCulloch v. Maryland*, 17 US 316, 419, 420 (1819).

37. *McCulloch v. Maryland*, 17 US 316, 423 (1819).

38. *McCulloch v. Maryland*, 17 US 316, 407 (1819).

39. Abram Shulsky's chapter in this volume points to some elements that might have gone into such a justification.

40. David S. Schwartz, "Misreading *McCulloch v. Maryland*," *University of Pennsylvania Journal of Constitutional Law* 18, no. 1 (October 2015): 62, https://papers.ssrn.com/sol3/papers.cfm?abstract_id=2572408.

41. Schwartz, "Misreading *McCulloch v. Maryland*."

42. *McCulloch v. Maryland*, 17 US 316, 401–02 (1819).

43. *McCulloch v. Maryland*, 17 US 316, 402 (1819).

44. In Chapter 6 of this volume, Adam White joins Schwartz in treating *McCulloch* as an exercise of judicial statesmanship. But canny tactics are not synonymous with prudence, and they cannot be justified without reference to the worth of their aims and effects. Whatever Marshall's aims may have been, the ultimate effect of his political maneuvering has been to help destroy the fundamental structure of the government established by the Constitution. Whether or not the Supreme Court's judicially manufactured constitution is better than the one it replaced, the legitimate way to make such alterations is through the procedures set out in Article V. Marshall himself recognized this elementary point when he observed, "The peculiar circumstances of the moment may render a measure more or less wise, but cannot render it more or less constitutional." Gunther, *John Marshall's Defense of McCulloch v. Maryland*, 190–91. Many among his legions of intense admirers do not share this view.

45. James Madison, Letter to Spencer Roane, September 2, 1819.

46. Madison did not find it necessary to provide a citation to Article V. Two centuries after *McCulloch*, I am not so sure that one can safely dispense with this formality.

47. At one point, Marshall argues that the states never had, and thus need not surrender, a right to tax the means by which the federal government executes its powers. Whatever the merits of this argument, Marshall immediately said that he was "waiving this theory for the present," and he never returned to it. I find the theory unpersuasive, but it hardly matters since Marshall himself treated it as obiter dicta. See *McCulloch v. Maryland*, 17 US 316, 430 (1819).

48. "It is of the very essence of supremacy to remove all obstacles to its action within its own sphere, and so to modify every power vested in subordinate governments as to exempt its own operations from their own influence. This effect need not be stated in terms." See *McCulloch v. Maryland*, 17 US 316, 427 (1819). Objects over which the sovereign power of a state does not extend are "upon the soundest principles, exempt from taxation." *McCulloch v. Maryland*, 17 US 316, 429 (1819). An attempt to tax "the means employed by the Government of the Union, in pursuance of the Constitution, is itself an abuse because it is the usurpation of a power which the people of a single State cannot give." *McCulloch v. Maryland*, 17 US 316, 420 (1819). "The States have no power, by taxation or otherwise, to retard, impede, burden, or in any manner control the operations of the constitutional laws enacted by Congress to carry into execution the powers vested in the General Government." *McCulloch v. Maryland*, 17 US 316, 436 (1819). "A tax on the operation of an instrument employed by the Government of the Union to carry its powers into execution . . . must be unconstitutional." *McCulloch v. Maryland*, 17 US 316, 436–37 (1819).

49. Accordingly, and in light of their context, the quotations in the previous note might be interpreted (though with great difficulty) to mean little more than that the states lack an absolute right (which Congress may not override) to impose a tax on federal operations.

50. For example, Marshall refers in general to the Constitution's power to restrain a state from imposing a tax "as is in its nature incompatible with, and repugnant to, the constitutional laws of the Union." *McCulloch v. Maryland*, 17 US 316, 425 (1819). He also refers to the federal government's "incidental privilege of exempting its own measures from State taxation." *McCulloch v. Maryland*, 17 US 316, 434 (1819).

51. US Const., art. VI, cl. 2.

52. See "A supplement to the act entitled, an act to incorporate a company to make a turnpike road leading to Cumberland, and for the extension of the charters of the several banks in the city of Baltimore, and for other purposes," January 27, 1814; and "An act to impose a Tax on all Banks or Branches thereof in the State of Maryland not chartered by the Legislature," February 11, 1818.

53. See John Thom Holdsworth and Davis R. Dewey, *The First and Second Banks of the United States* (Washington, DC: National Monetary Commission, 1910).

54. See Ellis, *Aggressive Nationalism*, 71.

55. Ellis, *Aggressive Nationalism*, 72.

56. Ellis, *Aggressive Nationalism*, 71.

57. *Arizona v. United States*, 567 US 387, 407–10 (2012), for example, invoked the doctrine of obstacle preemption when it forbade a state to arrest illegal aliens on the basis

of probable cause that they committed a public offense for which the aliens are removable from the United States under federal law. The Court so held notwithstanding that the federal government is required to take custody of criminal aliens and federal law specifically contemplates that states will cooperate in "the identification, apprehension, detention, or removal of aliens not lawfully present in the United States." See *Arizona v. United States*, 567 US 387, 426–27 (2012) (Scalia, J., dissenting); 567 US 387, 437–38 (2012) (Thomas, J., dissenting); and 567 US 387, 454–59 (2012) (Alito, J., dissenting).

58. *McCulloch v. Maryland*, 17 US 316, 436–37 (1819).

59. In Chapter 3 of this volume, Christopher Wolfe argues that Congress alone may decide questions that arise under the necessary and proper clause because judges are unfit to make decisions that involve questions of degree. But he thinks that courts are permitted to decide which taxes states may impose on federal instrumentalities: "Putting the onus [on Congress to make those decisions] seems unnecessary and not the ordinary implication of 'supremacy.'" The logic of this argument escapes me.

60. Jackson, "Veto Message on the National Bank."

61. *McCulloch v. Maryland*, 17 US 316, 405 (1819).

62. The Court has not selected them all. In *Home Building & Loan Association v. Blaisdell*, 290 US 398 (1934), for example, the Court refused to enforce the Constitution's prohibition against state laws "impairing the Obligation of Contracts." US Const., art. I, § 10, cl. 1. In response to a devastating dissent joined by four justices, the majority opinion said: "If by the statement that what the Constitution meant at the time of its adoption it means to-day, it is intended to say that the great clauses of the Constitution must be confined to the interpretation which the framers, with the conditions and outlook of their time, would have placed upon them, the statement carries its own refutation." *Home Building & Loan Association v. Blaisdell*, 290 US 398, 442–43 (1934).

63. The Court's first major harvest of judicially planted individual rights arose from controversies over slavery. See *Prigg v. Pennsylvania*, 41 US 539, 312–13 (1842), which purported to recognize a constitutional right of private slave catchers to abduct black residents in free states without proof that the captured people were fugitive slaves; and *Scott v. Sanford*, 60 US 393, 450 (1857), which purported to recognize a constitutional right of slaveholders to bring their peculiar form of property into federal territories, where Congress had outlawed slavery. Since that time, Supreme Court justices have conjured innumerable new individual rights from their own luxuriant imaginations.

64. US Const., art. I, § 8, cl. 3. "The Congress shall have Power . . . To regulate Commerce with foreign Nations, and among the several States, and with the Indian Tribes."

65. *NLRB v. Friedman-Harry Marks Clothing Co.*, 301 US 58 (1937).

66. *United States v. Darby*, 312 US 100 (1941).

67. *Heart of Atlanta Motel v. United States*, 379 US 241 (1964); *Katzenbach v. McClung*, 379 US 294 (1964); and *Daniel v. Paul*, 395 US 298 (1969).

68. *Wickard v. Filburn*, 317 US 111 (1942).

69. *Perez v. United States*, 402 US 146 (1971).

70. *United States v. Lopez*, 514 US 549 (1995).

71. *United States v. Morrison*, 529 US 598 (2000).

72. *United States v. Dorsey*, 418 F.3d 1038 (9th Cir. 2005); and *United States v. Danks*, 221 F.3d 1037 (8th Cir. 1999), cert. denied, 528 US 1091 (2000).

73. Compare with *United States v. Alderman*, 565 F.3d 641 (9th Cir. 2009), holding that the sale of body armor in interstate commerce creates a sufficient nexus between possession of body armor and commerce to allow for federal regulation under the commerce clause. The Supreme Court refused to review this decision over a dissent filed by Justice Thomas (and joined by Justice Scalia). *Milner v. Department of Navy*, 562 US 1163 (2011).

74. See *United States v. Lopez*, 514 US 549, 567 (1995), noting that there was "no indication that [the defendant] had recently moved in interstate commerce."

75. *United States v. Lopez*, 514 US 549, 561 (1995).

76. *Gonzales v. Raich*, 545 US 1 (2005).

77. *National Federation of Independent Business v. Sebelius*, 567 US 519 (2012).

78. Roberts acknowledged that the only reason to interpret the mandate-plus-penalty as a voluntarily incurred tax was to avoid holding it unconstitutional. *National Federation of Independent Business v. Sebelius*, 567 US 519, 2594 (2012). He also dismissed an objection that this would be a direct tax and thus subject to the constitutional requirement of apportionment. US Const., art. I, § 2, cl. 3. Oddly, Roberts suggested that the question was settled by an absence of prior precedents treating this unprecedented imposition as a direct tax. *National Federation of Independent Business v. Sebelius*, 567 US 519, 2598 (2012).

79. *McCulloch v. Maryland*, 17 US 316, 405 (1819).

80. *McCulloch v. Maryland*, 17 US 316, 407 (1819).

2

The Sound of the Third Hand Clapping: James Madison's Reading of the Necessary and Proper Clause

MICHAEL ZUCKERT

Two hundred years later, *McCulloch v. Maryland* is still one of the most widely read and discussed cases in American constitutional history. One of the most interesting aspects of the attention paid to *McCulloch* over the years is the degree to which the most relevant literature was written well before the case occurred. The most widely read commentary on *McCulloch* has been Alexander Hamilton's "Opinion on the Constitutionality of the Bank," written about 25 years before John Marshall wrote the Supreme Court's opinion in *McCulloch*.[1] The second most read is probably Thomas Jefferson's opinion, prepared, as was Hamilton's, at the behest of President George Washington, as he pondered whether to sign the recently passed congressional bill establishing the First Bank of the United States.[2] Jefferson and Hamilton are the "two hands clapping."

There was a third hand—or set of hands—that is surprisingly not among the most widely read and discussed early commentaries on the constitutional themes raised by the effort to charter the bank. This third hand is the opinion on the bank's constitutionality delivered by James Madison, at that time a representative from Virginia in the US Congress.[3]

The relative obscurity of Madison's opinion is surprising for a number of reasons: first, because of his stature—both in general and as an authority on the Constitution; second, because he was the first of the major authors to present a carefully worked out interpretation of the necessary and proper clause, the part of the Constitution most at stake in the debate over the bank; and third, because he opposed the bill in Congress, well before it was adopted and came to Washington for his approval.

Finally, and most importantly, Madison's argument not only differed from that of the other participants in the debate but also was arguably the most constitutionally correct of opinions then and since. Having said that, I must immediately qualify my claim by observing that Madison was a complicated player in this game. When the First Bank came up in Congress in 1791, he opposed it, but when the bill chartering the Second Bank of the United States came to his presidential desk in 1816, he signed it. His shift on the bank raises many interesting questions, but I am going to restrict my attention to his stance toward the First Bank.

The Sound of Two Hands Clapping

Another reason Madison's position on the bank has been more or less ignored derives, I suspect, from a tendency among scholars to assimilate his position to Jefferson's. This practice, in turn, is related to scholars' tendency to see Madison as, in effect, captured by his friend's political ideology. Madison did share with Jefferson certain fears of where Hamilton's expansive interpretation of the Constitution would take the nation. So in his congressional speech against the Bank Bill, Madison rejected any interpretation that "would give to Congress an unlimited power [and would thus] render nugatory the enumeration of particular powers."[4]

In somewhat more poetic language, Jefferson later made a similar point: "To take a single step beyond the boundaries thus specially drawn around the powers of Congress [by the 10th Amendment] is to take possession of a boundless field of power, no longer susceptible of any definition."[5] Both men wished to preserve limitations on Congress' powers and retain the meaningfulness of the enumeration of powers in Article I.

Nonetheless, their arguments concluding that the Bank Bill went beyond the Constitution and stepped onto that "boundless field of power" were quite different. Jefferson, as is widely known, took his stand mainly on the meaning of the term "necessary" in the necessary and proper clause. Jefferson said:

> The Constitution allows only the means which are "necessary" not those which are merely "convenient" for effecting the enumerated

powers. If such a latitude of construction be allowed to this phrase as to give any non-enumerated power, it will go to every one, for [there] is no one which ingenuity may not torture into a *convenience, in some way or other*, to *some one* of so long a list of enumerated powers. It would swallow up all the delegated powers, and reduce the whole to one [power]. . . . Therefore it was that the Constitution restrained [Congress] to the *necessary* means, that is to say, to those means without which the grant of the power would be nugatory.[6] (Emphasis added.)

This language of "means without which the grant of power would be nugatory" became central to the debate on the necessary and proper clause when Hamilton picked it as the chief target of his counterargument on that clause. Later, Chief Justice Marshall followed Hamilton in rejecting Jefferson's reading of the clause when it was used by the state of Maryland to assert that Congress had no power to charter the bank. But Madison's case against the bank did not depend on Jefferson's claim that "necessary" means "without which" or "absolutely necessary," as it was rephrased in various subsequent restatements.

Jefferson gives an essentially restrictive reading of the clause. Congress, he implies, has the right to use means to effectuate granted powers, but only those means without which the powers granted would be nugatory. But the placement of the necessary and proper clause strongly supports a less restrictive reading. It is the last of a long list of powers granted to the US government and seems intended to continue the process of adding powers that governed Article I, Section 8.

Moreover, Article I, Section 9 clearly shifts direction by enumerating a set of limitations on congressional powers. For example, Congress' exercise of its enumerated powers is limited by the prohibition that "no Bill of Attainder or ex post facto law shall be passed."[7] Jefferson's version of the necessary and proper clause fits better into Article I, Section 9 if restated as follows: No laws shall be made to effectuate the aforementioned powers unless the absence of which would render nugatory an enumerated power. Madison reads the necessary and proper clause as a grant or recognition of additional or implied powers. The two friends, Madison and Jefferson, shared an aversion to the Hamilton-Marshall rendition of implied powers, though they did not agree with each other on the correct reading of the clause.

Of course, the word "necessary," because it is contained in the necessary and proper clause, appeared frequently in Madison's speech, but it was never joined with the word "absolutely" or similar terms. Although the "unless nugatory" test is not central to Madison's exposition, it is a major part of Hamilton's. In Hamilton's opinion on the bank, he took strong issue with Jefferson's construal of the word "necessary" as implying the unless nugatory rule. According to Hamilton, "Neither the grammatical nor popular sense of the term ['necessary'] requires [the Jeffersonian] construction." Hamilton pointed out, "Necessary often means no more than needful, requisite, incidental, useful, or conducive to."[8]

Chief Justice Marshall, in his heavily Hamilton-influenced opinion in *McCulloch*, made a similar linguistic argument. He asked whether the Maryland or Jeffersonian equation of "necessary" with the "unless nugatory" principle holds up. "Does [the word 'necessary'] always import an absolute physical necessity so strong that one thing to which another may be termed necessary cannot exist without that other?" The chief justice thought not. As he put it, according to "its [common] use in the common affairs of the world or in approved authors, we find that it frequently imports no more than that one thing is convenient, or useful, or essential to another."[9]

The sound of two hands clapping is thus the cacophony produced by the different assertions about the meaning of "necessary." Each party to the debate developed a test to demarcate the line between what is or should be allowed under the clause and what should not be. For Jefferson, the test was the "unless nugatory" standard. No matter how limiting the warrant for implied powers under Jefferson's test, there still was room for some implied powers.

Hamilton insisted that no matter how much looser his reading of the necessary and proper clause, it did not justify unlimited implied powers as both Madison and Jefferson averred. As a counter to the accusations he faced, Hamilton laid down his famous test for legitimate derivation of implied powers: "The only question must be . . . whether the mean to be employed . . . has a natural relation to any of the acknowledged objects or lawful ends of the government."[10] This test delineates not only the scope of the necessary and proper clause but also its limitations. Hamilton illustrates the latter by distinguishing the legitimacy of Congress exercising an implied power to charter or incorporate the proposed First Bank of the

United States from a corporation "superintending the police of the city of Philadelphia, because they [Congress] are not authorized to regulate the police of that city."[11]

Chief Justice Marshall laid down a rule similar to Hamilton's.

> Let the end be legitimate, let it be within the scope of the Constitution, and all means which are appropriate, which are plainly adapted to that end, which are not prohibited, but consist with the letter and spirit of the Constitution, are Constitutional.[12]

The Third Hand Clapping

Responding in advance, so to speak, Madison took quite a different road from the debate over the meaning of "necessary." The congressional reporter restated Madison's chief point: "He here adverted to a distinction, which he said had not been sufficiently kept in view, between a *power necessary and proper for the government or union, and a power necessary and proper for executing the enumerated powers.*"[13] (Emphasis added.) With this observation, Madison introduced a different consideration into the debate. There are, Madison pointed out, two conceptually different kinds of necessary and proper or implied powers.

There is, first, power necessary and proper for the government or union. We might understand what Madison is getting at with this notion of necessary and proper power if we look at this issue from the point of view of constitution makers. Their task is to generate a constitutional scheme, including the structures of governing institutions and the empowerment of the government. If they aim, as the American founders did, at a government of enumerated and express powers, they must first figure out what powers (and how to allocate them) are necessary (and proper) for the successful operation of the government. They must begin by specifying for themselves just what the government must do and what it must accomplish. These were often called, by Madison and other founders, the "objects" of the government.

When Madison introduced the series of papers, *Federalists* 41–46, detailing the powers allocated to the general government, he affirmed that the detailed review of the "powers conferred . . . may be the more conveniently done" if they are "reduced into different classes as they relate to the following different objects."[14] The powers may be clustered into classes of objects because there is a relation between the powers and objects. He identified these clusters of powers with six different objects. We have no need for his entire list of objects, but a few of them will give a good idea of what the objects are and how they relate to the powers.

The first object Madison listed is "security against foreign dangers"; the fifth is "restraint of the states from certain injurious acts."[15] In this and the succeeding papers, he proceeded to list the enumerated powers that relate to those objects. In explaining the powers related to "security against foreign dangers," he identified such security as "one of the primitive objects of civil society. It is an avowed and essential object of the American union. The powers requisite for attaining it, must be efficiently confided to the federal councils."[16] Among those powers "necessary" to both civil society in general and the American union is not only "the powers of declaring war" but also the powers of "raising armies, and equipping fleets."[17]

Madison saw the relation between objects and powers as a relation of ends to means. The powers are necessary and proper means to achieve the objects. The constitution makers, in their task of empowering the government, begin by identifying the objects in view and then inferring the powers that are necessary and proper to achieve these objects. These inferred powers are then put into the Constitution. They are the first sort of necessary and proper powers adverted to in Madison's speech against the constitutionality of the bank.

The second type of necessary and proper power is one "necessary and proper for executing the enumerated powers."[18] Madison believed that two different sets of powers that could be necessary and proper were missed. The first set includes all those powers inferred from the objects of government. Constitution makers take this set of implied powers and transform it into enumerated powers by expressly putting them into their constitution.

As Madison made clear in *Federalist* 41, this process can also be reversed. A constitutional interpreter begins with an already existing constitutional text in which the constitution makers have put the powers they inferred from their identified objects. So Madison inferred the enumerated powers in classes or sets of powers that helped identify the objects sought by the constitution makers when they decided which powers expressly to include in their constitution. It is a process that can go both ways—for the constitution makers, down from the objects to the powers and, for the constitutional interpreter, up from the enumerated powers to the objects.

The other kind of implied powers works similarly but with an especially significant difference. The second kind of implied powers is derived from the first sort, but only when this first set has been expressly placed in the Constitution as enumerated powers. This second sort of implied powers is those inferred to be powers necessary and proper for executing the enumerated powers. Like the first kind of necessary and proper powers, these are derived as means of effectuating certain ends, in this case the effectuation of the enumerated powers.

The enumerated powers are those inferred means to achieving the ends known as objects. The enumerated powers then switch from being means to being ends. They in turn imply means to their achievement, which are the necessary and proper powers. These are then the ultimate means in the chain running from objects (ultimate ends) through enumerated powers (intermediate entities both means and their ends) and the necessary and proper powers per se (i.e., implied means to the enumerated powers).

As Madison rightly said, the distinction between the two sets of necessary and proper powers is absolutely essential for correctly interpreting and applying Article I, Section 8's necessary and proper clause. The wording of the necessary and proper clause, when read in light of Madison's explanation of the complex conceptual structure in play in the set of objects, enumerated powers, and implied power, becomes clear. This clause, we should now notice, provides that "the Congress shall have Power . . . to make all Laws which shall be necessary and proper for carrying into Execution *the foregoing Powers, and all other Powers vested by this Constitution in the Government of the United States, or in any Department or Officer thereof.*"[9] (Emphasis added.) The constitutionally implied powers are only those effectuating the enumerated powers, not the objects related to those enumerated powers.

Article I, Section 8 allows the derivation of further powers as means, but only further powers that are means to the enumerated powers, not to the objects of government of the union as such. Although we can infer from the enumerated powers a notion of these objects of government, inferring further powers from the objects as inferred from the enumerated powers is not authorized. Working from the examples Madison provided, we can see rather easily what the Constitution authorizes and what it does not.

Among the enumerated powers are many powers related as means to one of the major objects of the government, such as "security against foreign dangers."[20] Among the powers granted to the government to achieve that object is the enumerated power "to raise and support Armies."[21] There are, however, numerous ways in which an army can be raised. These are the powers needed to execute the vested, enumerated power to raise an army.

So, to raise an army, Congress might establish army recruiting stations throughout the United States. Congress would have the implied power to do so from the necessary and proper clause as written. But Congress could deploy other means as implied powers to the same end. It could, for example, set up a bounty system to procure soldiers.

The necessary and proper clause also sets limits to implied powers. Madison tells us that "no power therefore not enumerated [can] be inferred from the general nature of government" but only from the enumerated powers.[22] Constitution makers have the authority to conclude what powers are necessary and proper to achieve the objects of government *and* to include those powers as the enumerated powers in their constitution. Subordinate legislators, such as Congress, then have the power to derive further implied powers from the enumerated powers but not from the objects directly.

Madison provided a stunning example of what cannot be an implied power: "Had the power of making treaties, for example, been omitted, however necessary it might have been, the defect could only have been lamented, or supplied by an amendment of the constitution."[23] Implied powers can be derived from the enumerated powers but not from the objects or ends of the vested powers.

The difference between Madison's and Hamilton's construals of the necessary and proper clause is evident in the language they use to explain the necessary and proper clause. According to Hamilton, "The only question must be . . . whether the mean to be employed . . . has a natural relation to any of the acknowledged objects or lawful ends of the government."[24] This is to say that (according to Hamilton) legitimate implied powers are all those derived from the "objects or lawful ends of the government." Madison leads us to see that this is precisely not what the Constitution authorizes. Perhaps the Constitution would be a more rational document if it were as Hamilton construed it to be. But Madison's point is that constitutional interpreters and subordinate legislators are bound to the Constitution as it is rather than the Constitution as we would prefer it to be.

Madison weighs the actual enumeration of powers so heavily because the fact of enumeration identifies *a* or *the* leading feature of the Constitution—that its powers are enumerated, and if later interpreters had a right to amend (add powers) by constructing new powers (at the level of the enumerated powers), the overall character of the Constitution as one of enumerated powers would be lost. In distinguishing between the various necessary and proper powers, Madison points to a different approach to the necessary and proper clause from that taken by Jefferson, Hamilton, and Marshall. All three interpreters claimed that the issue at stake is *how necessary* the implied power is—"absolutely necessary," "conducive to," or something in between.

However, Madison conceptualized the matter entirely differently. It is not a matter of *how necessary* but *necessary for what*. An implied power may be one necessary for the government or union (i.e., the question the constitution maker is driven to ask) or one necessary for executing "the enumerated powers" (i.e., the question subordinate constitution makers and legislators are driven to ask).

In framing the decisive question as necessary for what, rather than how necessary, Madison was in one sense closer to Hamilton and Marshall than to Jefferson. Hamilton and Marshall also inquire into the "necessary for what" question, as when Hamilton set a standard for properly deducing implied powers. The reference points for Hamilton for judging the necessity of implied powers are "acknowledged objects."[25] Marshall similarly identifies the way to approach the "necessary for what" question as an inquiry into the legitimacy of the end for which the implied power is to be exercised. If the end is legitimate, the alleged implied power is constitutionally acceptable when "plainly adapted to that end."[26] Both Madison and Jefferson discerned this procedure to be an expansive avenue toward identifying new implied powers, in which the line between the enumerated and implied powers tends to blur if not dissolve.

As we have seen, Madison was opposed to the Hamilton-Marshall technique, in part because of its implications for the enumerated powers, but even more decisively because it was based on a clear misinterpretation of the necessary and proper clause. Had the constitution makers meant to create a constitution with Hamilton's and Marshall's meanings, they would have written their constitution differently. To begin with, the constitution makers could have drafted a necessary and proper clause in language different from what appeared in Article I, Section 8 of the Constitution: "Congress shall have the power to make all laws which shall be necessary and proper for achieving the objects and ends of this constitution." More radically, but in practice the same, the constitution makers could have forgone the enumerated powers altogether and merely listed the objects they had in mind and affirmed Congress' power to achieve them. These alternative ways of providing for implied powers would validate the Hamilton-Marshall approach of moving from expressly granted powers to inferred objects of those powers back down to enumerated powers, which are further means to the implied objects found by the expressly enumerated powers.

Madison's chief objection to the Hamilton-Marshall procedure derived from his observation that the Constitution's language is not compatible with their approach. The language of the necessary and proper clause does not fit their procedure: The clause explicitly validates implied powers to effectuate expressly granted powers. This rules out the direct appeal by the constitutional interpreters to the objects and ends. The constitution makers begin with a notion of objects and ends but do not directly grant all powers that might contribute to accomplishing those objects and ends.

The absence of some powers from the explicit grant of powers might have been quite intentional, and the Hamilton-Marshall approach might lead to serious distortions of what the constitution makers sought to accomplish. Madison used a hypothetical absence of an express power to make treaties. This may be a mere (though important) oversight, but it may not be. Granting that the constitution makers accepted "security against foreign dangers" as a valid intended object of the Constitution and that they provided many of the express powers that they did to achieve that object, it nonetheless does not follow that they would admit the validity of any or all unexpressed powers that arguably serve the end of security. We could take torture as an example of a power that could be taken to serve the purpose of security but one which the constitution makers could have meant to intentionally exclude from the powers granted for that purpose.

Apart from the specific language of the necessary and proper clause, Madison also found the Hamilton-Marshall approach not in accordance with the Constitution's overall character. Marshall famously said, "We must never forget that it is *a Constitution* we are expounding,"[27] to which Madison would add, "It is a constitution of enumerated powers." If later constitutional actors were free to appeal directly to the objects and ends that presumably guided the constitution makers in their making, then it made no sense for the constitution makers to have explicitly listed the powers of government.

Beyond the faults Madison's argument pinpoints in both the Hamilton and Jefferson approaches to the constitutional interpretation of the necessary and proper clause, Madison's own treatment of the question of the national bank and implied powers raises at least three major questions that continue to be of relevance. If, as Madison has it, we must either endure or amend without powers truly necessary for accomplishing acknowledged ends or objects of the government—for example, the treaty power—is this the sort of constitution we should feel stuck with? Could the constitution makers have truly meant to impose on us a constitution with this sort of limitation in it? Ought we to accept a less literal reading of Article I, Section 8 as the more effective and wise Constitution? Two hundred years after *McCulloch v. Maryland*, the continued importance of these questions—raised by the case itself and by the early commentaries authored by Hamilton, Jefferson, and Madison—contributes to its enduring importance in American constitutional history.

Notes

1. Alexander Hamilton, "Opinion on the Constitutionality of the Bank," in *The Founders' Constitution*, ed. Philip B. Kurland and Ralph Lerner (Chicago: University of Chicago Press, 1987).

2. Thomas Jefferson, "Opinion on the Constitutionality of the Bill for Establishing a National Bank," in *The Founders' Constitution*, ed. Philip B. Kurland and Ralph Lerner

(Chicago: University of Chicago Press, 1987).

3. James Madison, "Speech in Congress Opposing the National Bank," in *James Madison, Writings*, ed. Jack N. Rakove (New York: Library of America, 1999), 480–90.

4. Madison, "Speech in Congress Opposing the National Bank," 483.

5. Jefferson, "Opinion on the Constitutionality of the Bill for Establishing a National Bank."

6. Jefferson, "Opinion on the Constitutionality of the Bill for Establishing a National Bank."

7. US Const. art. I, § 9, cl. 3.

8. Hamilton, "Opinion on the Constitutionality of the Bank."

9. *McCulloch v. Maryland*, 17 US 316, 413 (1819).

10 Hamilton, "Opinion on the Constitutionality of the Bank."

11. Hamilton, "Opinion on the Constitutionality of the Bank."

12. *McCulloch v. Maryland*, 17 US 316, 421 (1819).

13. Madison, "Speech in Congress Opposing the National Bank," 488.

14. James Madison, "On the Powers of the National Government: An Analysis of Armies, Taxation, and the General Welfare Clause (Federalist XLI)," in *The Debate on the Constitution: Federalist and Antifederalist Speeches, Articles, and Letters During the Struggle over Ratification, Part Two: January to August 1788*, ed. Bernard Bailyn (New York: Library of America, 1993), 47–56.

15. Madison, "On the Powers of the National Government," 48.

16. Madison, "On the Powers of the National Government," 48.

17. Madison, "On the Powers of the National Government," 48.

18. Madison, "Speech in Congress Opposing the National Bank," 488.

19. US Const. art. I, § 8.

20. Madison, "On the Powers of the National Government," 48.

21. US Const. art. I, § 8, cl. 12.

22. James Madison, "The Bank Bill, House of Representatives," in *The Founders' Constitution*, ed. Philip B. Kurland and Ralph Lerner (Chicago: University of Chicago Press, 1987).

23. Madison, "The Bank Bill, House of Representatives."

24. Hamilton, "Opinion on the Constitutionality of the Bank."

25. Hamilton, "Opinion on the Constitutionality of the Bank."

26. *McCulloch v. Maryland*, 17 US 316, 421 (1819).

27. *McCulloch v. Maryland*, 17 US 316, 407 (1819).

3

McCulloch v. Maryland and John Marshall's Constitutional Interpretation

CHRISTOPHER WOLFE

In 1791, Congress passed a bill establishing the First Bank of the United States. The bank was proposed by Alexander Hamilton, passed over the constitutional objections of Thomas Jefferson and James Madison, and was signed into law by George Washington. That bank lasted until its charter expired in 1811 and, initially, was not renewed. The untoward consequences of the bank's demise led to the Second Bank of the United States, which passed Congress in 1815 and was signed into law by President James Madison.[1]

Maryland decided to tax this bank's bills in 1818.[2] James McCulloch, the cashier of the bank's Baltimore branch, refused to pay the tax, giving rise to *McCulloch v. Maryland*. After state courts upheld the tax, McCulloch appealed to the Supreme Court, which decided the case in 1819—just over 200 years ago.

In this chapter, I lay out the basics of Chief Justice John Marshall's opinion for the Court, in particular following his interpretation of the Constitution in the case. I then make observations on some key interpretive moves in the case and generally argue that Marshall's arguments are persuasive.

Marshall's *McCulloch* Opinion

Marshall's opinion for the Court, after reciting the facts, including the historical background, begins with a preliminary discussion regarding the rule of construction on the nature of the Constitution. The state of Maryland had argued that one should approach the interpretation of the

Constitution bearing in mind that the federal government (as we call it today) was a compact of states. Marshall responded that it was more than that: It was "emphatically and truly, a Government of the people. In form and in substance, it emanates from them. Its powers are granted by them, and are to be exercised directly on them, and for their benefit."[3] Marshall moved on to discuss the two key questions in the case: (1) Does Congress have the power to establish a national bank, and (2) can a state tax the operations of this federal instrumentality?

The Constitutionality of the National Bank

It is not immediately obvious why the first question is implicated by *McCulloch*. Presumably, the reason is that if Congress has no power to establish a national bank, the bank has no legal standing and does not derive any legal protection against state regulation from the Constitution.

Marshall began from the foundational principle that all accept: The federal government is a government of enumerated powers, not a government of general power. It cannot base its actions on the grounds that they are allegedly in the public interest in some indefinite way. The federal government's actions require some specific grounding in the powers granted by the Constitution.

But, Marshall said, "the question respecting the extent of the powers actually granted is perpetually arising, and will probably continue to arise so long as our system shall exist."[4] And, "in discussing these questions, the conflicting powers of the General and State Governments must be brought into view, and the supremacy of their respective laws, when they are in opposition, must be settled."[5] Marshall then invoked the principle "that the Government of the Union, though limited in its powers, is supreme within its sphere of action."[6]

There is no enumerated congressional power to establish a national bank, Marshall acknowledged. But that does not end the question. Marshall pointed to the absence in the Constitution (in the 10th Amendment) of any limitation of powers to those *expressly* delegated. This was probably omitted, he said, because of the embarrassments the framers experienced under the Articles of Confederation, and therefore whether a power has been delegated to the general government or reserved to the states is left to "a fair construction of the whole instrument."[7]

In one of his most famous passages, Marshall said:

> A Constitution, to contain an accurate detail of all the subdivisions of which its great powers will admit, and of all the means by which they may be carried into execution, would partake of the prolixity of a legal code, and could scarcely be embraced by the human mind. It would probably never be understood by the public. Its nature, therefore, requires that only its great outlines should be marked, its important objects designated, and the minor ingredients which compose those objects be deduced from the nature of the objects themselves.[8]

This principle is "not only to be inferred from the nature of the instrument"[9] but also supported by some specific limits on the federal government in Article 1, Section 9. Marshall had in mind, I think, something like the prohibition that "No Preference shall be given by any Regulation of Commerce or Revenue to the Ports of one State over those of another"[10]— a power that is not explicitly granted by the Constitution and is prohibited only because it would otherwise be an implied power respecting the enumerated power to regulate foreign and interstate commerce.[11]

Because the establishment of a national bank is not a specific or express enumerated power of the federal government, Marshall turned to the question of whether it is an implied power. In his discussion, he dealt (indirectly, without naming him) with Madison's argument (in the original debate on the bank) against considering the incorporation of a bank as an implied power, on the grounds that "the power of creating a corporation is one appertaining to sovereignty, and is not expressly conferred on Congress."[12] But Marshall argued:

> The power of creating a corporation, though appertaining to sovereignty, is not, like the power of making war or levying taxes or of regulating commerce, a great substantive and independent power which cannot be implied as incidental to other powers or used as a means of executing them. It is never the end for which other powers are exercised, but a means by which other objects are accomplished.[13]

To this point, Marshall's argument has been derived from general reasoning about the nature of the Constitution. But then he turned to the argument that the implied powers have not been left only to implication, since Congress has been given the power to pass "all Laws which shall be necessary and proper for carrying into Execution the foregoing Powers, and all other powers vested by this Constitution in the Government of the United States or in any department or Office thereof." Maryland had tried to enlist the necessary and proper clause in its own argument, especially by contending that this is a restriction of the power to legislate; it limits "the right to pass laws for the execution of the granted powers to such as are indispensable, and without which the power would be nugatory."[14]

Marshall began his response by noting that there are gradations of the meaning of "necessary" in common usage, proving this by reference to the use of the phrase "absolutely necessary" in Article 1, Section 10.[15] So, he concluded, it is necessary to construe the Constitution, to determine which meaning of necessary the framers intended. Appealing to common-law rules of interpretation, he said that, in doing this, "the subject, the context, the intention of the person using them are all to be taken into view."[16]

Marshall argued, "The subject is the execution of those great powers on which the welfare of a Nation essentially depends." This calls forth another of Marshall's most famous passages:

> It must have been the intention of those who gave these powers to insure, so far as human prudence could insure, their beneficial execution. This could not be done by confiding the choice of means to such narrow limits as not to leave it in the power of Congress to adopt any which might be appropriate, and which were conducive to the end. This provision is made in a Constitution intended to endure for ages to come, and consequently to be adapted to the various crises of human affairs. To have prescribed the means by which Government should, in all future time, execute its powers would have been to change entirely the character of the instrument and give it the properties of a legal code. It would have been an unwise attempt to provide by immutable rules for exigencies which, if foreseen at all, must have been seen dimly, and which can be best provided for as they occur. To have declared that the best means shall not be used, but

those alone without which the power given would be nugatory, would have been to deprive the legislature of the capacity to avail itself of experience, to exercise its reason, and to accommodate its legislation to circumstances.[17]

A narrow construction of the necessary and proper clause would "render[] the Government incompetent to its great objects," and Marshall provided several examples of this.[18] For example, there is no specific power to punish robbing the federal mail service, as there is for counterfeiting, and theoretically, a mail service would be possible without such federal punishment. And yet, that power is incidental and conducive to the exercise of the power to provide a federal mail service.

Marshall turned to context, noting the other words with which "necessary" is associated in the phrase. Regarding the word "proper," it would make no sense, he argued, if the word "necessary" were used in the strict sense for which Maryland contends "to add a word the only possible effect of which is to qualify that strict and rigorous meaning."[19]

Finally, Marshall turned to "the argument which most conclusively demonstrates the error of the construction contended for by the counsel for the State of Maryland"—namely, "the intention of the convention as manifested in the whole clause."[20] He emphasized two factors here. First, the placement of the clause (Article 1, Section 8) is among the powers of government, not—as would be more appropriate if Maryland were right that the use of the word "necessary" was to limit or restrict the powers of the general government—the limits on the powers of the federal government (which are contained in Article 1, Section 9). Second, the actual terms of the clause purport to enlarge, not diminish, government power. (For example, if Maryland were right, the appropriate terms would have been something like: "In carrying into execution the foregoing powers . . . no laws shall be passed but such as are necessary and proper."[21])

And so Marshall concluded the general discussion of the necessary and proper clause with:

Let the end be legitimate, let it be within the scope of the Constitution, and all means which are appropriate, which are plainly adapted to that end, which are not prohibited, but consist with the letter and spirit of the Constitution, are Constitutional.[22]

Marshall then applied the general principle to the questions of corporations and banks. He argued that there is nothing so special about a corporation that it needed to be specified.[23] Since it is considered not "a distinct and independent" power but "merely as a means, to be employed only for the purpose of carrying into execution the given powers,"[24] there was no reason to mention it particularly.

And there is no reason to exclude a bank as a means regarding the government's fiscal operations, since "that it is a convenient, a useful, and essential instrument in the prosecution of its fiscal operations is not now a subject of controversy. All those who have been concerned in the administration of our finances have concurred in representing its importance and necessity."[25]

Finally, Marshall concluded the first part of *McCulloch* by acknowledging the limits on Congress.

> Should Congress . . . under the pretext of executing its powers, pass laws for the accomplishment of objects not intrusted to the Government, it would become the painful duty of this tribunal, should a case requiring such a decision come before it, to say that such an act was not the law of the land. But where the law is not prohibited, and is really calculated to effect any of the objects intrusted to the Government, to undertake here to inquire into the decree of its necessity would be to pass the line which circumscribes the judicial department and to tread on legislative ground.[26]

(Marshall will have more to say on judicial determinations of "degree" later in the opinion, which I discuss below.)

The State's Power to Tax the Bank

Having defended Congress' power to establish the bank, Marshall turned to the second question: Can a state tax the Maryland branch of the bank? Marshall began by observing that the states, of course, retain a general power to tax under the Constitution. The power to tax is limited only insofar as the Constitution prohibits it or when, in its nature, it is incompatible with the union's constitutional laws. There is no explicit prohibition on states to tax a federal bank.

But the bank claims that the tax is precluded by a principle that pervades the whole Constitution—namely, that the Constitution and laws made in pursuance thereof are supreme. Marshall said that three corollaries are deduced from this principle: (1) the power to create implies the power to preserve; (2) the power to destroy, if wielded by a different hand, is hostile to and incompatible with the power to create and preserve; and (3) where this repugnancy exists, the supreme authority controls.

The power of taxing the bank may be exercised to destroy it (i.e., by a prohibitive tax). Maryland says that, short of an express prohibition, the power of taxation is left to the discretion of the sovereign state that exercises it. But, Marshall contended, it is clear that the Constitution does limit the power of taxation and "how far it has been controlled by that instrument must be a question of construction."[27] And supremacy demands that no construction "can be admissible which would defeat the legitimate operations of a supreme Government."[28] Maryland's argument is that the Constitution leaves the taxing power to the states, confident they will not abuse it.

Before taking up that argument, Marshall digressed into an examination of "the nature and extent of this original right of taxation, which is acknowledged to remain with the States."[29] He argued that the only security for its proper exercise (which is usually sufficient) is in the structure of government itself—namely, that the legislature is acting on its constituents, who exercise political control over it. So the people of the state give the state government power to tax themselves and their property.

But, Marshall pointed out, the means employed by the general government enjoy no such security from the states (since a given state's legislature is not subject to control by citizens in other states). So the states' right to tax a federal instrumentality is not sustained by the same theory. Those instruments or means are given by all people in the nation and should be subjected only to the government of all.

To the objection that state taxing power extends to not just citizens and their property but also any object brought within its jurisdiction, Marshall responded with a theory of taxation and sovereignty. "The sovereignty of a State extends to everything which exists by its own authority or is introduced by its permission," he said, but not to those "means which are employed by Congress to carry into execution powers conferred on that body by the people of the United States."[30]

In an important paragraph (which I will examine later), Marshall argued:

> If we measure the power of taxation residing in a State by the extent of sovereignty which the people of a single State possess and can confer on its Government, we have an intelligible standard, applicable to every case to which the power may be applied. We have a principle which leaves the power of taxing the people and property of a State unimpaired; which leaves to a State the command of all its resources, and which places beyond its reach all those powers which are conferred by the people of the United States on the Government of the Union, and all those means which are given for the purpose of carrying those powers into execution. We have a principle which is safe for the States and safe for the Union. We are relieved, as we ought to be, from clashing sovereignty; from interfering powers; from a repugnancy between a right in one Government to pull down what there is an acknowledged right in another to build up; from the incompatibility of a right in one Government to destroy what there is a right in another to preserve. We are not driven to the perplexing inquiry, so unfit for the judicial department, what degree of taxation is the legitimate use and what degree may amount to the abuse of the power.[31]

But then Marshall, after carefully proposing this theory, dismissed it, "waiving this theory for the present," to "resume the inquiry, whether this power [to tax federal instrumentalities] can be exercised by the respective States, consistently with a fair construction of the Constitution."[32]

Marshall returned to his earlier observation that "the power to tax involves the power to destroy" and therefore "may defeat and render useless the power to create," and "there is a plain repugnance in conferring on one Government a power to control the constitutional measures of another, which other, with respect to those very measures, is declared to be supreme over that which exerts the control."[33]

Marshall indulged in an unusual level of sarcasm in response to Maryland's argument: "But all inconsistencies are to be reconciled by the magic of the word CONFIDENCE" (in capital letters).[34] He asked whether the people of one state would let the people of another "control the most insignificant operations of their State Government."[35] Of course not. Why, then, would the people of the United States permit a single state to control an operation of the national government?

Only in the legislature of the union, which they control politically, would the people of the nation entrust control over the general government's operations. Maryland's interpretation, Marshall argued, would leave the possibility that the general government can be prostrated at the foot of states and that the power to tax could be used to defeat all ends of the general government. Moreover, if state supremacy regarding taxation is acknowledged, what about other operations (e.g., the mail, the custom house, and the judicial process)?

Marshall pointed out the argument does not work the other way: There is no constitutional principle that would prohibit federal taxation of state banks. That case is essentially different because all states are represented in Congress (while people outside a given state are not represented in a state legislature). There is a difference between the action of a whole on a part and the action of a part on the whole, and there is a difference between a supreme government and one that is not supreme.

Marshall concluded that the supremacy declared by the Constitution means that "the States have no power, by taxation or otherwise, to retard, impede, burden, or in any manner control the operations of the constitutional laws enacted by Congress to carry into execution the powers vested in the General Government."[36] So, the Maryland tax was unconstitutional.

Having given a broad argument against state taxation of federal instruments, Marshall walked it back a bit at the end of his opinion by making some important distinctions. Does Marshall's argument imply that a state tax on bank property, in common with all other property in the state, or a tax on Maryland citizens' interest from the bank would be unconstitutional? No. Because in those cases, the equality of property taxes imposed on state and federal property, or taxes on interest from the bank, means that the desired political check on the state legislature is in place—because the citizens of the state, in protecting their own rights, will protect the federal instrumentality from abusive state regulation as well.

Marshall's Constitutional Interpretation in *McCulloch*

In the second half of this chapter, I do three things: first, make some observations regarding the character and implications of Marshall's approach to constitutional interpretation in *McCulloch*; second, take up some of the criticisms of his constitutional interpretation; and third, briefly discuss whether, or in what sense, Marshall can be considered a "judicial activist."

***McCulloch* and Two Kinds of Constitutional Interpretation.** I want to begin my observations about Marshall's constitutional interpretation by examining a paragraph from the second part of Marshall's opinion in *McCulloch*, in which he argued:

> If we measure the power of taxation residing in a State by the extent of sovereignty which the people of a single State possess and can confer on its Government, we have an intelligible standard, applicable to every case to which the power may be applied. . . . We are relieved, as we ought to be, from clashing sovereignty; from interfering powers; from a repugnancy between a right in one Government to pull down what there is an acknowledged right in another to build up; from the incompatibility of a right in one Government to destroy what there is a right in another to preserve. We are not driven to the perplexing inquiry, so unfit for the judicial department, what degree of taxation is the legitimate use and what degree may amount to the abuse of the power.[37]

What Marshall said here helps explain some of the deep differences between traditional (pre-1890) and modern (post-1937) judicial review.[38] Why is the "degree of taxation" that is legitimate or an abuse a "perplexing inquiry" that is "so unfit for the judicial department"?

Why would Marshall even raise this question? One possible argument in defense of state taxes on federal instrumentalities might have been that, surely, relatively minor taxes that did not obstruct the operation of the federal instrumentalities were not constitutionally objectionable. Only if the taxing power were abused—by imposing a tax that obstructed federal action—would a problem arise.

This argument could have been taken in several different directions. Maryland could have said, as it did in *McCulloch*, that the Constitution simply had "confidence" that the states would not abuse their powers.[39] Marshall, of course, lavished some pretty heavy sarcasm on that contention. Alternatively, it might have been argued that judges could strike down taxes that abused the taxing power, leaving intact those that did not.

But Marshall thought the question about the degree of taxing that is legitimate or an abuse is not fit for judges. Why?

I think Marshall said this because judges, in deciding such questions of degree, would receive no guidance from the law or the Constitution. What would guide the judges in making such a judgment? Basically, they would have to make a judgment about what was "too big" a tax because it obstructed the action of the bank and what was OK because it did not obstruct it. But that is fundamentally a policy judgment, not a legal one. That is why it is so "perplexing" for the judges and so "unfit" for them.[40]

In ordinary common-law cases, judges sometimes did have to make such judgments.[41] But in those cases, judges were not employing the extraordinary power of judicial review—striking down laws or acts of the representatives in a democratic republic. There was general agreement in the early years of American government that such a power ought to be used rarely (if at all) and only when necessary, when a law clearly or manifestly violated the Constitution. But when the question was fundamentally one of degree—how big a tax had to be before it was an abuse—there would typically be no clarity. To wade into that morass of often arbitrary line drawing would be imprudent for judges.

So judges in the early, or traditional, era of American judicial review preferred to find an "intelligible standard," which usually was a question of evaluating the constitutional status of different *kinds* of power. That is why Marshall thinks the line could be drawn more clearly by relying on a theory of taxation—namely, that states could tax those objects over which they exercised sovereignty. But, at the same time—perhaps from the awareness of the controversial character of that theory—Marshall opted to rely on the principle that "the power to tax involves the power to destroy" and the idea that decisions about which taxes were destructive, and which were not, were not appropriate for judges to make.

I think Marshall's argument about the potential for questions of degree to force judges into making policy decisions rather than legal decisions has been borne out in US history, precisely because legal theorists and judges came to reject that approach and to institute a new, essentially different form of judicial review that entrusted judges precisely with questions of degree.

The rejection of Marshall's dictum in *McCulloch* that "the power to tax is the power to destroy"[42] is explicit in the justice who was the progenitor of the modern approach to judicial review, Justice Oliver Wendell Holmes Jr. Holmes argued, in a dissent in *Panhandle Oil Co. v. Miss. ex Rel. Knox* (in which the Court struck down application of a state gasoline tax to federal instrumentalities, such as the Coast Guard):

> It seems to me that the state court was right [in upholding the state tax]. I should say plainly right but for the effect of certain dicta of Chief Justice John Marshall which culminated in or rather were founded upon his often quoted proposition that the power to tax is the power to destroy. In those days it was not recognized as it is today that most of the distinctions of law are distinctions of degree. If the States had any power it was assumed that they had all power, and that the necessary alternative was to deny it altogether. But, this Court, which so often has defeated the attempt to tax in certain ways, can defeat an attempt to discriminate or otherwise go too far without wholly abolishing the power to tax. The power to tax is not the power to destroy while this Court sits.[43]

Holmes treats Marshall's opinion as the reflection of an earlier, more naive, and less sophisticated understanding of judicial power, one that simply "failed to recognize" that most legal distinctions are distinctions of degree. He is entirely comfortable with courts that "sit" to make these determinations of degree.[44]

As Holmes says, in the modern era, judges have no hesitation about deciding questions of degree. In fact, the most characteristic form of judicial review in the modern era is one that essentially depends on deciding such questions. Using the term in a broad sense (not in the narrow sense associated with Justice Felix Frankfurter), I think the typical modern form of judicial review is "balancing." The judge begins by identifying some broad general principle in the Constitution: liberty in the due process clause, equality in the equal protection clause, free exercise of religion, and so forth. None of these are absolute, of course. They are effectively broad presumptions in favor of the principles (liberty, equality, freedom of religion, etc.).

On the other side are the asserted state interests in limiting the presumption: It might be, for example, a state interest in educating children, in a case involving Amish refusal to send their children to high schools, as required by Wisconsin's compulsory education law.[45] The judge then has to evaluate (1) how much the state law impinges on the presumptive constitutional principle, (2) the importance or weight of the countervailing state interest, and (3) whether state interest outweighs the presumption.

Such a process is replete with judgments about degrees: How much is the presumptive constitutional value impinged on? (A lot? A little? In between?) How significant is the state interest? (Compelling? Important? Not so much?) In the end, the process actually parallels many judgments that one would expect, or hope, to find in the legislative process. But contemporary legal theorists and judges have a pretty low opinion of legislators, at least when civil liberties and equality are involved.[46]

This modern process cannot, in my opinion, reasonably be described as "interpretation of the Constitution." It is, more accurately, "specification of allegedly vague constitutional generalities or presumptions." It is effectively a new kind of power, a form of modern judicial legislation. And this is a point on which Justice Holmes—and most contemporary legal theorists, I think—would have no hesitation in concurring.

Judges using this approach today to strike down many laws, however, have to be a bit more circumspect about such politically charged assertions.[47] But the word is out, which is why the judicial confirmation process looks the way it does. It is unfortunate that the American legal profession ultimately turned its back on Marshall's prudent understanding of the limits of judicial power, embodied in his dictum in *McCulloch* that questions of degree are "so unfit for the judicial department."[48]

Criticisms of Marshall's Opinion

I want to turn briefly to two critiques of Marshall's opinion in this volume.

The Third Hand Clapping: Madison. Michael Zuckert takes James Madison's side in the congressional debate with Hamilton (and, by extension, Marshall) over establishing a national bank. Zuckert's main argument is that, according to Madison, Hamilton (and Marshall) said the bank is constitutional because it is a means to the objects of the general government, rather than focusing on whether it is a means to an enumerated power. The point is that the objects are broader and would authorize the general government to do more than what it could do if it confined itself to effectuating the enumerated powers.[49]

I do think the general objects of government lie in the background (or, in a sense, in the foreground, given the preamble) and may have some bearing on constitutional interpretation. For example, I think they support Marshall's description of the "subject matter" of the necessary and proper clause: "the execution of those great powers on which the welfare of a Nation essentially depends."[50] And I agree that laws have to be necessary and proper to carry out enumerated powers, not the general objects of the national government. I do not think, however, that Hamilton and Marshall tried to justify the national bank constitutionally by appealing to those general objects *independent of the enumerated powers*.

I think Madison's main argument against the bank rests on a distinction between merely "technical" means, which he seems to regard as uncontroversial, and "a distinct, an independent and substantive prerogative," such as a corporation (or at least this corporation).[51] But I believe this is a distinction that Madison read into the Constitution—except to the extent that he and Marshall agreed about the unconstitutionality of an alleged means that is not "plainly adapted to that end."[52] I think what Marshall meant by not "plainly adapted to that end" is what is not adapted to the end of carrying out the *enumerated powers*, not what might further the general objects of government *independent of* those enumerated powers. When Marshall said, "Let the end be legitimate,"[53] I do not think he was talking about the general objects of the Constitution (apart from the enumerated powers), but rather the objects *implicit in* the enumerated powers.

For example, Hamilton said in his opinion concerning the constitutionality of the national bank:

> It shall now be endeavored to be shown that there is a power to erect one of the kind [of corporations] proposed by the bill. This will be done by tracing *a natural and obvious relation between the institution of a bank and the objects of several of the enumerated powers of the government*; and by showing that, politically speaking, it is necessary to the effectual execution of one or more of those powers.[54] (Emphasis added.)

So the real difference between Hamilton and Marshall and Madison is whether the national bank is genuinely a means—a means plainly adapted—to carrying out the enumerated powers of the national government. That is an argument that Hamilton made powerfully, and perhaps that is why Marshall spent less time on it in his own opinion in *McCulloch*. Between Hamilton's opinion to Washington and the history of the bank, including the embarrassments resulting from the failure to renew it, Marshall thought the answer was plain.

> That [the bank] is a convenient, a useful, and essential instrument in the prosecution of [the government's] fiscal operations is not now a subject of controversy. All those who have been concerned in the administration of our finances have concurred in representing its importance and necessity.[55]

The reference to government's "fiscal operations" is a reference to the enumerated powers: especially "to lay and collect taxes, duties, imposts and excises, to pay the debts and provide for the common defense and general welfare of the United States" and "to borrow money on the credit of the United States."[56] Hamilton laid out at some length, in his opinion on the bank, the arguments for the importance of a bank as a means to collecting taxes and borrowing money. These may be right or wrong, as a matter of policy, but the constitutional question is whether they show that there is a plain adaptation of this end (the bank) to these enumerated powers (collecting taxes and borrowing money). I think Hamilton's argument is compelling.

The Destructive Legacy of McCulloch? Nelson Lund argues: "*McCulloch* was used to justify expanding federal power far beyond its proper constitutional bounds. Although Marshall's opinion lends itself to this use, the decision need not and should not be relied on as a precedent for such expansion."[57]

I could not agree with him more that the decision need not be used as a precedent for expanding federal power beyond its proper constitutional bounds—though I do not think "the opinion lends itself to this use."

Lund quotes Marshall in an earlier case, *US v. Fisher*.

> Congress must possess the choice of means, and must be empowered to use any means which are in fact conducive to the exercise of a power granted by the constitution.
>
> The government is to pay the debt of the union, and must be authorized to use the means which appear to itself most eligible to effect that object.[58]

Lund's response is: "Any means at all, no matter how unnecessary or improper they may be?"[59] To which I think Marshall would say: "Yes—because the judge has no legitimate power to evaluate how necessary or proper a means is. That discretion is left to Congress. The judge's discretion would go no further than evaluating whether a given means is 'plainly adapted' to a constitutional power."[60]

McCulloch, Lund believes, is somewhat more circumspect. But in the end, it still is too open-ended: "Marshall could be seen as suggesting . . . that the Court should rubber-stamp congressional exercises of power whenever there has not been 'a bold and plain usurpation.'"[61]

Actually, except for the pejorative language of "rubber-stamp," I think that has it just about right. Lund goes on to say:

> But there were some obvious reasons for doubting that this particular bank law was consistent with the spirit of the Constitution. The *McCulloch* opinion never mentions that Congress had not established a government agency but instead had incorporated an essentially private bank controlled by private shareholders who

sought profits for themselves. That institution, moreover, was given competitive advantages over state banks.

Shouldn't the Second Bank's lawyers at least have been required to justify these features of the law, perhaps with evidence that the government's ability to carry out its legitimate functions was threatened by deficiencies in the existing banks? And how did the Court know that the Second Bank was structured to serve the government's interests rather than a pretext to enrich the private shareholders? For example, did the bank's practice of establishing branches anywhere it chose serve any real purpose other than increasing private profits?[62]

I think Marshall would say these are *precisely* the things judges should *not* be considering in their evaluation of a case. Why should *Supreme Court justices* be evaluating whether Congress should have created a government agency rather than a private bank? Why should they evaluate "evidence that the government's ability to carry out its legitimate functions was threatened by deficiencies of existing banks?"[63] On what grounds should Supreme Court justices be evaluating whether "the Second Bank was structured to serve the government's interests rather than a pretext to enrich the private shareholders?" These are all important questions that the democratic representatives in Congress needed to consider. But I think they are a far distance from the legal judgments that judges should be making.

According to Lund, judges should be making those evaluations instead of "expatiating without any clear necessity on the political theory of the union."[64] But the political theory of the union, as embodied in the document, is what judges need to understand to interpret the Constitution. As Marshall says in *Gibbons v. Ogden*, there were people who wanted to render the Constitution inadequate to its purposes by reading it narrowly, against the fair reading of the document. Political theory matters.

Lund also attacks the second half of *McCulloch*, regarding Maryland's power to tax the national bank's notes.

Marshall seemed to think it was obvious that Maryland's tax violated the statute establishing the bank. That conclusion was not even close to being evident. The statute did not address the permissibility of

state taxes one way or the other, and Marshall offered no argument
for inferring that this tax was forbidden.[65]

Marshall may not have offered as detailed or effective an answer as
he could have, but it can hardly be said that he offered no argument. He
argued that national laws, such as the Constitution, were "supreme" and
that supremacy was incompatible with leaving to another hand (a potentially hostile one) the power to destroy the national government's instrumentalities. And everyone in America knew this was precisely the situation
in the bank dispute (though Maryland may actually have been one of the
more moderate states in its taxation). There was widespread hostility to
the national bank (and banks in general) at this time, and Marshall certainly had reasonable grounds to fear that the power to tax could be used
to destroy.

Should Marshall have issued an opinion simply indicating that Congress had the power to exempt its instrumentalities from taxation, rather
than one striking down this form of state taxation? This reminds me of
the Paperwork Reduction Act, which requires the federal government to
include statements about the act in its forms that waste a great deal of
paper and ink. Yes, Marshall could have required Congress to include in
all its legislation an explicit statement regarding the unconstitutionality of
state taxes on each federal instrumentality. But putting the onus, instead,
on Congress to anticipate, discover, and respond to state legislation hostile to federal laws (especially given the power of even minorities in Congress to stall or block legislation to undo mischievous state action) seems
unnecessary and not the ordinary implication of "supremacy."[66]

Marshall's discussion of the power to tax ultimately rejects the broad
assertion that all state taxes are unconstitutional. He readily concedes that
state taxes that apply evenhandedly to state and federal property are per-
fectly legitimate because there is an inherent check to prevent that kind of
tax from being used to undermine federal supremacy.

Lund's challenge to *McCulloch* ends with a lengthy description of modern Court decisions, and I concur with him in rejecting many of them,
especially those involving judicial inventions of new rights. I am much less
sure, given modern economic realities (that is, how little truly intrastate
commerce there is anymore), than he is that judges can find a judicially

manageable standard for intervention in commerce clause cases, at least those that actually involve commerce.

But there is one area where we particularly agree: that legislators have as much an obligation to enforce constitutional limits as judges do—and they (unlike judges) are not constrained by the requirement of avoiding questions of degree and the policymaking implicit in them, since that is their job. Whether or not there are judicially manageable standards for effectively limiting the federal government's power regarding most commercial activities, a conscientious legislator today, attuned to the importance of federalism in our Constitution, should often oppose, on *constitutional* grounds, legislation allegedly based on the commerce clause.[67]

Was Marshall an Activist Judge?

I think most scholars regard Marshall as a quintessentially activist judge, one who, in his opinions, read his Federalist principles into the Constitution. I want to make some distinctions about what it means to be an activist judge.[68]

One definition of judicial activism (generally along the lines of the constitutional theory of the "traditional era," of which Marshall is a great representative) is based on the relationship of the judicial interpreter to the constitutional text. An interpreter can either adhere to the text or treat it as a set of highly general presumptions requiring specification. The latter can also be thought of as the Constitution delegating a great deal of power to judges to fill in the content of constitutional principles. In this case, the interpreter moves beyond "interpretation" to some form of judicial legislation, which is a form of judicial activism.

With this definition of judicial activism, I believe that Marshall was not an activist. He adopted rules of construction that aimed to discern the legal principles in the constitutional text, with a view to maintaining a fidelity to the Constitution's principles.[69] If Marshall gave a Federalist reading of the Constitution, it was because the Constitution is a Federalist document.

Another idea of activism is quite different, focusing not so much on constitutional interpretation as on various features of judging. Several (overlapping) examples would include (1) the practice of writing opinions broader than is required to decide the case, (2) the extent to which a judge relies on and defers to precedent, and (3) the weight a judge gives to "case and controversy" questions (e.g., standing, political questions, ripeness, and mootness) and other procedural questions.

With this understanding of judicial activism, Marshall was certainly an activist in various ways. For example, he would sometimes offer an extensive analysis of one ground for deciding the case and then decide the case on a different (often much narrower) ground. For example, in *Gibbons v. Ogden* he undertook a lengthy discussion of the idea of "exclusivity" of the power to regulate interstate commerce (which precluded state regulation, even without federal regulation) and then decided the case on a much narrower ground—that is, that New York's regulation was inconsistent with a congressional statute.[70]

In *McCulloch*, as noted above, Marshall went into an extensive discussion of a particular theory of taxation (states could tax things over which they are sovereign) and then, "waiving this theory," decided the case on other grounds. And, of course, most famously, in *Marbury v. Madison*, he discussed the merits of Marbury's claim extensively before ruling that the Court had no jurisdiction.[71]

Marshall's penchant for broad opinions (including his opinion in *McCulloch*) stemmed from his sense that the United States was a young nation and that the principles of the Constitution (as he understood them—rightly, in my opinion) were still not broadly understood and accepted, and they were therefore vulnerable to being undermined. The classic statement of this concern is found at the end of *Gibbons v. Ogden*, where he said:

> Powerful and ingenious minds, taking as postulates that the powers expressly granted to the government of the Union are to be contracted by construction into the narrowest possible compass and that the original powers of the States are retained if any possible construction will retain them may, by a course of well digested but refined and metaphysical reasoning founded on these premises, explain away the Constitution of our country and leave it a magnificent structure indeed to look at, but totally unfit for use. They may so entangle and

perplex the understanding as to obscure principles which were before thought quite plain, and induce doubts where, if the mind were to pursue its own course, none would be perceived. In such a case, it is peculiarly necessary to recur to safe and fundamental principles to sustain those principles, and when sustained, to make them the tests of the arguments to be examined.[72]

This quotation captures Marshall's stance in *McCulloch v. Maryland*, a case in which he likewise provided extensive reasoning that, from his perspective, was necessary to not only understand the Constitution but also defend it.

Notes

1. James Madison had not changed his opinion on the abstract question of the bank's constitutionality, but he defended his acquiescence to the bill on the grounds of his unchanging sentiment that constitutional questions could be settled by government practice.

2. The law required that banks "without authority from the state" issue notes on only stamped paper provided by the state ($5 notes had a stamp of 10 cents, and stamps ranged up to $20 for a $1,000 note) or, in lieu of using the stamped paper, pay an annual tax of $15,000 (about $300,000 in 2019 dollars). Alfred Beveridge, *The Life of John Marshall* (Boston, MA: Houghton Mifflin Company, 1919), vol. IV, 283. A state official sued McCulloch for recovery of the draconian penalties ($500 for each offense, for each officer of the bank, and for anyone helping circulate the notes) for violating this law.

3. *McCulloch v. Maryland*, 17 US 316 (1819).

4. *McCulloch v. Maryland*, 17 US 316 (1819).

5. *McCulloch v. Maryland*, 17 US 316 (1819).

6. *McCulloch v. Maryland*, 17 US 316 (1819).

7. *McCulloch v. Maryland*, 17 US 316 (1819).

8. *McCulloch v. Maryland*, 17 US 316 (1819).

9. *McCulloch v. Maryland*, 17 US 316 (1819).

10. US Const. art. I, § 9.

11. US Const. art. I, § 9.

12. *McCulloch v. Maryland*, 17 US 316 (1819).

13. *McCulloch v. Maryland*, 17 US 316 (1819).

14. *McCulloch v. Maryland*, 17 US 316 (1819).

15. "No State shall, without the Consent of the Congress, lay any Imposts or Duties on Imports or Exports, except what may be absolutely necessary for executing it's inspection Laws." US Const. art. I, § 10.

16. *McCulloch v. Maryland*, 17 US 316 (1819).

17. *McCulloch v. Maryland*, 17 US 316 (1819).

18. *McCulloch v. Maryland*, 17 US 316 (1819).

19. *McCulloch v. Maryland*, 17 US 316 (1819).

20. *McCulloch v. Maryland*, 17 US 316 (1819).

21. In trying to discern intent, Marshall does not go to sources extrinsic to the Constitution, such as convention records, papers and letters of the framers, and so forth. He focuses primarily on the Constitution's text, rather than engaging in historical research of external sources, as some originalists have (e.g., Raoul Berger's detailed analysis of the records of the Congress that produced the 14th Amendment). Raoul Berger, *Government by Judiciary* (Indianapolis, IN: Liberty Fund, 1997).

22. *McCulloch v. Maryland*, 17 US 316 (1819).

23. "That a corporation must be considered as a means not less usual, not of higher dignity, not more requiring a particular specification than other means has been sufficiently proved. If we look to the origin of corporations, to the manner in which they have been framed in that Government from which we have derived most of our legal principles and ideas, or to the uses to which they have been applied, we find no reason to suppose that a Constitution, omitting, and wisely omitting, to enumerate all the means for carrying into execution the great powers vested in Government, ought to have specified this." *McCulloch v. Maryland*, 17 US 316 (1819).

24. *McCulloch v. Maryland*, 17 US 316 (1819).

25. *McCulloch v. Maryland*, 17 US 316 (1819).

26. *McCulloch v. Maryland*, 17 US 316 (1819).

27. *McCulloch v. Maryland*, 17 US 316 (1819).

28. *McCulloch v. Maryland*, 17 US 316 (1819).

29. *McCulloch v. Maryland*, 17 US 316 (1819).

30. *McCulloch v. Maryland*, 17 US 316 (1819).

31. *McCulloch v. Maryland*, 17 US 316 (1819).

32. *McCulloch v. Maryland*, 17 US 316 (1819).

33. *McCulloch v. Maryland*, 17 US 316 (1819).

34. *McCulloch v. Maryland*, 17 US 316 (1819).

35. *McCulloch v. Maryland*, 17 US 316 (1819).

36. *McCulloch v. Maryland*, 17 US 316 (1819).

37. *McCulloch v. Maryland*, 17 US 316 (1819).

38. The 1890–1937 period is a transitional period, in which the Court's actual approach to constitutional interpretation and judicial review had changed fundamentally but without any explicit understanding of, or theory of, that change. See Christopher Wolfe, *The Rise of Modern Judicial Review: From Judicial Interpretation to Judge-Made Law* (New York: Basic Books, 1986), Part Two.

39. *McCulloch v. Maryland*, 17 US 316 (1819).

40. This same argument is actually made by Marshall in the first part of *McCulloch* as well, when referring to the bank as a necessary means: "But were its necessity less apparent, none can deny its being an appropriate measure; and if it is, *the decree of its necessity, as has been very justly observed, is to be discussed in another place.* Should Congress . . . under the pretext of executing its powers, pass laws for the accomplishment of objects not intrusted to the Government, it would become the painful duty of this

tribunal, should a case requiring such a decision come before it, to say that such an act was not the law of the land. But where the law is not prohibited, and is really calculated to effect any of the objects intrusted to the Government, *to undertake here to inquire into the decree of its necessity would be to pass the line which circumscribes the judicial department and to tread on legislative ground.*" (Emphasis added.) *McCulloch v. Maryland,* 17 US 316, 423 (1819).

41. For the record, it could also happen in some constitutional questions—those concerning constitutional provisions that explicitly involve questions of degree (e.g., excessive bail or just compensation). Those questions tended to be particularized ones, and it is also unclear how readily traditional judges would have overridden legislative standards for such issues.

42. *McCulloch v. Maryland,* 17 US 316 (1819).

43. *Panhandle Oil Co. v. Miss. ex Rel Knox,* 227 US 218, 223 (1928).

44. For the record, I think Marshall, like Oliver Wendell Holmes, would also have dissented in that case, for the same reason that he goes on in *McCulloch* to say that a state property tax applied to the bank's property, in common with state property, would not be constitutionally objectionable. The application of a property tax had a political corrective built into it: If the property tax were abused, the abuse would fall on state and federal property, and the voters of the state could rein in the abuse. Likewise, a state gasoline tax applied equally to state citizens and federal instrumentalities had that built-in corrective to prevent abuse. So there was something that prevented *that* tax from being a power to destroy.

45. *Wisconsin v. Yoder,* 406 US 205 (1972).

46. It will be interesting to see whether, or how much, in our own era, more conservative judges will share an equally low opinion of legislators when economic or property rights are involved—as they once did, during the transitional era of judicial review from 1890 to 1937.

47. One of the factors that disguised the activist potential of Holmes' approach to judging was that he used it primarily to justify *deferring* to legislatures regarding new economic and industrial regulation in his time.

48. *McCulloch v. Maryland,* 17 US 316 (1819).

49. This is a passage from Madison on this point: "He here adverted to a distinction, which he said had not been sufficiently kept in view, between a power necessary and proper for the government or union, and a power necessary and proper for executing the enumerated powers. In the latter case, the powers included in each of the enumerated powers were not expressed, but to be drawn from the nature of each. In the former, the powers composing the government were expressly enumerated. This constituted the peculiar nature of the government, no power therefore not enumerated, could be inferred from the general nature of government. Had the power of making treaties, for example, been omitted, however necessary it might have been, the defect could only have been lamented, or supplied by an amendment of the constitution." James Madison, "The Bank Bill," National Archives, Founders Online, February 2, 1791, https:// founders.archives.gov/documents/Madison/01-13-02-0282. While it is a side issue, I think that Madison's contention that, if the treaty power had been omitted, the defect could only have been lamented (or added by amendment) must be wrong. It is good

that the Constitution provided for the treaty power because it involved complicated separation of powers questions—the relation between the executive and legislature in treaty matters. But, without a specific treaty power in the Constitution, the general government would have had that power simply by being a government, under the law of nations. As the Declaration of Independence says, "As Free and Independent States, they [the United States of America] have full Power to levy War, conclude Peace, contract Alliances."

50. *McCulloch v. Maryland*, 17 US 316 (1819).

51. "From this view of the power of incorporation exercised in the bill, it could never be deemed an accessary or subaltern power, to be deduced by implication, as a means of executing another power; it was in its nature a distinct, an independent and substantive prerogative, which not being enumerated in the constitution could never have been meant to be included in it, and not being included could never be rightfully exercised." Madison, "The Bank Bill."

52. *McCulloch v. Maryland*, 17 US 316 (1819).

53. *McCulloch v. Maryland*, 17 US 316 (1819).

54. Alexander Hamilton, "Opinion as to the Constitutionality of the Bank of the United States," Yale Law School, Avalon Project, http://avalon.law.yale.edu/18th_century/bank-ah.asp.

55. *McCulloch v. Maryland*, 17 US 316 (1819).

56. *McCulloch v. Maryland*, 17 US 316 (1819).

57. Nelson Lund, "The Destructive Legacy of *McCulloch v. Maryland*," in *McCulloch v. Maryland at 200*, ed. Gary J. Schmitt and Rebecca Burgess (Washington, DC: AEI Press, 2020).

58. *United States v. Fisher*, 6 US 358, 396 (1805).

59. Lund, "The Destructive Legacy of *McCulloch v. Maryland*."

60. Lund says, Marshall did, in fact, think that judges should consider the necessity and propriety of the means: "The court may be mistaken in the 'propriety and necessity' of [the bank]. I do not think so; but others may honestly entertain this opinion." Gerald Gunther, ed., *John Marshall's Defense of McCulloch v. Maryland* (Palo Alto, CA: Stanford University Press, 1969), 190. I think this refers not to the *specific* question of whether a bank is the necessary or proper means but to the more circumscribed question of whether it is a means "plainly adapted" to the end; that is, it is a bank in the broad general category of means that can be considered to be reasonably related to the end (leaving to Congress the decision as to whether this is the best means—necessary and proper—to achieve the end in these circumstances). I think that is more a legal judgment than a policy judgment.

61. Lund, "The Destructive Legacy of *McCulloch v. Maryland*."

62. Lund, "The Destructive Legacy of *McCulloch v. Maryland*."

63. Lund, "The Destructive Legacy of *McCulloch v. Maryland*."

64. Lund, "The Destructive Legacy of *McCulloch v. Maryland*."

65. Lund, "The Destructive Legacy of *McCulloch v. Maryland*."

66. Citing this sentence, Lund says: "Christopher Wolfe argues that Congress alone may decide questions that arise under the necessary and proper clause because judges are unfit to make decisions that involve questions of degree. But he thinks that courts

are permitted to decide which taxes states may impose on federal instrumentalities." That is true, but I also indicate that judges should avoid questions of degree regarding the state taxation and implied powers issues. A judge's job is not to consider policy questions of degree but only legal questions regarding the inherent compatibility of certain state action with the principle of federal supremacy.

67. For more on this approach, see Christopher Wolfe, "The Contemporary Supreme Court and Federalism," in *Federalism and the Constitution: A Symposium on Garcia* (Washington, DC: Advisory Commission on Intergovernmental Relations, 1987).

68. This section draws on arguments I made in Christopher Wolfe, *Judicial Activism*, revised ed. (Lanham, MD: Rowman & Littlefield, 1997), 2–5, 30–31.

69. One can take this view of Marshall even if one does not accept all his constitutional arguments or decisions. Originalists, in good faith, can come to different conclusions about some constitutional issues. For example, Marshall and Bushrod Washington, who were generally quite close in their constitutional interpretation, differed in *Ogden v. Saunders* on certain bankruptcy laws (and I incline to side with Washington on that issue).

70. *Gibbons V. Ogden*, 22 US 1 (1824).

71. Lund also gives an example of this argument. Noting that Marshall cites President Madison's signing of the second bank bill, Lund says: "Instead, Marshall went on to discuss the *hypothetical* case that would have been presented 'were the question entirely new.' Thus, he unnecessarily opened up questions that he then declined to address. This made for a much *broader* ruling than the case required according to Marshall's own analysis."

72. *Gibbons v. Ogden*, 22 US 1, 222 (1824).

4

"A Friend of the Constitution": John Marshall's Defense of *McCulloch v. Maryland*

ROBERT WEBKING

The Supreme Court's decision in *McCulloch v. Maryland* was delivered on March 6, 1819. Immediately, it was highly controversial because of the result: It permitted the Second Bank of the United States, an institution many at the time hated and feared. In Virginia, the strongest criticisms were not about the bank itself, but about the reasoning the Court used in reaching its unanimous decision. Chief Justice John Marshall wrote to his colleague Joseph Story that "the opinion on the Bank case has brought into operation the whole antifederal spirit of Virginia."[1]

This spirit took to the newspapers in two sets of essays, the first written by Virginia Judge William Brokenbrough under the pseudonym "Amphicytion" and the second, lengthier, more formidable, and more harshly critical by "Hampden," who was Spencer Roane, the most prominent judge on the Virginia Court of Appeals and an important Republican leader in the state. Marshall thought the essays were intended to "excite ferment" among the people and the Virginia legislature to harm the national judiciary and to impair the Constitution. They "grossly misrepresented" the opinion in the case and opposed its argument with, as Marshall saw it, "principles one would think too palpably absurd for intelligent men." But since "prejudice will swallow anything," Marshall found them dangerous.[2]

Fearing that the decision in *McCulloch v. Maryland* and the principles of the government under the Constitution on which it was based would go undefended against these attacks, Marshall took the extraordinary step of responding anonymously in the papers. His first effort as "A Friend to the Union" was to refute Amphicytion. Marshall wrote two essays that appeared in the *Philadelphia Union* in April 1819. Unfortunately, portions of these essays were mixed up in the publication, so neither seemed to be quite coherent and could not create the response Marshall intended.

When the stronger challenge came from Hampden in June, Marshall determined to respond again and waited until all four of Hampden's papers had been published to answer with nine of his own, placed in the *Alexandria Gazette* in June and July. My interest here is with Marshall's essays under the pseudonym "A Friend of the Constitution." Motivated by Hampden's relentless push to weaken the Constitution and reestablish confederacy, Marshall clarified and elaborated on the reasoning for the decision in *McCulloch v. Maryland*, and, in so doing, at times, challenged generally accepted beliefs on what the decision was about. Ultimately, his defense of that reasoning became a defense of the Constitution itself.

Introductions

Hampden's first essay about the Court's reasoning in *McCulloch v. Maryland* set out the issue and its importance and explained what was to come. It was a "most momentous subject" involving a threat to the very existence of the state governments and, therefore, to the American people's happiness.[3] Warfare was being conducted by the general government against the state governments, and it was taking a bolder and much more serious turn with the Supreme Court's decision in *McCulloch v. Maryland*.

Hampden was unrestrained in his language. He noted how the Court's decision was a coup de main, a sudden surprise attack that could succeed in a single blow to "tread under foot" all the limits in the Constitution to the powers of the federal legislature. The decision went far beyond the particular abuse of power that might have come from failing to rule the national bank unconstitutional and asserted a "general power of attorney" for Congress to violate state rights. Hampden reminded the public, quoting the well-known words from the Declaratory Act, that it was the British claim that Parliament could "legislate for us in all cases whatsoever" that made the people come together and act against the "British tyrant."[4]

He continued, ominously, to warn that "such a declaration is now at hand" in the Court's opinion in *McCulloch v. Maryland*. And he reminded his readers of the Declaration of Independence's statement that "all experience hath shewn that mankind are more disposed to suffer while evils are sufferable" to suggest that just as that point had been passed when the Revolution came, so it was passed again with *McCulloch v. Maryland.*[5] If the Pennsylvania farmer, in pointing out the grave danger of the Declaratory Act, began the process that ended in revolution, Hampden saw himself as taking the first steps to oust a new tyrant.

Marshall, as A Friend of the Constitution, responded to Hampden's first essay in kind. Although he waited until all of Hampden's essays appeared before publishing a response, Marshall went through them in order from first to last. He sought to grab the public's attention with forceful words, in this case about the great danger posed to their happiness and to the maintenance of their country by Hampden's incendiary writings. Where his opponent held up a usurping tyrannical general government, A Friend of the Constitution saw a government created by the people for their prosperity and happiness and succeeding. Opponents of that government were driven by the "unfounded jealousies" and "vindictive hate" of the defeated opponents of ratification of the Constitution.[6] They attacked the government of the union, aiming their assault at its weakest department, the judiciary.

The goal was to strip the government of its powers and to reestablish the confederation by construction of the Constitution. In doing its proper work, the Supreme Court could support the Constitution and the government it created, defending the powers bestowed on it by the people as "most conducive to public happiness and to public liberty."[7] A Friend of the Constitution countered Hampden's quotation of the Declaratory Act with the Preamble to remind the people of the Constitution's goals, which its opponents would undermine in the attempt to make the government inoperative by stripping it of its intended powers.

The Nature of the Instrument

As his first essay closed, Hampden set out his plan to prove the grave allegation *McCulloch v. Maryland* represented, in the phrase from Revelation, the "*Alpha and Omega*, the beginning and the *end*, the first and the *last*— of federal usurpations."[8] (Emphasis added.) He promised to demonstrate two points: that the Supreme Court had no jurisdiction over the case and that, in any event, the Supreme Court had decided the case wrongly.

Hampden took up the second of these in his second essay, addressing the merits of the decision by pointing out what he saw as its errors. Hampden based his analysis on three propositions, which A Friend of the Constitution took up in his second and third essays. The first was that the "constitution conveyed only a limited grant of powers to the general government, and reserved the residuary powers to the governments of the states, and to the people."[9] Marshall agreed wholeheartedly, adding a quotation from the opinion, and likened it to a mathematical axiom whose truth is universally admitted.

Marshall agreed also with Hampden's second proposition but then devoted his second and third essays to explaining how Hampden misunderstood the principle itself and its application to the issues of *McCulloch v. Maryland*. The proposition, quoted faithfully by Marshall, was that "the limited grant to congress of certain enumerated powers, only carried with it such additional powers as were *fairly incidental* to them, or, in other words, were necessary and proper for their execution."[10]

With this proposition Hampden attempted to show that the correct construction of any contract or agreement allows for only a limited range of incidental powers (what we also call implied powers) beyond those expressly included in the agreement. It was, he wrote, "a clear principle of universal law—of the law of nature, of nations, of war, of reason, and of common law—that the general grant of a thing or power, carries with it all those means (and those only) which are necessary to the perfection of the grant, or the execution of the power."[11] Hampden was most interested in applying the parenthetical "and those only" part to the Constitution and to the opinion in *McCulloch v. Maryland* and to show that this restrictive "true limitation" applied "to all cases whatsoever and is inflexible and universal."[12]

He referred to Emmerich de Vattel on the laws of nature and nations that an express provision in a treaty (e.g., to allow an invading enemy safe passage to return to its own borders) should include only those additional things without which the provision could have no effect—in this case that the army should have the provisions needed physically to make the return. The key is the crucial phrase "without which," which Hampden found in at least four places in Vattel, restricting the implied or incidental to the necessary, defined as that without which the thing cannot be done. Hampden then added quotations from common law, which, he said, also favored "a restricted construction of the incidental powers" to include only what is necessary and not what is "remotely necessary."[13]

A Friend of the Constitution took up this proposition and agreed, adding that it did not controvert the Supreme Court's opinion in *McCulloch v. Maryland*. Marshall was concerned, however, that the words quoted from Vattel would "mislead a careless reader" and offered a "more clear and distinct" understanding of what they meant. Hampden, he said, wished to show that the express grant of a specific power does not carry with it the incidents or means for giving the grant its "full and complete effect" and that only those incidental powers that are strictly necessary can be added to it. In this, Marshall said, Hampden had been "caught by the words 'necessary,' 'without which,' and 'only means'" in the text from Vattel, giving them an emphasis that Vattel did not, to infer a conclusion that incidental powers are limited to things "strictly necessary," which is far less than the "extensive" latitude allowed by the Court in *McCulloch v. Maryland*.[14]

Lifting these words from the larger context and argument, however, tends to lose the full meaning of Vattel's text. The "great and obvious error" on Hampden's part was that he changed an affirmative into a negative proposition. "He converts a declaration of Vattel, that a nation has a natural right to do certain things, into a declaration that a nation has no natural right to do other things."[15] To say, for example, that "a nation has a right to do everything *necessary* for is [*sic*] preservation" does not mean that it has no right to do other things with a view to happiness, convenience, interest, or power. In fact, Marshall continued, in the case of its preservation, a nation, Vattel recognized, has a right to do anything it judges might be useful in preventing its ruin, which is a broad field for "necessary" indeed.

Marshall added analysis of examples from Vattel that Hampden had raised, along with other passages that Hampden had passed over, to conclude that there was no rule from Vattel that powers accompanying those expressly stated in agreements must be restricted to the indispensably necessary and that in some cases they may include a range that was quite extensive. Indeed, Vattel wrote that "we can only make laws or treaties in a general manner, and the interpretation ought to apply them to particular cases conformably to the intention of the legislature and of the contracting powers."[16] Marshall concluded:

> In truth, the only principle which can be extracted from Vattel, and safely laid down as a general independent rule is, that pacts are to be understood according to the intention of the parties, and shall be construed liberally, or restrictively, as may best promote the objects for which they were made.[17]

Turning from Vattel and the laws of nature and nations to the common law, Marshall agreed with the passage Hampden quoted that "the incident is to be taken according to a 'reasonable and easy sense'" and took "reasonable" to mean no construction that is strained either to include or exclude incidental or implied powers, but a construction that follows the intention of the makers of the instrument. In achieving this, "The nature of the instrument, the words that are employed, the object to be effected, are all to be taken into consideration, and to have their due weight."[18]

With Marshall's guidance, Hampden's argument led away from what was allowed by a highly constrained view of implied powers to a need to understand the purpose of an instrument being construed to know how to assess the range of things that may accompany those expressly stated. Here there are great differences between the examples Hampden presented from Vattel and a constitution. Unlike a treaty ending a conflict or a promise of safe passage, a constitution is not an agreement between enemies seeking to destroy one another. Neither is it a contract between individuals on some particular object in which one's gain is the other's loss. Here is Marshall's characterization of its nature and object.

> It is the act of a people, creating a government, without which they cannot exist as a people. The powers of this government are conferred for their own benefit, are essential to their own prosperity, and are to be exercised for their good, by persons chosen for that purpose by themselves. The object of the instrument is not a single one which can be minutely described, with all its circumstances. The attempt to do so, would totally change its nature, and defeat its purpose. It is intended to be a general system for future times, to be adapted by

those who administer it, to all future occasions that may come within its own view. From its nature, such an instrument can describe only the great objects it is intended to accomplish, and state in general terms, the specific powers which are deemed necessary for those objects. To direct the manner in which these powers are to be exercised, the means by which the objects of the government are to be effected, a legislature is granted. This would be totally useless, if its office and duty were performed in the constitution. This legislature is an emanation from the people themselves. It is a part chosen to represent the whole, and to mark, according to the judgment of the nation, its course, within those great outlines which are given in the constitution. It is impossible to construe such an instrument rightly, without adverting to its nature, and marking the points of difference which distinguish it from ordinary contracts.[19]

In this passage, Marshall elaborated on the statement "it is a constitution we are expounding" from *McCulloch v. Maryland*. As in the opinion, he noted that a constitution can state only its "great objects," but not the specific things to be done in pursuit of them. Here he added that a constitution is created by mutual choice among citizens about how to pursue their positive good together. It is for the gain of each without incurring the loss of the other. It is not that act of mutually jealous state governments trying, above all, to maintain their independence and the powers of their officials. Neither is it the product of hard bargaining among its signatories to maximize individual advantage. Although it is specific about what the government is for and about the great powers it ought to employ to accomplish its objectives, it does not and cannot specify how the government is to make those powers effective in particular cases.

Indeed, Marshall said—calling to mind James Madison's comment in the Philadelphia Convention on June 26, 1787, that it is a "system we wish to last for the ages"[20]—a constitution should continue to affect the people into the future when conditions not imaginable and measures whose benefits could not now be seen would be appropriate for the citizens' prosperity. But if it does not declare what is to be done in particular, it should spell out who will do the deciding. It should create a legislature chosen by the people to represent the whole to make the judgments about specific measures to be taken to pursue the great objects for the benefit of the people. It intends for that legislature to have and accomplish meaningful duties in choosing the measures to benefit the people.

All this, then, is to be considered in deciding what the Constitution means. And at the very least, it concludes that claiming the Constitution intends to restrict the legislature to acts that are indispensably necessary to carry out the objects assigned to the government in the Constitution is not reasonable.

Marshall agreed with Hampden that the powers expressly included in the Constitution carry additional powers "fairly incidental" to them but then showed that Hampden did not understand what "fairly incidental" meant. Rather than accepting an artificially strict necessity, A Friend of the Constitution appealed "with confidence to the authority to which Hampden has introduced us"[21] to show that an agreement, when construed fairly, is construed according to its intention. And the intention of the constitution in question is to benefit the people who created it for their good and the good of generations to come in specific ways to be decided by the legislature it creates to pursue its great objects. Marshall took Hampden's appeal to crimp and confine the national government and turned it into a celebration of the popular nature of that government and a statement of its design to serve the people well by having the popularly elected legislature decide how best to accomplish the things the Constitution assigns to it for the people's benefit—and to do so well into the unforeseen future.

Marshall did not confront directly Hampden's likening of the Supreme Court's opinion in *McCulloch v. Maryland* to the Declaratory Act passed by the British Parliament in 1765, but the argument addressed the charge nonetheless. The Declaratory Act was offensive because it asserted that American colonists were ruled "in all cases whatsoever" by a Parliament in which they were not represented. As A Friend of the Constitution reminded his readers (if they needed reminding), the circumstance was the opposite in the United States under its Constitution created by the people with a legislature elected by the people to serve the people's good. It was the popular, representative system the patriots of the 18th century fought to establish and then did establish to replace the tyrannical Parliament of the Declaratory Act.

Misunderstanding *McCulloch v. Maryland*:
Incidental Powers and Means

After explaining the errors in Hampden's claims about the limits on incidental powers by showing the inapplicability of the examples Hampden used, Marshall turned to "a still more decisive objection to the exact application of the cases put by Hampden."[22] As he developed this point, Marshall showed that Hampden failed to grasp what the decision was really about. He misunderstood it in thinking it was about implied powers.

For us too, Marshall's explanation leads to a reexamination of the usual belief about what the opinion in *McCulloch v. Maryland* is about. The decision, we are usually taught, presents an analysis of the Constitution that allows a broad range of implied powers based on a reading of the necessary and proper clause. But Marshall wrote that this was not the case, for the decision was not about implied powers and did not depend on the necessary and proper clause to reach its conclusion on the bank. The key to this surprising claim is the explanation that the powers at issue in the bank case are not, in fact, additional ones that are "incidental," or implied, but merely "means of executing enumerated powers."[23]

Marshall's argument that challenges our beliefs may be unfamiliar and difficult, so it will be developed in careful steps, considering, first, the meaning of the distinction between incidental powers and means as treated by A Friend of the Constitution, followed by some important examples used to clarify it. Next comes a discussion of the importance of the distinction for the powers of Congress. This will be followed by an analysis of the distinction in the opinion in *McCulloch v. Maryland*, which will serve also to clarify it further. Finally, I will comment on the absence of the distinction in the history of constitutional law after Chief Justice Marshall.

The Distinction from A Friend of the Constitution. In his second essay Hampden explained that in common law the term "incident" is well established and well-defined and provides clear limits on implied powers. But the Supreme Court, he charged, seeks to avoid those limits by avoiding the word, instead "starting up" a new term, "means," which is "novel, undefined, and *general*" to "demolish the limits prescribed to the general government, by the constitution."[24]

Hampden was correct in saying that in the opinion, when writing of congressional powers, Chief Justice Marshall employed the term "means" heavily. Over the 18 pages of analysis on the topic, beginning with "among the enumerated powers, we do not find that of establishing a bank" and ending with "it is the unanimous and decided opinion of this Court that the act to incorporate the Bank of the United States is a law made in pursuance of the Constitution," the word "means" occurs 47 times, compared to seven for "incidental."

The matter was important to Hampden, who claimed that the enumerated powers carry with them only such others as are "fairly incidental" to them. And the meaning of that term is well established in common law and the law of nations: "The general grant of a thing or power, carries with it all those means (and those only) which are necessary to the perfection of the grant, or the execution of the power."[25] And "necessary" means something without which the power cannot have effect. This may not always mean "sheer" necessity, according to Hampden, but it "falls far short of the extensive range claimed" by the Supreme Court in *McCulloch v. Maryland*.[26] The Supreme Court, he charged, escapes this strict limit by avoiding the appropriate term for implied powers and inventing a new one, "means," which it then defines broadly to achieve much expanded powers for the general government.

A Friend of the Constitution took up Hampden's charge that the Court invented a new term to avoid the limits that come with the correct one with relish. He agreed on the definition of "incident" as "a thing appertaining to, or following another, as being more worthy or principal," but he denied the applicability to *McCulloch v. Maryland*, which is not about additional powers that may be implied by enumerated ones but about "the means by which a power expressly granted is to be executed."[27] Marshall disputed Hampden's claim that the terms "necessary" and "incidental powers" were uniformly used at the outset of the Constitution with measures not expressly included in the Constitution and that the Court invented the word "means" to use in their place. He mocked Hampden for his statement that the Court "trumps up" the term, repeating the phrase from Hampden four times.

In fact, Marshall wrote, both "incident" and "means" were well-known at the outset of the Constitution, and which one was used on a particular occasion depended on the meaning of the user, for they are different things. Incidental or implied powers are new ones, additional to those expressly included in the Constitution. Means are specific measures taken by the legislature not in exercising additional powers, but in implementing the ones that are included in the Constitution. The confusion, according to Marshall, was Hampden's.

Marshall noted Hampden's quoting of the *Federalist* to say that "powers *indispensably* necessary, are granted by the constitution" (Hampden's emphasis) and pointed out that in that essay (*Federalist* 44), while there is no mention of incidental powers, there are uses of the word "means." Indeed, though A Friend of the Constitution did not mention it, *Federalist* 44, by Madison, includes the statement that "no axiom is more clearly established in law, or in reason, than that wherever the end is required, the means are authorized."[28] Marshall added that the *Federalist* says the power to do something is the ability to employ "the means necessary to its execution."

In this passage from an essay about the necessary and proper clause, *Federalist* 33 uses the word "means" and not the word "incidental." In the debates in the first Congress about the bank bill, Marshall continued, both friends and opponents of the bill "continually" used the word "means." President George Washington's cabinet members, including the secretary of state and attorney general—Virginians Thomas Jefferson and Edmund Randolph who opposed the bank—used the word in discussing Congress' powers. And in Alexander Hamilton's "masterly argument" on the constitutionality of the bank, the word "means" was frequently used (about 20 times).

Hence, the term "means" is not a trumped-up modern invention, and it seems likely that Hampden would have known that. Perhaps, then, it is the other way around: that the "invention" of the term "means" was itself invented by Hampden to allow his allegation that the Supreme Court's conclusion about the bank and the reasoning supporting it were usurpations of authority not allowed by the Constitution. According to Marshall, use of the term "means" was not a deceptive way of avoiding known limits on creating additional implied powers, but an accurate way of discussing a different thing—permissible measures passed to execute established powers of the government.

Examples Clarify the Distinction. Marshall agreed with Hampden that an incidental power is an additional power that is deduced from or implied by another enumerated one. This is different from the means used to execute one of those expressly granted powers. Marshall made the point most clearly with several examples. The Constitution states that Congress has the power "to raise and support armies."[29] If in carrying out that task Congress makes provision for appointing officers, in doing so, it is not using some additional power to define officers that must be inferred as incidental to the first but only executing the power to raise and support armies. Appointing officers is part of raising and supporting armies, or a means to its execution. It is not another power.

The Constitution also gives Congress the power "to establish post offices and post roads."[30] The many laws setting up the particulars for such buildings and byways would be means to executing that power. By contrast, according to Marshall, the right to punish someone who robs the mail is not merely a means to establishing post offices, but an additional power, an incidental power, and "the question whether it is fairly deducible from the grant is open for argument."[31] Thus, it is easier to show the constitutional legitimacy of a measure that is genuinely employed pursuant to an existing power than it is to show that a power not expressly included in the Constitution is properly asserted.

Importance of the Distinction. With two more examples, A Friend of the Constitution showed not only the difference between incidental powers and means to executing existing powers but also that the distinction was of great importance because the standards to prove constitutional legitimacy were different in the two cases. With an incidental power, wrote Marshall, "we are always to enquire whether 'it appertains to or follows the principal'; for the power itself may be questioned."[32]

On the other hand, where it is established that a power is granted, the legislature may select any means to execute it. With the power "to constitute tribunals inferior to the supreme court,"[33] to pass a law to punish people who falsify records before such tribunals would be to assert an additional power, an incidental one, and Congress might be called on to prove that the power is properly inferred. But an act actually creating the tribunals and spelling out their jurisdiction and procedures is not asserting an incidental power, but merely using means to execute the enumerated power. If Congress should decide to change the number of tribunals or their jurisdiction, it may do so at will. "These laws are means, and the constitution creates no question respecting their necessity."[34]

Again, since the power "to make rules for the government of the land and naval forces"[35] is included in the Constitution, a law enacting articles of war, for example, "is the instrument or the means by which congress has chosen to execute it. With those means the doctrine of incidents has nothing to do."[36] Thus, tests that might apply to determine the constitutionality of implied powers need not be applied to means. "No court has a right to enquire whether the punishments inflicted by the articles of war are necessary or unnecessary."[37] At one point Hampden observed that all the Court had to decide in *McCulloch v. Maryland* was "whether the bank was 'necessary and proper,' within the meaning of the constitution."[38] But Marshall responded that it need not even decide that. The Court's ruling was that if the bank was created by Congress as a means to execute an existing power, then it was not required to be necessary in the Constitution's meaning, in Vattel's meaning, or in any other meaning to be permitted by the Constitution. It did not have to be proved that it was genuinely implied.

The relationship between incidental powers and means developed by A Friend of the Constitution is suggested in two other places. Marshall named the secretary of the Treasury's 1791 report on the constitutionality of the bank for using the term "means," and both his opinion for the Court and his argument as A Friend of the Constitution seem greatly indebted to Hamilton's. Hamilton wrote that a sovereign government must have "a right to employ all the means requisite and fairly applicable to the attainment of the ends of such power, and which are not precluded by restrictions and exceptions specified in the Constitution, or not immoral, or not contrary to the essential ends of political society." This right, he continued, exists "because it is incident to a general sovereign or legislative power to regulate a thing, to employ all the means which relate to its regulation to the best and greatest advantage."[39] Thus, Hamilton suggested that the right of a government to use any means not specifically prohibited in executing its powers is, itself, an incidental power that follows from the nature of sovereignty.

The same relationship appears in Justice Story's *Commentaries on the Constitution of the United States*. In writing about *McCulloch v. Maryland*, Story observed that "it is incident to the sovereign legislative power to regulate a thing, to employ all the means, which relate to its regulation, to the best and greatest advantage" and cited Hamilton on the point.[40] A Friend of the Constitution similarly argued that the right of Congress to select the means to execute its powers comes with the creation of a legislature, since "the very business of a legislature is to select the means."[41]

Of course, the right to select means may not be fraudulently used. "But if the means have a plain relation to the end—if they be direct, natural and appropriate, who, but the people at the elections, shall, under the pretext of their being unnecessary, control the legislative will, and directed understanding?"[42] That Congress may select means at its own discretion is, then, implied by the nature of legislative power. The incidental power involved here is not one to create a corporation or a bank, but a power that must belong to a legislature to decide on the means to execute the powers it is expressly given by the Constitution.[43] This appears also in Marshall's opinion in *McCulloch v. Maryland* when he wrote of the state of Maryland's wish to restrict "the general right which might otherwise be implied of selecting means for executing the enumerated powers."[44]

The Distinction in *McCulloch v. Maryland*. In the bank case the importance of the distinction between incidental powers and means became clear. Hampden objected to the bank based on the Constitutional Convention's reported rejection of a proposed power for Congress to erect corporations.[45] But the bank's constitutionality does not require an implied power—an incidental power—to create corporations. It requires only Congress' judgment that this particular corporation is a tool that helps execute at least one of the powers, such as the power to borrow money, which is included in the Constitution. To permit some means to a constitutional end requires executing a power in the Constitution that the Constitution does not prohibit. It does not require demonstration that it is an additional power "without which" the other cannot be executed or that it is "necessary and proper" to execute the enumerated power. It is part of the enumerated power itself.

The distinction between incidental powers and means is not explained in *McCulloch v. Maryland,* perhaps because there was no need to do so since, from the Supreme Court's point of view, the case is not primarily about implied or incidental powers. Still, as noted, both terms are used, though "means" appears much more frequently than does "incidental." And when the Court's opinion is read with the aid of the commentary from A Friend of the Constitution, it appears at least consistent with the distinction between the two and may even be taken to assume that distinction. The bank is held constitutional as a means to the execution of enumerated powers and not as an implied or incidental power.

In the sentence leading up to the statement of the famous test for determining whether a congressional act is permitted by the Constitution, the chief justice wrote that though the powers of the government are limited, "we think the sound construction of the Constitution must allow to the national legislature that discretion with respect to the means by which the powers it confers are to be carried into execution."[46] The test itself is about means and does not mention implied powers.

> Let the end be legitimate, let it be within the scope of the Constitution, and all means which are appropriate, which are plainly adapted to that end, which are not prohibited, but consist with the letter and spirit of the Constitution, are Constitutional.[47]

Since the bank is such a means to one or more enumerated power, it is constitutional.

In the argument leading to the "let the end be legitimate" test, Marshall addressed the necessary and proper clause not to find authorization for the congressional right to choose means but to show that the clause was not to be read, as the state of Maryland contended, as a limit on what Congress might otherwise do. Marshall argued that it did not make sense to see this as the founders' intention. He showed this first by addressing "the case under consideration," which involved "the execution of those great powers on which the welfare of a Nation essentially depends." The authors of the Constitution must have intended the "beneficial execution" of those powers, and this required leaving Congress the right to choose any means "which might be appropriate, and which were conducive to the end."[48]

The next paragraph begins: "If we apply this principle of construction [that 'necessary' must be taken as 'absolutely necessary'] to any of the powers of the Government, we shall find it so pernicious in its operation that we shall be compelled to discard it."[49] With this, the analysis shifts to "incidental powers," including the power to require oaths of office, to legislate the penal code, and to punish violations of congressional laws. These are not means used to execute any of the other powers, but additional powers, incidental ones implied by the words of the Constitution. In particular, Marshall introduced two examples that were the very same ones he offered three months later as A Friend of the Constitution. The powers to punish those who rob the mail and commit perjury are both presented by A Friend of the Constitution as things that are not means to the execution of enumerated powers—they do not help make post roads or establish inferior tribunals—but are nonetheless generally understood to belong to the national government. These incidental powers are different from the means used to execute powers. Consider this from the opinion:

> Take, for example, the power "to establish post-offices and post-roads." This power is executed by the single act of making the establishment. But from this has been inferred the power and duty of carrying the mail along the post road from one post office to another. And from this implied power has again been inferred the right to punish those who steal letters from the post office, or rob the mail.[50]

These implied powers are "inferred" from known ones—in the case of the power to punish mail robbers from an enumerated power. We learn of them and their constitutional legitimacy through a rational process. We think about the known power and what it is for and understand what appertains to it. Means, by contrast, are not inferred. They are not new things learned by thought about known things, but are specific measures employed to execute powers. They are not deduced, but chosen, adopted, selected, and devised because they are calculated to produce an effect.

Now, Marshall declared that Congress has the constitutional authority to use any means not prohibited by the Constitution in pursuit of ends established by the Constitution. But he also insisted that this does not permit Congress to do anything at all. Things done under this permission must be genuine means to constitutional ends. They must be "really calculated to effect any of the objects intrusted to the Government" and measures that are "appropriate, which are plainly adapted to that end."[51] A Friend of the Constitution wrote that "their constitutionality depends on their being the natural, direct, and appropriate means, or the known and usual means, for the execution of the given power."[52] If something is done under the "pretext" of being a means to a constitutional end, it would not pass constitutional muster, and the Court's responsibility would be to declare it not the law of the land.

The examples in *McCulloch v. Maryland* that Marshall returned to three months later as A Friend of the Constitution show that means and incidental powers are not the same and must be evaluated differently. In discussing the congressional power "to make rules for the government of the land and naval forces," A Friend of the Constitution wrote that had it not been expressly stated in the Constitution, "a law made for this purpose would have rested, for its support, on the incidental or implied powers of congress, and to a question respecting its constitutionality, the doctrines of implication would have applied."[53] As to what those doctrines are and how a court would apply them, A Friend of the Constitution declared himself "content" with Hampden's definition of an incident as an additional power "appertaining to or following another" that is "beside the main design" of that other. And we have seen his argument that in deciding whether things meet this definition one needs to take into account especially the nature of the instrument being applied.

But in *McCulloch v. Maryland* no test is developed for the legitimacy of implied powers as there is for the legitimacy of means used to implement the powers of government. As explained by A Friend of the Constitution, the argument about the necessary and proper clause is made to demonstrate that it does not prohibit Congress from having powers it would otherwise have, but Marshall also stated that it does not add to the powers that Congress would otherwise have. These include, according to Marshall, a "vast mass of incidental powers which must be involved in the Constitution,"[54] but the necessary and proper clause is irrelevant to determining what is included in that mass. According to the argument, if a power is legitimately an implied one, then it is necessary and proper, but whether it is implied is established another way. And there is no attempt in *McCulloch v. Maryland* to explain how it can be decided which particular powers are incidental to others. The case at hand does not require such a test for its decision. It is resolved by the conclusion that no implied power to establish a corporation need be deduced, since in this case the bank is used as a means to implement existing powers.

Still, there is some guidance as to what such a test for incidental powers might involve. In *McCulloch v. Maryland*, in addition to the examples of incidental powers that are not means, there is one important incidental power that is asserted and argued as the basis for the ruling on means: the implied power belonging to Congress under the Constitution to employ whatever means it chooses to execute its constitutional powers. The argument that this power is properly inferred is this:

> But it may with great reason be contended that a Government intrusted with such ample powers, on the due execution of which the happiness and prosperity of the Nation so vitally depends, must also be intrusted with ample means for their execution. The power being given, it is the interest of the Nation to facilitate its execution. It can never be their interest, and cannot be presumed to have been their intention, to clog and embarrass its execution by withholding the most appropriate means.[55]

In this argument, Marshall employed the standards of interpretation he developed as A Friend of the Constitution based on the nature of the instrument, its object, and its words. It "appertains to" a government created by a constitution that spells out its great powers and then creates a legislature to decide how to implement those powers to give that legislature its choice of means. The other incidental powers mentioned in *McCulloch v. Maryland*, by contrast, are implied not from the nature of the Constitution but from specific powers that point to goals of an effective postal service and the due administration of justice. None of these cases would be settled by the famous "let the end be legitimate" test. Hence, a way to resolve disputes about the constitutionality of powers claimed by Congress as implied that would account for both sorts of implication had yet to be formulated by the Supreme Court.

The Distinction Between Incidental Powers and Means After Marshall. At one point, A Friend of the Constitution noted that the distinction "between a power which is 'incidental' or 'additional' to another, and the means which may be employed to carry a given power into execution, though not perceived by Hampden, is most obvious."[56] If Marshall believed that, then it seems unlikely he discovered the distinction only after *McCulloch v. Maryland*, and it makes it less likely that he thought it necessary to explain it carefully in his opinion in the case since he would have expected others to perceive it. But whether he had formulated it before publishing the opinion in *McCulloch v. Maryland* or only in the three months following it, Marshall believed there was a key distinction between implied powers and means used to execute powers in the scope of the Constitution. They were two different paths to establishing the constitutionality of measures not included among the enumerated powers in the Constitution.

However, in his remaining 16 years on the Court, Marshall did not have occasion to clarify the difference. Since his death and the departure of his 1819 colleagues from the Court, the distinction has been lost, while *McCulloch v. Maryland* is seen, nonetheless, as authoritative on the question of implied powers. That authoritative *McCulloch v. Maryland*, however, is not the same as the one Marshall wrote and then explained in 1819. Consider what the opinion is taken to mean in two of the cases that treat it most extensively.

In 1862 Congress passed a law establishing paper money as legal tender in the United States. In 1869 in *Hepburn v. Griswold*, the Supreme Court held that a provision in the law requiring that money to be accepted in the payment of debts contracted before the law was passed exceeded Congress' powers and was unconstitutional. The next year, with two new members, the Court overruled itself in the Legal Tender Cases, holding that Congress did have the power to make the law. Chief Justice Salmon P. Chase, who wrote for the majority in *Hepburn* and in dissent in the second case, observed that in *Hepburn* there appeared to be no real difference of opinion on the Court as to the rule by which the existence of an implied power is to be tested, though there were differences as to how the rule applied in the case. In his majority opinion, he explained that the Constitution includes "extensive" incidental and ancillary powers and that

The rule for determining whether a legislative enactment can be supported as an exercise of an implied power was stated by Chief Justice Marshall, speaking for the whole court, in the case of *McCullough v. the State of Maryland*; and the statement then made has ever since been accepted as a correct exposition of the Constitution. His words were these: "Let the end be legitimate, let it be within the scope of the Constitution, and all means which are appropriate, which are plainly adapted to that end, which are not prohibited, but consistent with the letter and spirit of the Constitution, are constitutional."[57]

Chase continued to quote the passage from Marshall in *McCulloch v. Maryland* that the Court would have to intervene should Congress try to pass a law under the pretext of it being a means to an enumerated power.

But where the law is not prohibited, and is really calculated to effect any of the objects intrusted to the Government, to undertake here to inquire into the decree of its necessity would be to pass the line which circumscribes the judicial department and to tread on legislative ground.[58]

Still, having noted Marshall's comment that it is not the business of the Court to inquire whether legitimate means are necessary, Chase maintained that the rule in *McCulloch v. Maryland* is to establish what congressional measures are genuine implied powers because they are "necessary and proper."

There are at least two differences from what Marshall wrote in 1819. The source of the "vast mass of incidental powers" is not the necessary and proper clause, which Marshall concluded both as A Friend of the Constitution and in *McCulloch v. Maryland* neither adds to nor limits the powers that the government would otherwise have under the Constitution. The source for those powers is to be found in the nature and words of the Constitution. Next, Marshall's distinction between means and implied powers is not recognized, and the "let the end be legitimate" test for means is said to apply to implied powers. This leads to at least two problems from the perspective of Marshall's analysis.

First, most implied powers would not pass the test for means (when strictly applied as in the passage quoted by Chase), and, second, the test for means may be less rigorous than the requirements under the "doctrines of implication" for incidental powers. Recall the examples A Friend of the Constitution offered of a law regulating the jurisdiction of a lower court, which would be a means to constituting inferior tribunals and a law punishing perjury, which would be exercising an incidental power whose constitutional legitimacy could require proof that it can be "fairly deduced" from the document.

About 140 years later, the Supreme Court again presented an extensive review of what it took to be the argument on implied powers in *McCulloch v. Maryland* in *United States v. Comstock*. The issue concerned a congressional statute allowing the government to require the civil commitment of individuals already in federal custody. The lower court had ruled that Congress lacked the constitutional authority to pass the law, but the Supreme Court reversed it, ruling that the necessary and proper clause does allow the legislation.

In his opinion for the Court, Justice Stephen Breyer cited *McCulloch v. Maryland* to say that "the Necessary and Proper Clause makes clear that the Constitution's grants of specific federal legislative authority are accompanied by broad powers to enact laws that are 'convenient, or useful' or 'conducive' to the authority's 'beneficial exercise.'" He continued, saying that "in language that has come to define the scope of the Necessary and Proper Clause, [Marshall] wrote: 'Let the end be legitimate . . . are constitutional.'"[59]

Of course, in the opinion in *McCulloch v. Maryland*, this test is not presented as explaining the scope of the necessary and proper clause, but as a way to identify means that need not be proved necessary to be constitutionally permissible. It is not offered as a method to identify the "vast mass of incidental powers" that the clause points to. It serves to resolve the issue of the bank's constitutionality by showing that as means to the execution of enumerated powers it is permitted by the Constitution, necessary or not.

In his opinion in *Comstock*, while arguing for the congressional right to choose means to execute its given powers, Justice Breyer quoted from *McCulloch v. Maryland* to provide examples of the broad application of the means test to validate congressional use of implied powers. His examples, however, included the very ones—robbing the mail and perjury—that Marshall used to illustrate the difference between an incidental power and a means to the execution of a given power.[60] In *McCulloch v. Maryland,* Marshall presented these as inferences, and as A Friend of the Constitution, he wrote that these would not be found constitutional under the "let the end be legitimate" test exactly because they are not means, but additional powers inferred from enumerated powers. Breyer's misuse—from Marshall's perspective—of these examples shows that what the Supreme Court's ruling in *McCulloch v. Maryland* has come to be taken to mean is not what Marshall thought it meant, at least as explained in his commentary three months later. To Marshall, the case was not about implied powers, and its ruling on the bank was based on the distinction that says means are different from implied powers.

In his dissent in *United States v. Comstock,* Justice Clarence Thomas agreed that

> Chief Justice Marshall famously summarized Congress' authority under the Necessary and Proper Clause in *McCulloch,* which has stood for nearly 200 years as this Court's definitive interpretation of that text: "Let the end be legitimate . . . are constitutional."[61]

Justice Thomas argued that the majority in the case had not applied the test well and concluded that the legislation in question in *Comstock* failed it and so was beyond the power of Congress.

But the "let the end be legitimate" test was not presented as an interpretation of the necessary and proper clause. Marshall wrote that the congressional right to choose means was independent of it.

> To waste time and argument in proving that, without it, Congress might carry its powers into execution would be not much less idle than to hold a lighted taper to the sun. As little can it be required to prove that, in the absence of this clause, Congress would have some choice of means. That it might employ those which, in its judgment, would most advantageously effect the object to be accomplished. That any means adapted to the end, any means which tended directly to the execution of the Constitutional powers of the Government, were in themselves Constitutional.[62]

And as Marshall explained it as A Friend of the Constitution and seemed to have assumed in *McCulloch v. Maryland*, the only conclusion that can follow from applying that test is that the legislation in question is or is not constitutional because it is or is not a means to a constitutional end. If it is not such a means, it might still be constitutional as an exercise of a legitimate incidental power as determined by applying the doctrines of implication—as are the powers to punish perjury and mail robbing. Nowhere did Marshall claim that the only powers of Congress that are legitimate beyond the enumerated ones must come through the means test, but only that some legitimate acts are determined that way. From Marshall's perspective, the Supreme Court after he left made the same logical error that he identified in Hampden in converting a holding in *McCulloch v. Maryland* that power of Congress may be found legitimate in one way into a holding that a power of Congress may be found constitutional in no other way.

Conclusion on Incidental Powers and Means. Now return to A Friend of the Constitution's introduction to his discussion of the difference between incidental powers and means and the promise that it would provide a decisive objection to Hampden's application of the rules on incidental powers to *McCulloch v. Maryland*. In his first essay, Marshall noted that Supreme Court decisions "must sometimes depend on a course of intricate and abstruse reasoning, which it requires no inconsiderable degree of mental exertion to comprehend, and which may, of course, be grossly misrepresented."[63] This distinction between means and incidental powers (though obvious to Chief Justice Marshall) involves, perhaps, just such a course of reasoning, and it is one that Marshall went through in more detail as A Friend of the Constitution than he did in the Court's opinion.

However, it does prove to be much more decisive in explaining Marshall's view of the legitimacy of Congress' action in creating the bank and of the Court's decision that the law is constitutional than does reviewing the exact meaning of incidental powers in the law of nations and common law. For it shows that the question of Congress' authority to make the bank is not about implied powers and, therefore, need not be judged by a standard that requires arguments about the meaning of "necessary." It also provides an example of just how important "abstruse" judicial reasoning can be for the well-being of a nation. In a broader sense, it shows also that

McCulloch v. Maryland is not about a broad range of implied powers based on a reading of the necessary and proper clause.

The Necessary and Proper Clause

Recall that at the outset of his second essay Hampden set out three propositions in arguing that *McCulloch v. Maryland* was decided wrongly. The third is that "the insertion of the words 'necessary and proper,' in the last part of the 8th section of the 1st article, did not enlarge the powers previously given, but were inserted only through abundant caution."[64] After giving extensive treatment to the proposition on implied powers, this one receives a scant paragraph's discussion from Hampden. For his part, A Friend of the Constitution was also quite brief, saying simply that the Supreme Court agreed with the proposition and said so explicitly in the opinion.

This exchange calls our attention again to the fact that the entire discussion of implied powers and means to the execution of enumerated powers takes place without reference by either Hampden or A Friend of the Constitution to the Constitution's necessary and proper clause. It was not a factor in the analysis. And now, when the discussion of that clause comes, we find the two agreeing that it is not relevant to the question, that it does not change what the Constitution would allow in its absence.

The Supreme Court's position on the necessary and proper clause and the discretion that Congress has under the Constitution to choose the means for executing its expressly granted powers is summed up in this passage from A Friend of the Constitution, an elaboration of the "let the end be legitimate" test in *McCulloch v. Maryland*:

> The general principles maintained by the supreme court are, that the constitution may be construed as if the clause which has been so much discussed, had been entirely omitted. That the powers of congress are expressed in terms which, without its aid, enable and require the legislature to execute them, and of course, to take means for their execution. That the choice of these means devolve on the legislature, whose right, and whose duty it is, to adopt those which are most

advantageous to the people, provided they be within the limits of the constitution. Their constitutionality depends on their being the natural, direct, and appropriate means, or the known and usual means, for the execution of the given power.[65]

The discussion of the meaning of the necessary and proper clause in the Court's opinion and in the essay by A Friend of the Constitution is not about whether the clause allows Congress to choose how to execute its powers, for Congress would have that right without the clause. It is about the part that says Congress may choose means as it sees fit "provided they be within the limits of the constitution." For the state of Maryland had argued that the necessary and proper clause is meant as a limit on Congress, removing discretion on how to execute its powers. Hampden, however, insisted that the Court uses the clause as justification for its usurpations. His third essay is devoted to parts of the opinion that he called erroneous, that contribute to a claim that the necessary and proper clause increases congressional powers over what would be there without it. This is despite Hampden's noting that the Court "admits" that the necessary and proper clause does not enlarge the powers of Congress.

In his fourth and fifth essays, A Friend of the Constitution addressed these criticisms and the false or misleading statements about the opinion on which they are based. While the Court never departed from its position that the necessary and proper clause does not enlarge on the powers the Constitution already gives to the legislature, it also strongly countered the claim by the state of Maryland that it limited those powers: "The words prohibit nothing to the general government."[66] Hampden took several points in that argument against the Maryland position as claims by the Court that the clause enlarges Congress' powers beyond what it otherwise would be, and then he delights in his efforts to knock down the straw men he has created.

For example, in arguing that the clause is not meant to limit congressional power, the Court notes that it is included in Article I, Section 8, not Section 9. In addition, the Court takes note of the extent of the republic in discussing Congress' powers. Also, the Court points out that the necessary and proper clause is stated in the form of a power and not of a limit. In each case, Hampden portrayed the point as a claim for greater power through the clause than would otherwise be there, when, in fact, the position of the Court is that the clause cannot be meant to restrict the powers that the Constitution gives Congress without it.

A Friend of the Constitution's essay is peppered with quotations from the opinion countering false assertions from Hampden. Marshall wrote, "No man, I think, who will even glance at the opinion, will fall into the error into which Hampden would lead him," and "any man of the most ordinary understanding" would not believe that Hampden could have so misunderstood the meaning of the Supreme Court.[67] Why, then, does A Friend of the Constitution repeat several times but slightly differently, "Has Hampden attempted thus plainly to pervert this opinion, and to ascribe to it doctrines which it clearly rejects?"[68]

At the beginning of his discussion of the necessary and proper clause, Marshall raised the question of Hampden's misrepresentations in a way that suggested the answer: "Why then does he seek indirectly to impress upon the minds of his readers this idea known to himself to be incorrect?"[69] After reviewing some of the distortions and misstatements, Marshall noted that "Hampden knows well that prejudices once impressed upon the public mind, are not easily removed; and that the progress of truth and reason is slow."[70] The observation reminds us of Madison's comment in *Federalist* 49 that "the most rational government will not find it a superfluous advantage to have the prejudices of the community on its side."[71] In this case, however, according to A Friend of the Constitution, the aim is to turn the prejudices of the people against the Constitution and the government it creates.

Marshall wrote that Hampden's "grand objection to the opinion" is that it construes the necessary and proper clause as "an enlargement of the enumerated powers" and so extends Congress' power to "prostrate all the barriers to the unlimited powers of the general government."[72] Marshall showed what he believed was abundantly clear in the opinion itself that this is simply false. Hampden converted points made to refute Maryland's claim that the necessary and proper clause narrowed Congress' right to choose how to execute its powers into a design actually to extend those powers so thoroughly as to make them unlimited.

Marshall's charge, then, was that Hampden made the individual errors about the opinion to be able to reach the grand conclusion that the

Court and, by extension, the general government are usurping unlimited power. Hampden was seeking to nurture the prejudice among the people that the national government under the Constitution was grabbing power it did not rightfully have, and, therefore, it was harmful and ought to be changed. His is "a grand effort to impair the constitution of our country by construction," wrote A Friend of the Constitution, and in this effort "the doctrine 'that the end will justify the means,' seems not to be entirely exploded."[73]

Hampden noted that the Supreme Court twice says that the "general government"—the Court calls it the government of the union or the government of the United States—though limited in its powers, is supreme. And Hampden objected that "this word 'supreme' does not sound well in a government which acts under a limited constitution. The people only are supreme."[74] Again, Hampden was working to create the prejudice that the Court and the government it is a part of are engaged in a power grab that threatens tyranny. Hampden did not mention that the word "supreme" is not of the Court's invention since it comes from the supremacy clause of the Constitution, but Hampden's criticism of the term, and of the relationship between the nation and the states it creates, comes in the context of his previous paragraph, which explains that the Constitution is not perfect and could be amended.

The full sentence to which Hampden referred in *McCulloch v. Maryland* is: "If any one proposition could command the universal assent of mankind, we might expect it would be this—that the Government of the Union, though limited in its powers, is supreme within its sphere of action."[75] A Friend of the Constitution charged Hampden with simply not understanding the language, as he "would seem to have confounded *supremacy* with *despotism*."[76] (Emphasis in original.) "Supreme," he continued, means highest in authority, and there must be a highest authority under any constitution; in the United States, the Constitution makes unmistakably clear that the highest authority is the government of the union. It is, wrote A Friend of the Constitution, "the language of truth."[77]

It is a truth that Hampden wanted to change. He insisted that the Constitution does not make the general government supreme in fact and that the great error of *McCulloch v. Maryland* is that its reasoning would strengthen that government. Hampden pronounced that "I principally make war against the declaratory decision of the supreme court, giving congress power to 'bind us in all cases whatsoever.'"[78] And in this war he waved the symbols to rally the troops: He raised the specter that the construction in *McCulloch v. Maryland* "would even give congress a right to disarm the people" and is as broad as that "which brought the memorable sedition act into our code."[79] He suggested that it allows the people of Connecticut "to make laws, on the subject of our Negro population"[80] and repeatedly likened it to the Declaratory Act.

In response, Marshall noted Hampden's objection that the principles of the decision "prostrate all the barriers to the unlimited power of the general government"[81] and showed his readers the false and misleading statements Hampden employed in reaching this dire conclusion. On the bank itself Marshall commented that the need for it was widely admitted and that even "the most intelligent original enemies of the measure have admitted it,"[82] pointing out that the Second Bank was legislated by a Congress with a Republican majority, the law was signed by a Republican president, and the constitutionality of the act was affirmed by a unanimous Supreme Court, five of whose seven members had been appointed by Republican presidents.[83]

Hampden's principle that would hamper Congress in its choice of means to execute its powers greatly weakens the government of the union and leaves it unable to accomplish what it was made to do, which is to provide for, as A Friend of the Constitution quoted from the opinion, "the happiness and prosperity of the nation."[84] If the Constitution is not construed as the Court construes it, then the legislature is unable to execute its powers to make the government of the whole union effective. This would make Congress have to rely on the state legislatures to enforce its laws, so that "it would, in a great measure, reinstate the old confederation."[85] And that was what Hampden promoted.

Thus, Hampden worked to create prejudice against the government of the union and for confederation and, therefore, had to condemn *McCulloch v. Maryland*. A Friend of the Constitution and the Supreme Court speak for the Constitution and the government it creates as beneficial for the people and explain the importance of the ruling in the bank case if the Constitution is to operate as intended. On that defense of the Constitution, there is more to come.

Jurisdiction

In his final essay, Hampden developed the claim that the Supreme Court had no jurisdiction over the dispute in *McCulloch v. Maryland*. He noted earlier that in judicial proceedings it is appropriate to address jurisdictional issues first, for when a court is found to lack jurisdiction the case cannot continue. Hampden said that he would not do that since he wanted to make his arguments against the decision on the merits. Now, in his final essay, as he addressed the issue, we find that it is far from a technical legal point and actually presents his case against the Supreme Court and the government under the Constitution at its boldest and most fundamental level. Hampden related the dispute in *McCulloch v. Maryland* to the question of the nature of the Constitution and the union. In doing so, he presented A Friend of the Constitution with the opportunity to argue the case for the Court's decision at a level deeper than the meaning of the laws and the Constitution, as Marshall portrayed the benefits of union and of the government that were created by the people of the United States for their welfare. The jurisdictional issue, Marshall said, "concerns the prosperity of the union, the due execution of its laws, and even its preservation."[86]

The first premise of Hampden's argument is that the Constitution is a league or alliance, a confederation among the several states. The assumption used to establish the premise is that the Constitution must either be a consolidation of the states or a confederation of states. If it is not one, then it is the other. But, Hampden reasoned, since the Constitution recognizes the states and does not abolish their individual separate organization, and since it was created by the states that chose to ratify it, the Constitution cannot be a consolidation, so it is a confederation. Furthermore, since a confederation is not a national government and there could be a national government only with consolidation, the Constitution does not create a national government. The general government, he wrote, "is as much a federal government, or a 'league,' as was the former confederation. The only difference is, that the powers of this government are much extended."[87]

A Friend of the Constitution took up this argument in his sixth essay, noting that Hampden alleged that the Supreme Court's stance on the question of confederation is "indistinct" but that its actions seem to show the belief that the government under the Constitution is a consolidation.

This, Hampden wrote, is because the Court seems to think that "the states were not known in the establishment of the constitution" and from "their considering the government as no alliance or league."[88] So, Hampden concluded, the "doctrines" of the Court "show the government to be, in the opinion of the court, a consolidated and not a federal government."[89] Marshall responded flatly that this assertion is "neither true nor innocent." The issue was not raised by counsel on either side in *McCulloch v. Maryland*, he said, and consequently it was not addressed thematically in the case.

Nonetheless, Marshall maintained, the position the Court took is clear, although that clarity is obscured by the faulty argumentation from Hampden. That argument assumes that "national" is synonymous with "consolidated" and that a government may be consolidated or federal, but not both. Consolidated, in turn, implies abolition of the states, whereas the continued existence of the states means "federal." A part of this that is not "innocent" is that it enabled Hampden to claim that since the Court denies that the Constitution is a league or confederation, it must think it is a consolidation and, therefore, must favor destruction of the states.

Marshall cut through this thicket by exposing the logical flaws in Hampden's claims. He showed the false dichotomy between consolidation and confederation. He denied that "national" is synonymous with "consolidated," showing, for example, that in *Federalist* 39 the system under the Constitution is described as "neither a national nor a federal constitution, but a composition of both."[90] He showed that it is not impossible, as Hampden would have it, for the people to be both citizens of the United States and citizens of a state.

Yet in a sense, the dispute here is not about what the Supreme Court in *McCulloch v. Maryland* takes to be the case, but about what is the case. A Friend of the Constitution wrote that "the point to which all of [Hampden's] arguments tend is that the Constitution is 'an alliance or a league.'" To establish this as a fundamental principle, "an unnatural or restricted construction of the constitution is pressed upon us, and a fair exercise of the powers it confers, is reviled as an infraction of state rights."[91]

Whether the Constitution is a league is not a question discussed in the Court's opinion, but the belief that it ought to be is the moving force behind Hampden's bitter criticism of the decision and his efforts to reverse its ruling that the Constitution intends to provide for effective execution of the powers it gives to the government of the union. Thus, working to forestall that prejudice and to counter the effort "which would reduce the constitution to a dead letter," A Friend of the Constitution went outside the opinion in *McCulloch v. Maryland* to show the falsity of the principles that "render the terms American people and national government, odious."[92] The aim was not merely or even mainly to defend the Supreme Court's decision but to explain and celebrate the country's decision to replace the Articles of Confederation with the Constitution. As Supreme Court justice, Marshall's role was to act as the Constitution instructs. As commentator on *McCulloch v. Maryland*, however, Marshall was free to go outside the legal record to engage in argument about the virtues of confederation and national government and to defend the Constitution and what it is meant to do.

Marshall was firm: "But our constitution is not a league. It is a government." The nature of the instrument makes it clear. In contrast to the confederation, the Constitution creates legislative, executive, and judicial departments, and its government acts directly on people and not through the state governments. The congress under the articles was "a corps of ambassadors" that could propose things and pass resolutions, "but they could, by their own power, execute nothing." A government, by contrast, "carries it resolutions into execution by its own means, and ours is a government."[93] Indeed, it is this defining characteristic of a government that Hampden wished to destroy to remove the supremacy of the national government. And it is because a government must be able to execute its own resolutions that the right of Congress to select the means to execute its powers that is explained in *McCulloch v. Maryland* is essential under the Constitution. Without that right, it is not the government it is intended to be.

Marshall asked his reader to recall that there is good reason for the people of the United States to wish to maintain that national government and not replace it with the league Hampden desired. They had a confederation once, and it was an "awful stage in our history." He referred to *Federalist* 15 and its description of "the last stage of national humiliation" and continued to say that the "wisdom and patriotism of our country" led to the choice to abandon confederacy and replace it with "effective government."[94]

To return to Hampden, having established (to his satisfaction) the premise that the Constitution is a confederation, that its government is a "continuation of the *former* federal government . . . an expansion of the principles contained in the articles of confederation,"[95] he was prepared to reason that the Court has no jurisdiction in *McCulloch v. Maryland*. The conclusion does not follow from the terms of the Constitution, but from the nature of confederacies. Referring again to Vattel on the law of nations, Hampden wrote that a confederacy is made up of equal sovereigns and that the members do not give up sovereignty to a general government. When there is a disagreement among these sovereignties about a treaty they have made, no one of them can have the authority to decide it, since they are equal, and no one should have the right to be judge in its own case.

In the bank case, there was a disagreement between two of the equal contracting parties: the general government and the sovereign state of Maryland. Neither recognize a common superior, and neither should be judge in its own case. The Supreme Court is but a department of one of those parties, so it cannot rightfully decide the controversy. Hence, it has no jurisdiction. The founders, Hampden lamented, did not foresee the need to provide for an impartial tribunal to decide on such clashes between equal governments. Perhaps, he suggested, the confederacy should turn to a foreign power, maybe Russia, to arbitrate the dispute.

In the last two of his nine essays, A Friend of the Constitution easily disposed of this jurisdictional question. It proceeds from what Marshall had already shown to be an error, that the Constitution is a league or compact. This is nothing but a "delusion." Thus, the argument Hampden produced from Vattel about "sovereigns who acknowledge no superior"[96] does not apply. The Constitution is not a compact between the government of the union and the governments of the states, but a government created by the whole American people for their own good. Where the measures of a league are carried out by the governments of the member sovereigns, those of the government created by the Constitution are executed by that government itself without requiring the assistance of state governments (the very feature of the Constitution that is central to the decision in *McCulloch v. Maryland*). While the representatives of the sovereigns in a league are wholly subordinate to those various sovereigns, the Constitution creates a government of the union that is "supreme" over those of the member states in its sphere of action, and the Constitution explicitly says so.

Moreover, the government of the United States is not a party to any contract with the state governments, since the US government did not exist until the people created it with the Constitution. That Constitution is not an agreement among state governments, but the act of a single party, the people of the United States "assembling in their respective states, and adopting a government for the whole nation."[97]

Hampden's jurisdictional argument was fundamentally flawed. It was based on a premise that was demonstrably false. It embraced a view of what it wanted the Constitution to be—or not be—which did not correspond to what it is. In a court of law that would be enough quickly to dispose of a bad, perhaps frivolous, objection. But the newspapers were not a court, and Hampden was not trying to convince a judge. His aim was to influence opinion about what the Constitution ought to be, and because that was the objective, Marshall's response went beyond the simple rejection that would be called for in court.

A Friend of the Constitution was not a judge needing only to decide the case at hand, but a teacher of public opinion himself, working to educate people to avoid a dangerous prejudice. At the beginning of his treatment of Hampden's argument on jurisdiction, Marshall commented that in *McCulloch v. Maryland*, counsel for the state of Maryland "made every point which judgment, ingenuity, or imagination could suggest, on which a decent self-respect would permit them to insist," but it did not raise this jurisdictional claim.[98] Perhaps Marshall pointed this out to indicate that he understood that Hampden, on this score, was not really talking about *McCulloch v. Maryland*, but about the larger point: about the prejudice he would like to build against the government of the union and for confederation. It was not a campaign against the bank, but a campaign against the Constitution.

And so, A Friend of the Constitution worked to show not only that the Supreme Court has jurisdiction in the dispute between Maryland and James McCulloch, but that it is good that it does and that it decided the case as it did. Those are good because the people wisely decided to establish the Constitution with its supreme national government. Rather than going to Vattel and to an analysis of a hypothetical case that differs in basic ways from the one at hand, Marshall turned to the text that most certainly applies and to an analysis of the system it creates. The Constitution is the act of the people of the United States. It makes a government that includes a judicial department. This national tribunal was created to decide all national questions, questions in their nature that it makes no sense to refer to local tribunals.

The language of the Constitution is clear: "The judicial power shall extend to all cases in law and equity arising under this constitution, the laws of the United States & treaties made or to be made under their authority."[99] *McCulloch v. Maryland* involves a claim that an act of Congress is unconstitutional and, therefore, arises under the Constitution and laws of the United States, so the Court has jurisdiction over it.

Marshall wrote that "this is not now a question open for consideration. The constitution has decided it."[100] Still, he entertained the question of whether the Constitution decided it well, which Hampden answered with a resounding "no." If we were now making a constitution, Marshall asked, where would the duty of deciding disputes arising under it be safely and wisely placed? Should the laws be simply ignored if someone or some state chooses to disobey (as with the old confederation)? Should they be enforced by the sword? Hampden suggested asking a foreign government to serve as an arbiter. Marshall countered that it would be far better for such disputes to be submitted to a domestic tribunal "composed of American citizens, selected by the man in whom the American people have reposed their highest confidence, approved by the representatives of the state sovereignties, and placed by the people themselves in a situation which exempts them from all undue influence."[101]

To Hampden, however, this constitutionally created way of settling important disputes is a mistake by the founders because it allows a party to dispute between the general government and state government to decide in its own case. He reasoned that the judicial department is but a deputy of the general government and the general government is merely one of the "contracting parties" in the Constitution. To A Friend of the Constitution, this reasoning must stem from someone "inattentive to the constitution of his country," so consumed by hostility to the judicial department as knowingly to speak falsehoods.[102] First, there is no "general government" that is a contacting party to the Constitution. In fact, it is not clear what that government would be. If Hampden meant to call Congress the government, then certainly the judiciary is not its deputy. And Congress is not the government, which consists of three departments, none of which is a deputy to another or to some other whole apart from them all.

Under the guise of instructing Hampden, Marshall took the opportunity to explain separation of powers and the virtue of the system the Constitution created. Each of the three departments is confined to a particular sphere of action. "The legislature and executive can no more unite with the judiciary in deciding a cause than the judiciary can unite with them in making a law, or appointing a foreign minister."[103] Each of the departments in this government was "created by, and for, the people of the United States," and each is "filled by citizens of the several states."[104] It is not the foreign, despotic monolith that Hampden wanted people to fear, but a carefully designed government of the people working to serve the people's interest.

Hampden's claim that the Court has no legitimate jurisdiction is based, in part, on a principle that no party should be able to decide its own cause. But Marshall noted that, applied to governments, this principle makes no sense. If it were to be followed strictly, then no government could enforce its own criminal laws or resolve any issue involving the power of the legislature. The great basic duty of any government to provide for peaceful resolution of controversies would need to be abandoned. A good government must decide these issues and decide them well in the interest of the people it serves.

Marshall showed that the judicial department under the Constitution is designed to do just that. The judges are chosen from the great body of the people, and then they are made independent of political pressures. "They have no personal interest in aggrandizing the legislative power. Their paramount interest is in the public prosperity, in which is involved their own and that of their families."[105] This, then, is not a party deciding its own case, but a department of the government that the people have created judging the actions of another department of the same government with its only interest being that the departments act as the people intended. Hampden branded the justices appointed by Republican presidents who voted with the unanimous Supreme Court in the bank case as "turn-coats and apostates."[106] So, it was Hampden who expected the judges to act in their own partisan interest. But A Friend of the Constitution showed that they do not do so because the Constitution is built to motivate them to act in the people's interest.

In arguing about jurisdiction, Hampden stated what he took to be the issue in a way designed to inflame prejudices against the US government. He challenged whoever might disagree with him to show "*haec verba*," or in these exact words, where the Constitution gives the Supreme Court the right "to change the government: to convert a federal into a consolidated government."[107] Having shown that the dichotomy between confederation and consolidation that Hampden posed is false, Marshall did not step into the trap, but he did take up the challenge as an occasion to show that (1) the Constitution directly gives the Court the responsibility of deciding the case, (2) the Constitution makes the justices of the Court independent of political pressures and thereby motivates them to make the decision well, (3) the Constitution enables the judicial department to perform its function in a government characterized by separation of powers, and (4) the Court did its job in *McCulloch v. Maryland* by ruling according to the nature, words, and intention of the Constitution that Congress may select the means it finds useful in employing the powers it is charged with, while doing its part within that system of separation of powers.

Hampden sought to create an ineffectual legislature by denying it the means to execute its powers, and he attempted to accomplish that denial by arguing that the judicial branch decided wrongly and that, in any case, it had, or should have had, no right to decide at all. Thus, he would undermine one branch of the national government by denying the constitutional responsibility of another and, with that, threaten the happiness and prosperity of the American people.

With the jurisdiction issue, Hampden raised the dispute to its most important ground. He sought a constitution that is no more than a league of independent states, not fundamentally different from the Articles of Confederation. In the ninth essay, A Friend of the Constitution argued carefully in response that Hampden's claims

> advance[d] principles which go, in my judgment, to the utter subversion of the constitution. Let Hampden succeed, and that instrument will be radically changed. The government of the whole will be

prostrated at the feet of its members; and that great effort of wisdom, virtue, and patriotism, which produced it, will be totally defeated.[108]

That Congress may use means of its selection to carry out its powers under the Constitution is essential to the government of the union created by "the law which unites us as a nation"[109] by and for the people of the United States. Thus, the decision in the bank case is required by the Constitution and supported by the American people's desire for their happiness, prosperity, and liberty.

Notes

1. Charles Hobson, ed., "From John Marshall to Joseph Story, 28 April 1819," in *The Papers of John Marshall Digital Edition* (Charlottesville, VA: University of Virginia Press, 2014).

2. Charles Hobson, ed., "From John Marshall to Joseph Story, 27 May 1819," in *The Papers of John Marshall Digital Edition* (Charlottesville, VA: University of Virginia Press, 2014).

3. Gerald Gunther, "Roane's 'Hampden' Essays," in *John Marshall's Defense of McCulloch v. Maryland* (Stanford, CA: Stanford University Press, 1969), 107.

4. Gunther, "Roane's 'Hampden' Essays," 110, 112.

5. Gunther, "Roane's 'Hampden' Essays," 110–12.

6. John Marshall, "A Friend of the Constitution," in *John Marshall, Writings*, ed. Charles F. Hobson (New York: Library of America, 2010), 468.

7. Marshall, "A Friend of the Constitution," 472.

8. Gunther, "Roane's 'Hampden' Essays," 114.

9. Gunther, "Roane's 'Hampden' Essays," 114.

10. Gunther, "Roane's 'Hampden' Essays," 115.

11. Gunther, "Roane's 'Hampden' Essays," 117.

12. Gunther, "Roane's 'Hampden' Essays," 118.

13. Gunther, "Roane's 'Hampden' Essays," 121.

14. Marshall, "A Friend of the Constitution," 475.

15. Marshall, "A Friend of the Constitution," 475.

16. Marshall, "A Friend of the Constitution," 478.

17. Marshall, "A Friend of the Constitution," 477.

18. Marshall, "A Friend of the Constitution," 480.

19. Marshall, "A Friend of the Constitution," 481–82.

20. James Madison, *Notes of the Debates in the Federal Convention of 1787* (Athens, OH: Ohio University Press, 1985), 194.

21. Marshall, "A Friend of the Constitution," 478.

22. Marshall, "A Friend of the Constitution," 482.

23. Marshall, "A Friend of the Constitution," 482.

24. Gunther, "Roane's 'Hampden' Essays," 122.

25. Gunther, "Roane's 'Hampden' Essays," 117.

26. Note that "necessary" here is as understood in common law and Vattel and not the "necessary" in the Constitution's necessary and proper clause. As discussed below, both Hampden and Marshall find that clause to be irrelevant to the determination of incidental or implied powers under the Constitution.

27. Marshall, "A Friend of the Constitution," 482.

28. *Federalist*, no. 44 (James Madison).

29. US Const. art. I, § 8.

30. US Const. art. I, § 8.

31. Marshall, "A Friend of the Constitution," 483.

32. Marshall, "A Friend of the Constitution," 484.

33. US Const. art. I, § 8.

34. Marshall, "A Friend of the Constitution," 483–84.

35. US Const. art. I, § 8, cl. 14.

36. Marshall, "A Friend of the Constitution," 483.

37. Marshall, "A Friend of the Constitution," 483.

38. Gunther, "Roane's 'Hampden' Essays," 110.

39. Avalon Project, "Hamilton's Opinion as to the Constitutionality of the Bank of the United States: 1791," Yale Law School, https://avalon.law.yale.edu/18th_century/bank-ah.asp.

40. Joseph Story, *Commentaries on the Constitution of the United States, Volume 3* (Boston, MA: Hilliard, Gray, and Company, 1833), Chapter XXV, sec. 1257.

41. Marshall, "A Friend of the Constitution," 484.

42. Marshall, "A Friend of the Constitution," 484. Spencer Roane sent copies of his Hampden essays to James Madison. In his lengthy reply Madison made little substantive comment on Hampden's arguments, but he did address the opinion in *McCulloch v. Maryland*. Madison showed that he understood the Court's argument was about means, and his great concern was that the principle the Court developed would come to be abused in time by Congress. According to the Court's doctrine, he wrote, "The expediency & constitutionality of means for carrying into effect a specified power, are convertible terms; and Congress are admitted to be judges of the expediency." And while the Court says that the means Congress chooses must be related to an express power and that it may not violate the limits in the Constitution in selecting means, Madison feared that Congress would have the ingenuity to get around these things, so that its power could become nearly unlimited. Madison, then, did not share Hampden's objection to the use of the word "means," but he argued that the way it is used to give such great latitude to Congress is dangerous. James Madison, "From James Madison to Spencer Roane," National Archive, Founders Online, September 2, 1819, https://founders.archives.gov/douments/Madison/04-01-02-0455.

43. Again, note the emphasis on the people selecting the legislature through elections as showing the fundamental difference between the British Parliament of the Declaratory Act and the government of the United States under the Constitution.

44. *McCulloch v. Maryland*, 17 US 316, 421 (1819).

45. This was reported by James Madison in his speech in the House of Representatives on the bank bill on February 2, 1791.

46. *McCulloch v. Maryland*, 17 US 316, 421 (1819).

47. *McCulloch v. Maryland*, 17 US 316, 420–21 (1819).

48. *McCulloch v. Maryland*, 17 US 316, 416 (1819).

49. *McCulloch v. Maryland*, 17 US 316, 416 (1819).

50. *McCulloch v. Maryland*, 17 US 316, 417 (1819).

51. *McCulloch v. Maryland*, 17 US 316, 421, 423 (1819).

52. Marshall, "A Friend of the Constitution," 495–96.

53. Marshall, "A Friend of the Constitution," 483.

54. *McCulloch v. Maryland*, 17 US 316, 421 (1819).

55. *McCulloch v. Maryland*, 17 US 316, 408 (1819).

56. Marshall, "A Friend of the Constitution," 484.

57. *Hepburn v. Griswold*, 75 US 603, 614 (1869).

58. *Hepburn v. Griswold*, 75 US 603, 615 (1869).

59. *United States v. Comstock*, 560 US 126, 133, 134 (2010).

60. *United States v. Comstock*, 560 US 126, 136, 146 (2010).

61. *United States v. Comstock*, 560 US 126, 160 (2010).

62. *McCulloch v. Maryland*, 17 US 316, 419 (1819).

63. Marshall, "A Friend of the Constitution," 468.

64. Gunther, "Roane's 'Hampden' Essays," 115.

65. Marshall, "A Friend of the Constitution," 195–96.

66. Marshall, "A Friend of the Constitution," 490.

67. Marshall, "A Friend of the Constitution," 490–91.

68. Marshall, "A Friend of the Constitution," 495.

69. Marshall, "A Friend of the Constitution," 489.

70. Marshall, "A Friend of the Constitution," 495.

71. *Federalist*, no. 49 (James Madison).

72. Marshall, "A Friend of the Constitution," 499.

73. Marshall, "A Friend of the Constitution," 496.

74. Gunther, "Roane's 'Hampden' Essays," 130.

75. *McCulloch v. Maryland*, 17 US 316, 405 (1819).

76. Marshall, "A Friend of the Constitution," 496.

77. Marshall, "A Friend of the Constitution," 497.

78. Gunther, "Roane's 'Hampden' Essays," 135.

79. Gunther, "Roane's 'Hampden' Essays," 134.

80. Gunther, "Roane's 'Hampden' Essays," 129.

81. Marshall, "A Friend of the Constitution," 499.

82. Marshall, "A Friend of the Constitution," 499.

83. Hampden wrote that it means nothing about the constitutionality of the bank law that it was created by Republicans, saying that they were acting according to "the pressure of the times" and not from a conviction that it would be constitutional. Gunther, "Roane's 'Hampden' Essays," 137. Marshall responded that "if the 'pressure of the times' when this bill was passed, rendered it necessary, I am at a loss to conceive how it can be repugnant to that constitution which was made for all times. The peculiar

circumstances of the moment may render a measure more or less wise, but cannot render it more or less constitutional." Marshall, "A Friend of the Constitution," 499. Of the Republican Supreme Court justices, Hampden assumed that they have been corrupted by power: "They have undergone the common fate attending the possession of power. Few men come out from high stations, as pure as they went in." Gunther, "Roane's 'Hampden' Essays," 151. Hampden noted that all those who possess political power "will not fail to 'feel it and forget right.'" Gunther, "Roane's 'Hampden' Essays," 130. Of course, Spencer Roane held considerable political power in Virginia.

84. Marshall, "A Friend of the Constitution," 493; and *McCulloch v. Maryland*, 17 US 316, 408 (1819).

85. John Marshall, "A Friend to the Union," in *John Marshall, Writings*, ed. Charles F. Hobson (New York: Library of America, 2010), 457.

86. Marshall, "A Friend of the Constitution," 508.

87. Gunther, "Roane's 'Hampden' Essays," 146.

88. Gunther, "Roane's 'Hampden' Essays," 139.

89. Marshall, "A Friend of the Constitution," 500; and Gunther, "Roane's 'Hampden' Essays," 139.

90. Marshall, "A Friend of the Constitution," 502.

91. Marshall, "A Friend of the Constitution," 506.

92. Marshall, "A Friend of the Constitution," 506.

93. Marshall, "A Friend of the Constitution," 507.

94. Marshall, "A Friend of the Constitution," 508.

95. Gunther, "Roane's 'Hampden' Essays," 146.

96. Marshall, "A Friend of the Constitution," 509.

97. Marshall, "A Friend of the Constitution," 511.

98. Marshall, "A Friend of the Constitution," 509.

99. Marshall, "A Friend of the Constitution," 511.

100. Marshall, "A Friend of the Constitution," 516.

101. Marshall, "A Friend of the Constitution," 516.

102. Marshall, "A Friend of the Constitution," 517.

103. Marshall, "A Friend of the Constitution," 517.

104. Marshall, "A Friend of the Constitution," 517.

105. Marshall, "A Friend of the Constitution," 518.

106. Gunther, "Roane's 'Hampden' Essays," 113.

107. Gunther, "Roane's 'Hampden' Essays," 152.

108. Marshall, "A Friend of the Constitution," 521.

109. Marshall, "A Friend of the Constitution," 515.

5

How an Economist Might View
McCulloch v. Maryland

ABRAM N. SHULSKY

This chapter's task is somewhat different from that of the others; it is to look at *McCulloch v. Maryland* not with regard to its crucial role in the development of US constitutional law, but rather from the point of view of financial and economic theory and practice. Viewed through this latter lens, the relative importance of various aspects of the case appear differently than they do to students of constitutional law or than they did to the litigants in 1819. Following this discussion of the case, the chapter briefly discusses how the issues involved in the case relate to the subsequent financial and economic history of the United States.

An Economist's *McCulloch v. Maryland*

In this first part of the chapter, the focus is on the economic and financial questions raised in the case, viewed as economists might view them now. In some cases, the terminology has changed, and the chapter tries to bridge the gap between how the issues might have been discussed in the early 19th century and how they would be discussed now.

Can Congress Create a National Currency? In economic and financial terms, the First Bank of the United States was primarily intended to provide the young nation with a credible paper currency that would be accepted everywhere in the country and the volume of which could be to some extent adjusted. When Alexander Hamilton lists the advantages of a bank in his "Report on a National Bank," the first item he mentions is "the augmentation of the active or productive capital of a country."[1] In our terms, this was equivalent to claiming that a national bank of the type proposed would make possible an increase in the country's money supply.[2]

For us, who are used to fiat currency (i.e., government-issued paper money not backed by precious metal[3]), increasing the money supply appears to be a simple matter of (metaphorically) speeding up the printing presses. But in past times, money meant primarily specie—that is, gold or silver minted into coins or otherwise held as a monetary asset. A paper currency could, under those circumstances, have credibility only if it was backed in specie—that is, if the bearer of the note had the right to redeem it on demand for specie at a fixed rate (e.g., 1/35th of an ounce of gold per dollar)—and if it was generally believed that the issuer of the currency had sufficient specie on hand to meet any such demands.

Thus, the outflow of gold and silver from a country or region, due to an unfavorable balance of trade or for any other reason, threatened to contract the money supply. Unless a paper currency could compensate for the absence of specie, the inevitable result was a slowing of commercial activity and a fall in prices (i.e., deflation), which made it hard for debtors to meet the payments due on their loans and mortgages.

This was precisely the situation the United States found itself in after the Revolutionary War ended in 1783. Because of British trade restrictions, the US could no longer export foodstuffs and other commodities to the British colonies in the West Indies; at the same time, it remained dependent on Britain for many manufactured goods that were not produced domestically. The result was an unfavorable balance of trade, which had the effects described above.

As noted, the paucity of specie could be handled by a credible paper currency, but how to produce such a currency was the problem. During the Revolutionary War, the Congress had issued a fiat currency, called the Continental Dollar, but was unable to maintain its value. The currency depreciated rapidly, giving rise to the phrase "not worth a Continental." The Congress attempted to support the value of the currency by accepting it from the states in payment of a state's allocated share of the national government's expenses. However, under the Articles of Confederation, Congress had no power to force states to pay up, and they were often delinquent. As a result, by the end of its existence in the 1790s, the Continental had lost 99 percent of its original value.[4]

This experience was not unique. Before and under the Articles of Confederation, the various colonies/states had issued their own currencies, called bills of credit. The fates of these currencies varied, but the temptation to solve fiscal problems by issuing too much paper was a constant.[5] For example, Rhode Island's currency depreciated rapidly in the 1780s, forcing the state, in 1789, to give up on its attempt to make its currency legal tender at par and recognize that it was only worth 1/15th of its face value.[6]

This experience explains why Hamilton believed the government could not be trusted to provide a paper currency to make up for the paucity of specie. As he emphatically asserted in his "Report on a National Bank," the power of a government to emit a paper currency is "of a nature so liable to abuse—and, it may even be affirmed, so certain of being abused,—that the wisdom of the government will be shown in never trusting itself with the use of so seducing and dangerous an expedient."[7]

More generally, Hamilton argued that any entity charged with emitting a paper currency must be "under the guidance of *individual interest*, not of *public policy*."[8] (Emphasis in original.) Only private owners, he suggested, could be trusted to resist the temptation to overissue currency, since a resulting run on the bank would ultimately render their investment in the bank worthless. On the other hand, "it would, indeed, be little less than a miracle, should the credit of the bank be at the disposal of the government, if, in a long series of time, there was not experienced a calamitous abuse of it."[9]

Instead, Hamilton favored a national bank to create the national currency and increase the amount of it in circulation (thus making up for the shortage of specie) without running the risks of overissuance inherent in a governmental (or fiat) currency. As he noted:

> It is a well-established fact, that banks in good credit can circulate a far greater sum than the actual quantum of their capital in gold and silver. The extent of the possible excess seems indeterminate; though it has been conjecturally stated at the proportions of two and three to one.[10]

Thus, theoretically, the relevant congressional power for forming the First Bank of the United States would be that of "coin[ing] money [and] regulat[ing] the value thereof."[11] Surprisingly, in the list of enumerated powers (i.e., the powers granted to Congress under Article I, Section 8 of the US Constitution) cited by Chief Justice Marshall as the basis of his opinion, he omits this very power; he mentions instead what he calls the "great powers, to lay and collect taxes; to borrow money; to regulate commerce; to declare and conduct a war; and to raise and support armies and navies."[12] Marshall then argues that the incorporation of the First Bank of the United States is a permissible means of carrying into execution these enumerated powers.[13]

Despite Marshall's omission of the "coining" power, he does not discuss in any detail how the bank relates to carrying into execution of the "great powers" that he does mention. As for the connection between the implementation of these powers and the establishment of a bank, the most detailed argumentation we have is that contained in the memorandum Hamilton prepared for President George Washington to rebut the views of Secretary of State Thomas Jefferson and Attorney General Edmund Jennings Randolph that the creation of the First Bank of the United States represented a congressional usurpation of power.[14]

For example, Hamilton argues that power to tax implies the power to determine "the *money* or *thing* in which taxes are to be paid" and that this may include "bills issued under the authority of the United States."[15] (Emphasis in original.) But it seems a stretch to say that this implies the power to incorporate a bank so that Congress could permit the use of its bills to pay taxes.

Similarly, Hamilton argues that the congressional borrowing power implies a power to stimulate economic activity and the circulation of capital to ensure that, when the government needs to obtain large sums of money (e.g., to prosecute a war), it can borrow funds expeditiously. But this conflates a constitutional power to borrow money with the actual ability to do so; the latter, of course, depends on the government's credit in the markets, something a constitution cannot guarantee. Rather, the point of the power in question—"to borrow money on the credit of the United States"[16]—is to make clear that Congress is authorized to pledge what we now call "the full faith and credit of the United States" to the repayment of a debt.[17]

More generally, Hamilton regards the congressional power to regulate commerce among the states and foreign trade[18] not so much as a power to make the rules under which commerce will be conducted, but rather as a power to promote trade. In fact, this appears to be the primary meaning he attributes to the clause.

> Such only are the regulations to be found in the laws of the United States whose objects are to give encouragement to the enterprise of our own merchants, and to advance our navigation and manufactures. And it is in reference to these general relations of commerce, that an establishment which furnishes facilities to circulation, and a convenient medium of exchange and alienation, is to be regarded as a regulation of trade.[19]

Marshall's own discussion of the relationship of these powers and the establishment of the bank is much less detailed than Hamilton's. After mentioning the underlying powers, Marshall refers in passing to the powers of taxation and raising armies to argue that the Constitution should not be construed as to make their implementation more difficult. But his rhetorical strategy seems to involve the notion that the United States is destined to become a continental republican empire.

> Throughout this vast republic, from the St. Croix to the Gulf of Mexico, from the Atlantic to the Pacific, revenue is to be collected and expended, armies are to be marched and supported. The exigencies of the Nation may require, that the treasure raised in the north should be transported to the south that raised in the east, conveyed to the west, or that this order should be reversed. Is that construction of the Constitution to be preferred which would render these operations difficult, hazardous and expensive?[20]

One can imagine the dismay such a picture of the new country would cause among the old-time Jeffersonians. Although Jefferson himself set the stage for such a view of what the United States would become (through the Louisiana Purchase of 1803), this particular vision of the future would probably have come as something of a shock.

Given Marshall's failure to mention the congressional power to "coin money and regulate the value thereof," it would seem that, at the time, this power was generally believed to be confined to the actual minting of gold and silver into coins and had nothing to do with a "currency" of the sort the bank would create—or, for that matter, of the sort we have now. Underlying this notion was the view that true money had to be specie— that is, something whose value was independent of the government.

This view was expressed in the post–Civil War Greenback cases by those who argued that Congress did not have the power to make the Greenbacks (unbacked paper currency issued during the Civil War) legal tender—that is, the equivalent of specie for the payment of debts. (The market value of the Greenbacks varied during and after the war depending on the military prospects of the Union government and the amount issued; at its low point, it took $2.58 in Greenbacks to buy one dollar of specie.)

Chief Justice Salmon Chase, dissenting in *Knox v. Lee*,[21] described the congressional power to coin money as follows:

> The power conferred is the power to coin money, and these words must be understood as they were used at the time the Constitution was adopted. And we have been referred to no authority which at that time defined coining otherwise than as minting or stamping metals for money; or money otherwise than as metal coined for the purposes of commerce. . . .
>
> It is true that notes issued by banks, both in England and America, were then in circulation, and were used in exchanges, and in common speech called money, and that bills of credit, issued both by Congress and by the States, had been recently in circulation under the same general name; but these notes and bills were never regarded as real money. . . .
>
> The power to coin money was a power to determine the fineness, weight, and denominations of the metallic pieces by which values were to be measured.[22]

This view may seem quaint in an era of fiat currency, but it must have reflected a widespread view of the time, which would explain Marshall's omission of this power from his list of enumerated powers.

Of course, Chase's view lost out. While during the Civil War the introduction of a fiat currency may have been understood as an emergency measure, in the post–Civil War Greenback cases, it eventually became accepted that Congress had the power to create a national currency of whatever kind. In the last of these cases, *Juilliard v. Greenman*, in 1884, the court supported this congressional power as follows:

> Under the power to borrow money on the credit of the United States, and to issue circulating notes for the money borrowed, its power to define the quality and force of those notes as currency is as broad as the like power over a metallic currency under the power to coin money and to regulate the value thereof. *Under the two powers, taken together, congress is authorized to establish a national currency*, either in coin or in paper, and to make that currency lawful money for all purposes, as regards the nation government or private individuals.[23] (Emphasis added.)

Issues Related to Incorporation. Separate from the issue of creating a national currency, the bank raised the question of whether Congress could create a *corporation*. As Marshall, and all other participants in this debate, agreed, "Among the enumerated powers [of Congress], we do not find that of establishing a bank or creating a corporation."[24] So the question became whether creating a bank is a "necessary and proper" means (in the words of Article I, Section 8, Clause 18 of the Constitution) for "carrying into execution" the enumerated powers. Marshall rejected the contention of the bank's opponents that "necessary" should be understood to mean "absolutely necessary"; he denied that "necessary means" included only means such that "without [them] the power would be nugatory."[25]

But the bank's opponents objected not only to the permissive interpretation of the word "necessary" but more specifically to its extension to include the power to create a corporation. In our day, when the corporate form of organization is widespread and the granting of a corporate charter is essentially a ministerial act on the part of a state government bureaucrat, it is easy to underestimate how important this issue was to the bank's opponents. However, at the time, the creation of a corporation typically required a special act of the state legislature and was regarded as anything but routine. In many cases—and indeed in the case of both the First and Second Banks of the United States—a corporate charter contained an element of monopoly; this was explicit in the laws establishing the banks, both of which contained the provision that "no other bank shall be established by any future law of the United States, during the continuance of the corporation hereby created; for which the faith of the United States is hereby pledged."[26]

In political terms, given that obtaining a corporate charter required a political act that was not common or ordinary, corporations carried a whiff of crony capitalism—that is, the use of governmental power to enrich favored individuals. In European monarchies, kings often used corporate charters for precisely that purpose by granting favored subjects the exclusive right to trade in a certain commodity; the recipients could then exploit their monopoly status to earn extraordinary profits. With the Bank of the United States, arguably it was technically not a monopoly, since the states could and did charter banks that competed with it. However, the bank's legislation contained the provision that its "bills or notes . . . payable . . . on demand, in gold or silver coin, shall be receivable in all payments to the United States."[27] This was clearly an advantage that the Bank of the United States had relative to any competitors.

That government-granted monopolies were a sensitive issue at the time may be seen in the wording of the congressional power concerning what we now call patents and copyrights.[28] This is the one time that Congress is explicitly granted the power to award a private citizen a monopoly on some item of commerce; perhaps aware that this matter might raise suspicions on the part of the populace, the drafters were careful to include both the rationale for the power ("to promote the progress of science and useful arts") and significant limitations on it. (The monopoly may be granted only to "authors and inventors" and only for a "limited" time.)[29]

In addition, a corporation grants the investors the benefit of limited liability—that is, the investors in a corporation cannot be held liable for the debts of the corporation itself. This again could be seen as giving favored individuals a privilege not shared by the general population.

More generally, the bank's opponents feared it would become, thanks to the concentration of wealth that it represented, a political force to be reckoned with, one that might become a danger to republican institutions.[30] Opponents could look to the Bank of England, which some saw as a source of corruption. Our current concerns with lobbying activity in Washington and the role of money in politics reflect this same unease with concentrations of financial power.

All this was wrapped up in the concern over the creation of corporations. That this particular corporation would play a central role in the nation's financial life only exacerbated the concern.

"Privatization" of Policymaking. The constitutional argument about the bank centered on whether Congress had the power to incorporate a national bank. There does not seem to have been much debate at the time about the propriety of "privatizing" such an important matter of public policy as the creation and regulation of the national currency.[31]

As noted above, the congressional power "to coin money [and] regulate the value thereof"[32] was not relied on by Marshall (or, in the main, by Hamilton) to justify the bank's creation. Literally, of course, the bank did not "coin money" or "regulate [its] value." But if the power is read more expansively as a power to create a national currency for the United States, then arguably Congress had delegated to a group of private citizens the authority to exercise this vital power of the national government.

Constitutionally, this could raise the issue of whether, and to what extent, Congress can delegate its powers to other institutions or agencies, an issue that came to the fore when the Supreme Court struck down a section of the National Industrial Recovery Act (NIRA) of 1933 as "an unconstitutional delegation of legislative power."[33] Indeed, the bank represents an even more extreme case, since the power in question was being delegated to a privately owned corporation rather than to the president, as was the case in the NIRA.

Interestingly, Joseph Hopkinson, one of Maryland's attorneys, raised this issue of delegation, but only with respect to a side issue—whether it was constitutional to give the bank (assuming Congress had the power to incorporate it in the first place) the authority to establish branches "in the several states, without the direction of congress, or the assent of the states."[34] While Hopkinson denies the constitutionality of the establishment of bank branches at all (as not being necessary for implementing any of Congress' enumerated powers), he argues that "if these branches are to be supported, on the grounds of the constitutional necessity,"[35] then Congress should have to decide where they are to be established. He contends that "if this power belongs to congress, it cannot be delegated to the directors of a bank, any more than any other legislative power may be transferred to any other body of citizens."[36] Lurking in the background is the presumption that the bank directors can be expected to decide on branch locations not on grounds of any governmental necessity or convenience but based on what would maximize the bank's profitability.

Marshall, in his opinion, gives the delegation issue short shrift: "It would have been unwise to locate [the branches] in the charter, and it would be unnecessarily inconvenient to employ the legislative power in making those subordinate arrangements."[37] Marshall contends that "the bank itself may, we think, be safely trusted with the selection of places where those branches shall be fixed,"[38] without addressing the point that the bank's decisions would likely be based on profitability rather than the needs of the government. (This latter point is obliquely recognized in the proviso Marshall adds to the phrase just quoted: "reserving always to the Government the right to require that a branch shall be located where it may be deemed necessary."[39])

Taxation Issue. Ultimately, *McCulloch v. Maryland* concerned whether Maryland could tax the First Bank of the United States; the Supreme Court, guided by the premise that "the power to tax is the power to destroy," decided in the negative. Interestingly enough, Hopkinson, arguing for Maryland, agreed with the premise, if not with the decision. Observing that any power may be abused, he dismissed the danger that states might use their taxing power to destroy the institutions of the federal government by arguing that "whenever the states shall be in a disposition to uproot the general government, they will take more direct and speedy means; and until they have this disposition, they will not use these."[40]

However, Hopkinson also made statements that pointed in a different direction. He asked, rhetorically, "Can the bank and its branches . . . claim to be exempt from the *ordinary and equal taxation of property*, as assessed in the states in which they are placed?"[41] (Emphasis added.) This would suggest a possible rule: A state may tax instrumentalities of the federal government as long as the taxation is imposed equally on federal and nonfederal institutions—in this case, on the First Bank of the United States and the state-chartered banks. However, Hopkinson does not pursue this line of argument, presumably because the Maryland law he was defending in fact applied only to bank branches established "without authority from the state,"[42] of which the Baltimore branch of the First Bank of the United States was the only one. The record of the case does not show that the taxes imposed by this law were higher than those imposed on banks chartered by Maryland, although Hopkinson's silence on the matter implies that they were.

Hopkinson's implicit suggestion was countered explicitly by William Pinkney, one of the bank's attorneys.

> A criterion which has been proposed, is to see whether the tax has been laid, impartially, upon the state banks, as well as the Bank of the United States. Even this is an unsafe test; for the state governments may wish, and intend, to destroy their own banks. The existence of any national institution ought not to depend upon so frail a security.[43]

Marshall did not have to consider this possibility, since the Maryland law applied only to the Bank of the United States. After *McCulloch*, Maryland could have recast its law to tax equally all banks in the state, however chartered. One cannot predict how Marshall would have reacted to such a move. (One suspects he would have sided with Pinkney and rejected it.) But it is worth noting that, at present, states routinely tax, for example, salaries paid to their citizens by the federal government, at the same rate as other similar income. By a strict application of Marshall's reasoning, this should be questionable: If the power to tax is indeed the power to destroy, a state could tax federal salaries at 100 percent, thus effectively making it impossible for the US government to hire employees in the state, thereby impeding Congress' enumerated power to establish post offices.[44]

The key to this conundrum is Marshall's absolutist understanding of "the power to tax is the power to destroy." The implication is that, once it is admitted that a state may tax some form of property or income, there can be no constitutional limits on how that power is exercised. Today, of course, the Supreme Court would probably be more open to various limits on a state's power to tax. That a state's taxes should not discriminate against property or income connected with the federal government (e.g., federal salaries or transfer payments) would not seem an impossible requirement.

The Role (and Absence) of a Central Bank in
US Economic and Financial Development

McCulloch settled the issue of the constitutionality of the First Bank of the United States, but it could not, of course, guarantee the bank's future. One decade later, Andrew Jackson's election as president represented the political victory of the view—going back to Jefferson's tenure as secretary of state in the first Washington administration—that the bank represented an oligarchic deviation from true republican principles. After Jackson vetoed Congress' 1832 attempt to extend the charter of the Second Bank, he ordered the removal of government funds from it, thus ensuring its demise when its charter expired in 1836.

From then until 1914, the United States lacked a central bank.[45] When the financial system received a shock, the result could be a banking panic, in which note holders and depositors all tried to convert their notes into specie or withdraw their deposits at the same time. Without a mechanism for supplying additional liquidity at such junctures, the result could be bank failures and economic depression. From the 1830s onward, the US economic situation was vulnerable to such crises, and it was such a banking panic in 1907 that set in motion the chain of events that ultimately produced the Federal Reserve system with which we are familiar.[46]

Thus, a strange feature of US financial history is that the nation had a more sophisticated financial system in its first four decades than it had in the succeeding eight. This was primarily due to Alexander Hamilton, who was evidently familiar with financial developments in Great Britain, especially the Bank of England. During the 18th century, the Bank of England provided what seemed to onlookers as almost unlimited credit to the British government, enabling it to fight that period's many wars. This financial strength was generally recognized as a key component of Britain's geopolitical power. Hamilton understood the role of the Bank of the United States in similar terms, as a source of emergency funding for the government when required.

> And while this mass [of capital] is always ready, and can at once be put
> in motion, in aid of the Government, the interest of the bank to afford
> that aid, independent of regard to the public safety and welfare, is a

sure pledge of its disposition to go as far in its compliances, as can in prudence be desired.[47]

As noted, Hamilton's first reason for a national bank was so a national currency could be created in an adequate amount to allow the national economy to grow and flourish. The key issue was how to create public confidence in that currency; as we have seen, the first effort to create such a national current—the Continental Dollars issued by the Continental Congress during the Revolutionary War—was an abject failure. Hamilton believed that, in the long run, no government could be trusted with the power to issue a currency.

> The stamping of paper is an operation so much easier than the laying of taxes, that a government in the practice of paper emissions would rarely fail, in any [great and trying] emergency, to indulge itself too far in the employment of that resource, to avoid, as much as possible, one less auspicious to present popularity.[48]

Hamilton's solution was to have a banking system in which the banks issued notes that could serve as currency. Since the notes could be redeemed in specie (gold or silver), the self-interest of the bankers could serve as a check on the amount of currency they issued. If too many note holders tried to redeem their notes at the same time, the bank could run out of specie and fail. At the apex of this system was the First Bank of the United States, which could discipline the other banks (chartered by the various states) by holding or buying up a state bank's notes and threatening to present them for redemption in specie.

Hamilton also recognized the necessity of a "lender of last resort"—that is, some mechanism for injecting liquidity into the financial system to stave off a panic in which depositors and note holders all attempted to withdraw their money from the banks at the same time. As noted above, a characteristic of banking is that a given amount of reserves serves as backing for deposits and notes several times as large. Thus, the banking system is always vulnerable to a shock that causes a loss of confidence in the banks, thus possibly precipitating a run on the bank.[49] Although the bank may be solvent (that is, its assets are greater than its liabilities), it may be illiquid (that is, it cannot feasibly convert those assets into cash fast enough to meet its immediate obligations to creditors). Thus, a panic is possible, in which, as financial institutions try to sell off assets quickly enough to meet their creditors' demands, the price of those assets falls precipitously, thus ultimately rendering the institutions insolvent, as well as illiquid.

To handle this situation, there must be a lender of last resort, either to lend money against the assets of the financial institutions or, if necessary, to buy them up to prevent their decline to "fire sale" prices. In the first years under the new US Constitution, the country faced two such situations, a smaller crisis in August–September 1791 and then a larger one in March–April 1792.[50] In both cases, the US Treasury, under Hamilton, acted as a classic lender of last resort, injecting liquidity into the securities markets. Hamilton could do this because his plan for consolidating and funding the US debt included a provision for a "sinking fund" that was authorized to purchase US debt securities on the market.[51] Although the ostensible purpose of the sinking fund was to reassure the public that the government planned to extinguish the debt, Hamilton may have had the alternative purpose in mind when he proposed it.[52]

Indeed, it has been argued that, in handling these crises, Hamilton developed the theory of the lender of last resort, which is usually attributed to Walter Bagehot,[53] who formulated it 80 years later in his famous book *Lombard Street: A Description of the Money Market.* According to this view, Hamilton robbed himself of the distinction of having invented the theory by expressing his ideas only in letters to the officials of the Bank of New York and the Bank of the United States, in which he instructed them to buy securities on behalf of the Treasury or encouraged them to lend liberally. Some of the relevant information has only recently become available to scholars; it is unlikely, for example, that Bagehot would have been aware of Hamilton's activity when he formulated his rules.

Following the expiration of the Second Bank of the United States in 1836, the US no longer had a system for controlling the issuance of notes by state banks. It has been observed that "most state banks . . . were pleased with the BUS's [Bank of the United States'] demise because it meant the shuttering of its clearing and collection functions, which had served as a check on their own lending and note issues."[54] The US also had no lender of last resort, and the country experienced a succession of banking crises throughout the remainder of the 19th century. Of course, at the same time, for reasons unconnected with these financial developments, the country grew economically at a rapid pace. The underlying factors—the abundance of land, technological developments, and immigration—were not negated by the periodic financial problems.

During the Civil War—the type of emergency in which a highly developed national banking system's ability to lend large sums to the government would have been most helpful—the government was forced to issue US notes, the so-called Greenbacks, to cover its deficits. While the Greenbacks were declared legal tender for payment of debts and taxes (except for import duties), they were not backed in specie (i.e., the government did not promise to redeem them for gold or silver). Consequently, they depreciated in market value relative to gold, varying with the fortune of the Union armies and the dollar amount issued. (At their lowest point, it required 258 Greenbacks to purchase 100 dollars in gold on the open market; by the end of the war, Greenbacks had risen to the point that 150 were equivalent to 100 dollars in gold.) Eventually, Congress in 1875 mandated the redemption of Greenbacks at par by 1879.[55]

It is impossible to say whether a national bank such as the Second Bank of the United States, had it continued in existence until the Civil War, would have enabled the government to finance the war without issuing a fiat currency. Similarly, one cannot know whether a national bank could have avoided the secular deflation from the 1870s onward that eventually led to the populist movement and the demand for free coinage of silver in the 1890s. The silver movement was essentially a call for inflation to reverse the deflation and thus relieve the debt burden, primarily on agricultural interests. To some extent, the issue was defused by the large gold finds in the Yukon and South Africa in the 1890s, which stemmed deflation and produced inflationary pressures by the end of the decade.

As noted, the banking panic of 1907 led to the creation of the Federal Reserve system in 1914. The Fed, unlike the Bank of the United States, is essentially part of the federal government: Its Board of Governors, which exercises control over the system, is appointed by the president with the consent of the Senate. Technically, the individual Reserve Banks (of New York, Chicago, etc.) are owned by the national banks in their districts; however, the "owner" banks receive only a fixed payment based on their capital contribution, and all remaining profits are (after payment of the Reserve Systems expenses) remitted to the US Treasury.

However, in one important sense, the cautious spirit of Alexander Hamilton lives on: The Fed jealously guards its independence of the executive and legislative branches of government.

Notes

1. Alexander Hamilton, "Report on a National Bank," in *Alexander Hamilton's Papers on Public Credit, Commerce and Finance*, ed. Samuel McKee Jr. (New York: Liberal Arts Press, 1957), 54.

2. It was a matter of not only increasing the money supply but also creating a currency that could circulate easily throughout the country. A currency issued by a state-chartered bank (or, before the ratification of the Constitution, by a state) might be accepted at par in its home state, but it would lose value further away from its place of issue. Thus, a merchant in Boston might be hesitant to accept a currency emanating from North Carolina; he would need to know whether those with whom he did business, in Boston or elsewhere, would accept it and, if so, at what rate.

3. It is sometimes said that fiat currencies such as the dollar are "unbacked" simply, but this is not strictly true, since the federal government levies taxes and accepts dollars in payment of them. (The federal government has also declared the dollar legal tender for private debts.) An example of a simply unbacked currency would be bitcoin, which no one is obligated to accept.

4. In the 1790 act that funded the outstanding debt of the United States, Continentals were accepted at 1 percent of their face value. An Act Making Provision for the Debt of the United States, 1st Cong., 2nd sess., chap. 34, § 3. While key elements of the US financial system were being established in 1790 and 1791, revolutionary France was beginning its experience of a paper currency system, the *assignats*, which were in principle backed by lands confiscated from the Church but which, due to the large magnitude of the amounts issued, eventually lost all their value.

5. The Constitution put an end to this temptation by prohibiting the states from emitting bills of credit. US Const. art. I, § 10.

6. For a thorough discussion of fiat currencies issued by colonies/states before the ratification of the US Constitution, see Arthur J. Rolnick, Bruce D. Smith, and Warren E. Weber, "In Order to Form a More Perfect Monetary Union," *Quarterly Review* 1741 (Fall 1993): 2–13, https://www.minneapolisfed.org/research/quarterly-review/in-order-to-form-a-more-perfect-monetary-union. The example of the Rhode Island currency is on page 5.

7. Alexander Hamilton, *Alexander Hamilton's Papers on Public Credit, Commerce and Finance*, ed. Samuel McKee Jr. (New York: Liberal Arts Press, 1957), 72.

8. Hamilton, "Report on a National Bank," 83.

9. Hamilton, "Report on a National Bank," 83.

10. Hamilton, "Report on a National Bank," 55.

11. US Const. art. I, § 8, cl. 5.

12. *McCulloch v. Maryland*, 17 US 316, 407 (1819).

13. See *McCulloch v. Maryland*, 17 US 316, 411 (1819). These are the same powers that Hamilton stressed in his memorandum to President Washington in his "Opinion as to the Constitutionality of the Bank of the United States." Alexander Hamilton, "Opinion as to the Constitutionality of the Bank of the United States," in *Alexander Hamilton's Papers on Public Credit, Commerce and Finance*, ed. Samuel McKee Jr. (New York: Liberal Arts Press, 1957), 100–37. Hamilton's listing of the relevant congressional powers appears on pages 122–23. Later in the same document, however, Hamilton mentioned the "coining" power in passing in the context of a more general discussion of the "manifest design and scope of the Constitution," which he claims is "to vest in Congress all the powers requisite to the effectual administration of the finances of the United States." Hamilton, "Opinion as to the Constitutionality of the Bank of the United States," 134.

14. Hamilton, "Opinion as to the Constitutionality of the Bank of the United States," 100–37.

15. Hamilton, "Opinion as to the Constitutionality of the Bank of the United States," 123. Emphasis in the original.

16. US Const. art. I, § 8, cl. 2.

17. This seems unexceptional to us, but at the time, key figures such as Thomas Jefferson believed there was something improper—politically and morally—in one generation's presumption in saddling future generations with obligations to whose assumption they had no opportunity to consent. The ultimate result, they feared, would be a class of government creditors who would use their influence to exact high taxes from the common man to pay the interest on the debt. In 1798, Jefferson expressed the wish that the Constitution be amended to take away Congress' power to borrow money. Thomas Jefferson, letter to John Taylor, November 26, 1798, https://founders.archives.gov/documents/Jefferson/01-30-02-0398.

18. US Const. art. I, § 8, cl. 3.

19. Hamilton, "Opinion as to the Constitutionality of the Bank of the United States," 128.

20. *McCulloch v. Maryland*, 17 US 316, 408 (1819).

21. *Knox v. Lee* upheld Congress' power to issue Greenbacks and make them legal tender for all debts. *Knox v. Lee*, 79 US 457 (1871).

22. *Knox v. Lee*, 79 US 457, 583–84 (1871).

23. *Juilliard v. Greenman*, 110 US 421, 448 (1884). This fundamentally laid the issue to rest, although it resurfaced briefly in the Depression-era Gold Clause Cases, which upheld the federal government's right to abrogate provisions of contracts that called for calculating the amount owed under the contract in terms of a fixed amount of gold, rather than dollars.

24. *McCulloch v. Maryland*, 17 US 316, 406 (1819).

25. *McCulloch v. Maryland*, 17 US 316, 413 (1819).

26. An Act to Incorporate the Subscribers to the Bank of the United States, 1st Cong., 3rd sess., chap. 10, § 12 (1791); and An Act to Incorporate the Subscribers to the Bank of

the United States, 14th Cong., 1st sess., chap. 44, § 21 (1816).

27. Bank Bill of 1791, 1st Cong., § 10 (February 25, 1791); and Act for a National Bank, 14th Cong., § 14 (April 10, 1816). The latter section contains, however, the proviso "unless otherwise directed by Act of Congress."

28. US Const. art. I, § 8, cl. 8.

29. Perhaps the bank's opponents could have argued that this provision implies that granting monopoly rights is an exceptional act, one that requires explicit constitutional sanction. Thus, according to this argument, Congress would not be empowered to grant a monopoly in any other circumstance. There is no evidence that the opponents made this argument, although they did point out that the Constitutional Convention rejected a proposal to empower Congress to grant charters of incorporation to promote the construction of canals. Hamilton notes this action by the Constitutional Convention but evades the problem on the grounds that its precise nature or the reasons for rejecting it were not accurately known. Hamilton, "Opinion as to the Constitutionality of the Bank of the United States," 113.

30. As early as May 1792, Jefferson told President Washington that there was a public belief that bank's wealth and issuance of paper currency "has furnished effectual means of corrupting a portion of the legislature." Thomas Jefferson, *Writings*, ed. Merrill D. Peterson (New York: Literary Classics of the United States, 1984), 986. Jefferson claimed the ultimate aim of those engaged in corrupting the legislature was to create in America a monarchy on the English model. Jefferson, *Writings*, 987.

31. By contrast, President Andrew Jackson's veto message against the rechartering of the Second Bank of the United States emphasized that the granting of monopoly privileges to the bank "operated as a gratuity of many millions to the stockholders." Andrew Jackson, "Veto Message," July 10, 1832, Avalon Project, Yale Law School, http://avalon.law.yale.edu/19th_century/ajveto01.asp. Hamilton, as discussed above, argued that the power to issue paper money could not safely be given to the government.

32. US Const. art. I, § 8, cl. 5.

33. *A. L. A. Schechter Poultry Corp. v. United States*, 295 US 495, 542 (1935).

34. *McCulloch v. Maryland*, 17 US 316, 334 (1819).

35. *McCulloch v. Maryland*, 17 US 316, 335 (1819).

36. *McCulloch v. Maryland*, 17 US 316, 336 (1819).

37. *McCulloch v. Maryland*, 17 US 316, 424 (1819).

38. *McCulloch v. Maryland*, 17 US 316, 424–25 (1819).

39. *McCulloch v. Maryland*, 17 US 316, 425 (1819).

40. *McCulloch v. Maryland*, 17 US 316, 349 (1819).

41. *McCulloch v. Maryland*, 17 US 316, 337 (1819).

42. *McCulloch v. Maryland*, 17 US 316, 320 (1819).

43. *McCulloch v. Maryland*, 17 US 316, 392 (1819).

44. US Const. art. I, § 8, cl. 7.

45. Technically, neither the First nor the Second Bank of the United States was a full-fledged central bank, in the sense of being a lender of last resort with responsibility for maintaining the viability of the financial system. Nevertheless, thanks to the sophistication of Alexander Hamilton and some of his successors as secretary of the Treasury, it could function somewhat in that role.

46. During the 1907 crisis, J. P. Morgan, by far the richest man in the US at the time, played to some extent the role of a central bank, investing his own money at crucial points and corralling the main New York City banks into providing liquidity to threatened financial institutions. These events are discussed in Ellis W. Tallman and Jon R. Moen, "Lessons from the Panic of 1907," *Economic Review* (May/June 1990): 2–13.

47. Hamilton, "Report on a National Bank," 57–58. The second sentence deals with the opponents' complaint that, as a privately held corporation, the bank would be within its rights to refuse to lend money to the government.

48. Hamilton, "Report on a National Bank," 72.

49. The existence of deposit insurance through the Federal Deposit Insurance Corporation has made the classic "run on the bank" a thing of the past in the US. However, similar events can occur wherever financial institutions are funded by credits that can be withdrawn at any time; in 2008, for example, some money market funds came under pressure as investors rapidly withdrew large sums.

50. Both involved speculation that drove prices to unsustainably high prices: in the first case, in the Bank of the United States scrip (essentially, options to buy shares in the bank) and, in the second case, the newly issued securities of the US (the government debt issued under Hamilton's plan for consolidating and funding the debts inherited from the government under the Articles of Confederation).

51. For a discussion of these events, see Richard Sylla, Robert E. Wright, and David J. Cowen, "Alexander Hamilton, Central Banker: Crisis Management During the U.S. Financial Panic of 1792," *Business History Review* 82, no. 1 (Spring 2009): 61–86.

52. Sylla, Wright, and Cowen, "Alexander Hamilton, Central Banker," 66–67. Jefferson and James Madison accused Hamilton of regarding the public debt as a "blessing" and having no intention of ever extinguishing it. As noted above, Jefferson regarded the existence of the debt as a threat to republicanism and the investors and traders in it as an oligarchic faction that would feed off high taxes to be paid by the rest of the society.

53. Sylla, Wright, and Cowen, "Alexander Hamilton, Central Banker," 79–81.

54. Howard Bodenhorn, "Federal and State Commercial Banking Policy in the Federalist Era and Beyond," in *Founding Choices: American Economic Policy in the 1790s*, ed. Douglas A. Irwin and Richard Sylla (Chicago: University of Chicago Press, 2011), 164.

55. In 1877, the secretary of the Treasury earmarked sufficient gold for the redemption of the outstanding Greenbacks, after which they circulated at par.

6

McCulloch v. Maryland and John Marshall's Judicial Statesmanship

ADAM J. WHITE

John Marshall is "universally referred to as 'the great Chief Justice,'" as his more recent successor, William Rehnquist, aptly observed.[1] But was the great chief justice a judicial *statesman*? Was his opinion for the unanimous Court in *McCulloch v. Maryland* an act of judicial statesmanship?

It is not unreasonable to suggest, as Justice Felix Frankfurter did, that *McCulloch* was Marshall's "greatest single judicial performance."[2] But to declare it an act of judicial *statesmanship* requires us to ascertain what "judicial statesmanship" is—indeed, to ascertain that constitutional judges can and should be "statesmen" at all.

Notions of statesmanship fit uneasily with our view of judges. It is one thing to observe that a judge's personal qualities are statesmanlike; it is quite another to suggest that the judge's *jurisprudence* is statesmanlike.[3] If we see the judge's work as "lawyers' work," requiring only "a close examination of the text, history of the text, traditional understanding of the text, and so forth,"[4] then it is not obvious how notions of statesmanship could ever be relevant to the judge's work, let alone virtuous. Circumscribing the work of a constitutional judge in such terms, any judicial effort to conserve a court's "political capital" in light of public opinion "will itself detract from the very political capital that judicial statesmanship seeks to preserve," as one thoughtful scholar recently contended.[5]

But as Publius recognized, the judge's work is not merely a matter of interpretation narrowly conceived, but a matter of judgment by which the courts adjudicate cases by interpreting and applying the laws with an eye to the proper and limited constitutional role of courts in our constitutional republic.[6] In this we see room for a form of judicial statesmanship, one roughly akin to the statesmanship of Edmund Burke—and one that Marshall's opinion for the Court in *McCulloch* exemplifies.

On Judicial Statesmanship

Discussions of "judicial statesmanship" start from particular (and particularly recent) notions of both statesmanship and the judicial office. But to best understand judicial statesmanship, we should begin with older and better notions of both.

Tocquevillian Judging and Judicial Statesmanship. As with so many other matters, notions of judicial statesmanship can be traced to the "perceptive Frenchman,"[7] Alexis de Tocqueville. Reporting on the young American republic, Tocqueville concluded that federal judges "must not only be good citizens" but must even be statesmen.

> Federal judges . . . must not only be good citizens, educated and upright men—qualities necessary to all magistrates—*one must also find statesmen in them*; they must know how to discern the spirit of their times, to confront the obstacles they can defeat, and to turn away from the current when the flood threatens to carry them away with the sovereignty of the Union and the obedience due its laws.[8] (Emphasis added.)

Tocqueville's assessment of federal judges followed from his assessment of the Supreme Court's then-seven justices. His account sometimes risks grandiosity: "In the hands of seven federal judges rest ceaselessly the peace, the prosperity, the very existence of the Union," such that while "the president can fail without the state's suffering," the corruption of the Supreme Court could well bring "anarchy or civil war."[9] But if Tocqueville's rhetoric occasionally went too far, the heart of his assessment of judges was subtle, realistic, and accurate: Their power is "immense; but it is a power of opinion. They are omnipotent as long as the people consent to obey the law; they can do nothing when [the people] scorn it."[10]

And, he warned, the people would be more likely to scorn judges' decisions in controversial cases if the people saw the judges as willfully and eagerly reaching out for matters to decide, instead of waiting passively for cases to reach them—a risk that seems particularly significant in a nation where, as Tocqueville famously observed, "almost no political question in the United States . . . is not resolved sooner or later into a judicial question."[11]

For Tocqueville, then, the key to a judge's self-preservation is ultimately his self-restraint and subtlety in service of a republican rule of law. Because the judge does not "take the initiative" or "attack laws in a theoretical and general manner," he does not "[enter] onto the political stage with a bang." Instead, "when the judge attacks a law in an obscure debate and over a particular application" in cases brought to him by parties, "he in part hides the importance of the attack [on a statute] from the regard of the public."[12]

In sum, by Tocqueville's appraisal, "the American judge is led despite himself onto the terrain of politics. He judges the law only because he has to judge a case, and he cannot prevent himself from judging the case."[13] But even against the backdrop of judicial self-restraint, the Tocquevillian judge is a "statesman" only to the extent that he can successfully "discern the spirit of their times, to confront the obstacles they can defeat, and to turn away from the current when the flood threatens to carry [them] away."[14]

Largely absent from Tocqueville's seminal account of judicial statesmanship, however, is an account of judicial interpretive methodology. Tocqueville recognizes that the Constitution is "the first of laws" and thus commands judges' obedience above all other law,[15] but he specifies no interpretive methodology for judges to apply in the adjudication of cases under the Constitution. This silence on judicial interpretive methodology places Tocqueville at a remove from modern debates over the Supreme Court's work; in the era of textualism, methodology is at the center of debate, and increasingly it is the exclusive focus.

20th-Century Judicial Statesmanship. "Let me timidly suggest caution in the use of the word *statesmanship* with regard to judges," Justice Oliver Wendell Holmes wrote to Professor Felix Frankfurter in 1923, for "the word suggests a more political way of thinking than is desirable and also has become slightly banal."[16] (First emphasis added; second emphasis omitted.) Perhaps Holmes was gently rebuffing Frankfurter's suggestion, just months earlier in a tribute to Holmes himself, that the Supreme Court's development of "constitutional law," especially on questions of federalism and the separation of powers, "plainly" requires the justices to "move in the field of statesmanship."[17] What Frankfurter meant precisely by this "statesmanship" is not obvious: Sometimes he applies the term in service of syrupy sycophancy;[18] elsewhere he undercuts his own cause by dubiously or at least imprudently bestowing the title "statesman" on the infamous Chief Justice Roger Taney, whose "statesmanship on the Bench has unfortunately been obscured by the tragic dicta of the *Dred Scott* case."[19]

But in the final analysis, Frankfurter seems to define judicial statesmanship as something untethered to constitutional text. He declares the Court's commerce clause decisions to be unambiguous "acts of statesmanship," for the Court "has drawn its lines where it has drawn them because it has thought it wise to draw them there. The wisdom of its wisdom *depends upon a judgment about practical matters and not upon a knowledge of the Constitution.*"[20] (Emphasis added.)

Frankfurter's own nebulous view of judicial statesmanship echoes throughout his other writings, but he did not venture a coherent and complete analysis of the subject. Collecting some of these scattered fragments, Gary Jacobsohn observes that while "Frankfurter's stand on the *importance* of judicial statesmanship is thus clear[,] his views on *how* a jurist might fulfill the statesman's role are considerably less so."[21] (Emphasis added.)

Decades later, Neil Siegel offered a more thorough account of judicial statesmanship, one defined in terms of the law's "social legitimacy." Siegel proposed that "judicial statesmanship charges judges with approaching cases so as to facilitate the ability of the legal order to legitimate itself over the long term" by accomplishing two objectives: "expressing social values as social circumstances change and sustaining social solidarity amidst reasonable, irreconcilable disagreement."[22] Siegel traces the former goal, the expression of social values, to the mid-20th-century legal process school of Henry Hart, Herbert Wechsler, and Albert Sacks[23]; he traces the latter goal, sustaining social solidarity, to John Rawls and others.[24]

Defined in these terms, Siegel's judicial statesman labors to bring legal texts forward to catch up with social progress—approaching cases "so as to enable the legal system to maintain pace with those changes, to 'bring the public administration of justice into touch with changed moral, social, or political conditions.'"[25] Yet at the same time, the judicial statesman "must shape and refine as he expresses," claiming responsibility for "authoritatively expressing certain values and not others, with putting the power and prestige of the law behind the ones they embrace in an effort to 'sort out the enduring values of a society.'"[26] To that end Siegel quotes Alexander Bickel's *Least Dangerous Branch: The Supreme Court at the Bar of Politics*, although his vision of statesmanship seems not entirely consistent with Bickel's own approach, which has the court "keeping pace with" social change instead of leading the people by cooling the passions of a public that would "ordinarily prefer to act on expediency rather than take the long view."[27]

Siegel, anticipating the criticism that his judicial statesman is unmoored from actual law, reassures the reader that "this is hardly to suggest that 'anything goes' in the realm of judicial statesmanship."[28] But to define the set of what "goes," he offers only a tautology: "The Court labors under the obligation to succeed."[29] (Quotation marks omitted.) If his entire approach suffers from "vagueness," then it cannot be helped because "vagueness is to be expected when the purposes of law that statesmanship seeks to accomplish are multiple and relate paradoxically."[30] And in the end, Siegel joins Frankfurter in defining "judicial statesmanship" in conflict with originalist interpretation of statutory text: "Statesmanship can take some of the pressure off of" otherwise originalist judges such as Antonin Scalia, whose resort to stare decisis as a brake on pure textualism suggests to Siegel that "judges cannot proceed with strictly originalist premises because law *must* express evolving social values."[31] (Emphasis added.)

In the decades between Frankfurter and Siegel, however, Professor Harry Clor attempted to connect judicial statesmanship to constitutional interpretation somewhat more directly. Writing near the end of the Warren Burger Court, still in the wake of the Earl Warren Court, Clor recognized that "embattled adversaries of an aggressive, policy-making judiciary tend to shun, when they do not positively denigrate, the concept that judges can be statesmen."[32] Yet while sharing much of the criticism of progressive judicial activism, he did not share the aversion to judicial statesmanship and instead advanced a version of statesmanship that rooted judicial discretion in the country's tradition.

Starting from Tocqueville's own aforementioned writings on judging and judicial statesmanship, Clor embraces a view of the Supreme Court that "hardly looks like a simple court of law" but which "must possess and exercise considerable political judgment, including judgment about the temper of public opinion and consequently about what is possible or impossible to accomplish (or dangerous to attempt) by judicial decisions."[33] Clor restates Tocqueville's observations as an argument that "the power of the courts depends upon public respect for the law," which in turn "depends upon the moral authority of the idea of law."[34] This in turn requires the Court to promote, not impair, the public's respect for the law. That final task requires not just the skills of interpreting legal documents but also the capacity for "political prudence" and "the need for judges who can be moral educators" akin to Ralph Lerner's circuit-riding "republican schoolmasters."[35]

Clor recognizes that judicial invocation of values outside the legal text itself requires the striking of a delicate balance: Reliance on certain "regime considerations" is necessary to lend the Court's decisions the ballast of political support and sustainability, but there must not be too much of a good thing for "frequent and dramatic reliance upon constitution-transcending norms is likely to disrupt the continuity or stability of the law and undermine the people's confidence that the law is ruling."[36] (On this point Clor's approach resembles Publius' warning that if the courts are seen as "substitut[ing] their own pleasure to the constitutional intentions of the legislature," then they risk the courts' own political legitimacy.[37]) But this, then, is the judgment that undergirds judicial statesmanship: to grapple "to discern that *this* is or is not the appropriate time (or case), and to discern *how* the ethical standard can be incorporated in the law without injury to it—these are tasks calling for something more than the capacities of a good lawyer."[38] (Second emphasis added.)

For much of the analysis, Clor harkens to Chief Justice Marshall's example. On the question of state power and private rights in *Fletcher v. Peck*,[39] for example, Marshall faced a challenge that called "for something more persuasive than an ordinary legal judgment based on technical analysis of the language of constitutional clauses," but rather "for an appeal to large principles which are common to our free institutions . . . to preserve respect for the Constitution as law while periodically calling attention to the political theory which supports and guides the law."[40] Clor contrasts his approach with the then-contemporary "non-interpretivist doctrines" prevailing on the left, especially the "democratic process rationale" advanced by John Hart Ely's *Democracy and Distrust: A Theory of Judicial Review* and the moral-right rationale of Ronald Dworkin's *Taking Rights Seriously*.[41] All these approaches, Clor concludes, "reflect very little disposition to preserve; they are, for the most part, strikingly present-oriented or forward-looking doctrines."[42]

But, perhaps more importantly, Clor also contrasts his approach with the proto-textualism of conservatives such as Professor Raoul Berger, who "would confine the Supreme Court Justice almost entirely to the role of a legal and linguistic historian," which Clor sees as insufficient for judicial resolution of questions arising from at least the more "amorphous constitutional provisions," if not even the ones (such as the Fourteenth Amendment) that Berger saw as straightforward.[43] For Clor, judicial statesmanship arises when "recourse must be had to considerations beyond the written Constitution" and "the judge is obliged to take his direction from regime principles."[44]

This conservative argument for judicial statesmanship spurred a conservative response. Matthew Franck's disagreement with Clor traces to a deeper disagreement with Tocqueville over whether Supreme Court justices should attempt statesmanship at all. Franck agrees with Clor's reading of Tocqueville as describing a "judicial statesmanship" that demands significant "political judgment." But Franck, unlike Clor, finds Tocqueville's own approach to be profoundly misguided[45] because judges must not "attend to the state of [public opinion] when rendering judgment."[46]

Franck roots his own rejection of judicial statesmanship in an understanding of the *Federalist* that locates statesmanship in the president and the Senate, not the courts.[47] True, Publius indicates in *Federalist* 78 that judges must be (in Franck's words) "men a cut above the ordinary," but this is not to say that the judges would be *statesmen* exercising political judgment.[48] Rather, *Federalist* 78 calls for judges who are "faithful guardians of the Constitution," ensuring "inflexible and uniform adherence to the rights of the Constitution, and of individuals, which we perceive to be indispensable in the courts of justice."[49] Thus, Franck concludes, any theory of "judicial 'statesmanship'" that relies on judicial consideration of values not bound up in the constitutional text itself "is not only ungrounded in the Framers' thought but is an impeachable offense."[50]

Franck's account differs starkly from the others in his appraisal of judicial statesmanship, seeing a vice where Frankfurter, Siegel, and Clor see virtue. But he agrees with them on a more fundamental premise: that judicial statesmanship, as they see it, is a matter of *supplementing* constitutional text with other values to reach a decision that brings the court and thus the country beyond the limits of constitutional text to a judicial decision that cannot be justified by constitutional text alone. Frankfurter's judicial statesmanship justifies commerce clause decisions at odds with the clause's original meaning; Siegel stresses that judicial statesmanship cannot be squared with any version of originalism save for the most faint-hearted[51] variety, in which originalism expressly concedes the point to other values; Clor's judicial statesmanship occurs when "recourse must be had to considerations beyond the written Constitution" and "the judge is obliged to take his direction from regime principles."[52]

Franck agrees with them, and for that very reason he finds judicial statesmanship at odds with a judge's exercise of the Constitution's judicial power because judges violate the Constitution when they purport to add to it.[53] But what if all of them, in their unanimity, are unanimously wrong? That is, what if we think of statesmanship not as a matter of *assertion*, but as a matter of *restraint*?

Judicial Statesmanship and Restraint. In his *Thoughts on the Cause of the Present Discontents*, Edmund Burke begins on a hesitant note: "It is an undertaking of some degree of delicacy to examine into the cause of public disorders."[54] In this description of the danger Burke faced, Professor Harvey C. Mansfield finds not an "accidental" vagueness, but the "intended and studied" vagueness of a statesman.[55]

For as Mansfield observes, Burke's "statesmanship must lack candor and use rhetoric."[56] Burke's restraint, Mansfield explains, reflects a statesmanship that differs from that of Frankfurter and the rest, though as we shall see later on, it seems much more reflective of Marshall's approach in *McCulloch*. Mansfield's statesmanship begins similarly to the others: "Statesmanship is the capacity to do what is good in the circumstances, a capacity in which men, as individuals, are variously accomplished."[57] But the similarity between his statesmanship and the others' ends there.

As Mansfield further observes, Burke's own goal of establishing respectable party government required a particular type of statesmanship: that which is capable of winning good men's support for "honest principle," to which end the statesman "shocks no sensibilities" but instead "sacrifices some of the clear discernment" that he might otherwise employ were it not politically counterproductive.[58] This is not a matter of the statesman casting principles aside, but rather a matter of the statesman presenting those principles in a way that is not counterproductive.

> It is not that a statesman is unprincipled or above principle; it is rather that his principle loses its refinement in the translation to public speech, and thence to party program. In such translation, a principle must be defensible as well as practicable; and defensible not to a public ready to be impressed by great statesmen, but to a party eager to correct a seeming unconformity and to a public taught to reward partisanship.[59]

Burke himself admits this, as Mansfield emphasizes, from the outset of his *Thoughts on the Cause of the Present Discontents*. "The temper of the people amongst whom he presides ought therefore to be the first study of a statesman."[60]

So, when Burke ventures to "radically [reinterpret]" Britain's limited monarchy to more closely approach popular government, for example, Burke "does not go so far as to" actually "give it a new name, popular government."[61] Unlike James Madison's arguments in the *Federalist*, Burke presents his own program in a way that "never flaunts its novelty."[62] If Burke violates "the usual rule of prudence in private men with regard to politics" (i.e., "silence"), he at least recognizes "the general duty of reserve."[63]

By resolving older notions of statesmanship to newer necessities of party government, Burke "reduced statesmanship to the rules of prudence, in order to serve the needs of party government." Thus, even when Burke's new statesman agrees with others as to certain ends, he might differ significantly from them in his assessment of how best to further those ends. Burke's new statesman recognizes the need "to further [one's] ends less precipitously."[64] As we shall next see, the same can be said of Chief Justice Marshall's opinion for the Court in *McCulloch v. Maryland.*

The Great Chief Justice's Restrained Opinion for the Court in *McCulloch v. Maryland*

We are by now well accustomed to accounts of *McCulloch v. Maryland* that exalt the great chief justice in the grandest terms—if not world historic, then at least nation defining. For example, *McCulloch* arrived with Marshall's other later opinions, such as *Gibbons v. Ogden*, "like thunderbolts from on high"—with Marshall, "the American Law Giver, proclaim[ing] to all Americans what thou *shalt* and *shalt* not do."[65] Others said *McCulloch* was "a ringing restatement of national supremacy," whose "eloquent phrases have been invoked repeatedly by later generations . . . to justify the expansion of national authority at the expense of the states."[66] Or, *McCulloch*'s approval of Congress' power to charter a national bank "was nothing less than a universal touchstone to constitutional interpretation . . . a transcendent opinion that guaranteed" Marshall's place in history.[67] Finally "what was really at stake in *McCulloch*, with respect to the implied powers issue, was not whether Congress could create national banks but whether the Court would find Congress's unenumerated but implied sovereign powers to be vast."[68]

But while *McCulloch* was indeed one of the most significant decisions in Supreme Court history, such exalted characterizations of Chief Justice Marshall's handiwork obscures the crucial self-restraint that genuinely defines Marshall's accomplishment. And here I mean not the self-restraint of a Court deferring to Congress' interpretation of the breadth of its powers (for which *McCulloch* is commonly understood), but rather the self-restraint of a chief justice and Court quietly eschewing much broader and more aggressive arguments in favor of national power, resting instead on narrower and subtler grounds.

David Schwartz highlights this in his deft and compelling article challenging century-old conventional wisdom about *McCulloch*. In "Misreading *McCulloch v. Maryland*," his 2015 study of the chief justice's opinion for the Court and the legal arguments that gave rise to it, we see clearly a chief justice silently eschewing the most controversial argument proffered by the bank's proponents.[69] And with that in mind, we can best understand this as a chief justice exemplifying self-restraint in a spirit of Burkean statesmanship, looking first to what Marshall said and then to what he left unsaid.

The Bank and the Broader Debate. The Court's decision in *McCulloch* resolved a debate that had begun three decades earlier, with Alexander Hamilton's thorough proposal for a national bank in his *Second Report on the Further Provision Necessary for Establishing Public Credit*. Hamilton's report advanced myriad justifications for a national bank: It would be a source of emergency liquidity for the government and would facilitate the payment of taxes to the government, it would grow national wealth, and it would help control the money supply.[70] His arguments moved Congress to pass the Bank Bill in 1791, over the constitutional objections of Rep. James Madison, who at the Constitutional Convention four years earlier had unsuccessfully proposed to empower Congress to "grant charters of incorporation where the interest of the U.S. might require."[71]

When Attorney General Edmund Randolph and Secretary of State Thomas Jefferson supplied President George Washington with memoranda criticizing the constitutionality of a national bank, Hamilton replied with yet another memorandum of his own, adding yet another argument in favor of the bank—namely, that Congress' power to charter a national bank is, like its power to construct lighthouses and other aids to navigation, a power granted not expressly by the constitutional text but allowed by the Constitution's commerce clause, its necessary and proper clause, and the "sound maxim of construction namely, that the powers contained in a constitution of government, especially those which concern the general administration of the affairs of a country, its finances, trade, defence &c ought to be construed liberally, in advancement of the public good."[72] Finally, Hamilton argued that the power to charter a national bank followed from the Constitution's grant of power to tax, spend, borrow, and coin money, and even that the power to charter a national bank inhered in the sovereignty of all nations.[73]

Washington signed the Bank Bill in 1791. Twenty-five years later, after the bank's first charter expired, the bank was rechartered by legislation signed by the bank's previous critic, President Madison, who by 1916 saw the bank as justified in light of present exigencies, if not necessary and proper for all times. The legislative debate was marked by Rep. John C. Calhoun's Hamiltonian arguments, contending that a national bank was justified by Congress' constitutional power to tax, its power to coin money, and "the broad claim that currency control is an inherent attribute of sovereignty."[74]

Accordingly, when the Supreme Court received the litigation over the bank's constitutionality—arising from Maryland's lawsuit attempting to force the bank to pay taxes and penalties under state law—Marshall knew well the arguments for and against the bank. Indeed, his *Life of George Washington* recounted the debates for and against the bank, including Hamilton's arguments.[75]

And, as Schwartz observes, Marshall was well acquainted with not just the constitutional arguments raised during the decades-long debates around the national bank's constitutional legitimacy but also the much larger debates over national power, of which the bank debate was just one iteration. In that respect, legal debates surrounding the bank were recognized as reflecting arguments over internal improvements and the rest of Henry Clay's "American System," including the debate over whether Congress had implicit power to build internal improvements pursuant to the Constitution's commerce clause or other provisions.

"The arguments pro and con had been extensively debated in Congress and between Congress and three successive presidents," Schwartz writes. "The Bank controversy itself cannot be fully understood without reference to the rest of the American System," for "the arguments for congressional power embraced or ignored in the Bank debate"—especially with respect to the proper interpretation of Congress' enumerated constitutional powers and the breadth of its implied constitutional powers—"would also have had implications readily apparent to lawmakers at the time for the internal improvements question." As Marshall himself observed in *The Life of Washington*, "this great and radical division of opinion" over the bank "would necessarily affect every other question on the authority of the national legislature."[76]

When the bank issue reached the Supreme Court in *McCulloch*, for oral argument over nine days, the bank's lawyers—William Pinkney, Daniel Webster, and Attorney General William Wirt—did not hesitate to assert the broad arguments for constitutionality that had obvious ramifications for internal improvements.[77] Thus, when the case arrived at Court, the bank issue, however momentous it might have been, was overshadowed by the still greater issues of internal improvements and federal power that possibly hinged on the Court's eventual decision. Yet the chief justice, writing for the Court, took a markedly different approach.

The Court's Opinion: What Chief Justice Marshall Said. "No tribunal can approach such a question without a deep sense of its importance, and of the awful responsibility involved in its decision."[78] From its first paragraph onward, Chief Justice Marshall's opinion for the Court evoked a sense of obligation, self-restraint, and respect for settled institutions. In all this, the words that Chief Justice Marshall offered in explaining the Court's judgment exemplified Tocquevillian judicial statesmanship. Without reciting the Court's opinion in full, a few aspects deserve particular attention.

Marshall's opinion begins by recognizing the gravity of the matter, the parties' dispute cutting all the way down to the first principles of American constitutionalism: "The Constitution of our country, in its most interesting and vital parts, is to be considered, the conflicting powers of the Government of the Union and of its members, as marked in that Constitution, are to be discussed, and an opinion given which may essentially influence the great operations of the Government."[79] But upon emphasizing the gravity of the case, Marshall immediately turned to *minimizing* the Court's place in the dispute, framing the Court not as powerful but as constrained—not as *empowered* to act but as *obligated* to act.

> No tribunal can approach such a question without a deep sense of its importance, and of the awful *responsibility* involved in its decision. But it *must* be decided peacefully, or remain a source of hostile legislation, perhaps, of hostility of a still more serious nature; and if it is to be

so decided, by this tribunal alone can the decision be made. On the Supreme Court of the United States has the Constitution of our country devolved this important *duty*.[80] (Emphasis added.)

Marshall returned to this theme—accepting obligations, disclaiming power—at the end of his opinion's first part. Having explained why the bank is constitutional (for reasons to which I will turn shortly), Marshall emphasized that if the bank were not justified, then "it would become the painful *duty* of this tribunal" to declare the bank unconstitutional.[81] (Emphasis added.) And he even casted the bank's *critics*, rather than its proponents, as the ones urging the Court to aggrandize power to itself.

> But where the law is not prohibited, and is really calculated to effect any of the objects intrusted to the Government, to undertake here to inquire into the decree of its necessity would be to pass the line which circumscribes the judicial department and to tread on legislative ground. *This Court disclaims all pretensions to such a power*.[82] (Emphasis added.)

In all this, Marshall's approach exemplifies Tocqueville's description of judges wielding political power reluctantly, being led into the political arena not by their own ambition: "The American judge is led despite himself onto the terrain of politics. He judges the law only because he has to judge a case, and he cannot prevent himself from judging the case."[83]

Having set the stage, Marshall justified the bank's constitutionality by responding to Maryland's arguments against it. Here, too, Marshall's analysis is one of constraint rather than empowerment because he presented the Court as largely constrained by the weight of decades of precedent surrounding the institutions of government, which place obligations on courts.

> Has Congress power to incorporate a bank?
> It has been truly said that this can scarcely be considered as an open question entirely unprejudiced by the former proceedings of the Nation respecting it. The principle now contested was introduced at a very early period of our history, has been recognised by many successive legislatures, and has been acted upon by the Judicial Department, in cases of peculiar delicacy, as a law of undoubted obligation.

It will not be denied that a bold and daring usurpation might be resisted after an acquiescence still longer and more complete than this. But it is conceived that a doubtful question, one on which human reason may pause and the human judgment be suspended, in the decision of which the great principles of liberty are not concerned, but the respective powers of those who are equally the representatives of the people, are to be adjusted, if not put at rest by the practice of the Government, ought to receive a considerable impression from that practice. An exposition of the Constitution, deliberately established by legislative acts, on the faith of which an immense property has been advanced, ought not to be lightly disregarded.[84]

Among those who "said . . . that this can scarcely be considered as an open question" were President Madison, a critic of the First Bank of the United States but now a proponent of the Second Bank. He made this point in his 1815 veto message to Congress, explaining why an earlier version of the Second Bank was bad policy but not unconstitutional: "The question of the constitutional authority of the Legislature to establish an incorporated bank" was "precluded, in my judgment, by repeated recognitions, under varied circumstances, of the validity of such an Institution, in acts of the Legislative, Executive, and Judicial branches of the Government, accompanied by indications, in different modes, of a concurrence of the general will of the nation."[85] Madison's 1815 statement, though seemingly at odds with his opposition to a national bank decades earlier in the first Congress, exemplified his recognition in *Federalist* 37 that the Constitution's words are often best understood in light of the actual practice of government: "All new laws, though penned with the greatest technical skill, and passed on the fullest and most mature deliberation, are considered as more or less obscure and equivocal, until their meaning be liquidated and ascertained by a series of particular discussions and adjudications."[86]

Having presented himself as doubly obligated—first by his duty to hear the momentous case and second by his duty to defer to the weight of historical precedent—the chief justice then proceeds to the merits of the constitutional question. But even here, Marshall further frames the question by the past several decades of the nation's actual governance and institutional weight. Marshall understands that the Constitution is one of "enumerated powers" and that enumeration includes no power "of establishing a bank or creating a corporation," but he concludes that incorporating the bank was Congress' reasonable means for carrying into execution the other "great powers" of government: "to lay and collect taxes; to borrow money; to regulate commerce; to declare and conduct a war; and to raise and support armies and navies."[87] And he invokes these powers not as abstractions, but in the concrete terms of the nation's decades of growth and governance.

> Throughout this vast republic, from the St. Croix to the Gulf of Mexico, from the Atlantic to the Pacific, revenue is to be collected and expended, armies are to be marched and supported. The exigencies of the Nation may require that the treasure raised in the north should be transported to the south that raised in the east, conveyed to the west, or that this order should be reversed. Is that construction of the Constitution to be preferred which would render these operations difficult, hazardous and expensive? Can we adopt that construction (unless the words imperiously require it) which would impute to the framers of that instrument, when granting these powers for the public good, the intention of impeding their exercise, by withholding a choice of means?[88]

From these premises, Marshall undertakes his seminal analysis of the bank as being Congress' "necessary and proper" means for executing the Constitution's "great powers." Focusing not on an abstraction of national banking power but on the actual bank embodying decades of practical experience, and then situating that bank in the "vast republic" as it then existed, Marshall's justification for the bank reflected not abstractions but institutional weight and practical reality.

This was the frame in which the chief justice engaged Maryland's arguments. The Constitution lacked an express legislative power to incorporate a bank, but the bank was "a means by which other objects [of the Constitution] are accomplished."[89] And the bank was a sufficiently "necessary and proper" means to administering the legislative branch's constitutionally granted "great powers"—putatively the maintenance of armies and navies and the transportation of federal funds[90]—because Congress was not unreasonable in choosing the bank as a means to its ends.[91] When Maryland urged the Court to construe "necessary and proper" in the strictest possible sense of "necessary," the Court preserved room not just for Congress' "capacity to avail itself of experience, to exercise its reason, and to accommodate its legislation to circumstances"[92] but also for "the good sense of the public" to endorse operations of government as constitutionally necessary and proper though not *strictly* necessary.[93]

In all this, the chief justice presented himself not just doubly obligated but triply so. As noted above, he expressly observed that he was obligated to decide the case and that he owed deference to the weight of historical precedent. But his legal analysis, rooted firmly in the actual functioning of government, conceded his obligation to decide the case in light of the concrete choices faced by Congress and the people that elected it.

The Court's Opinion: What Chief Justice Marshall Left Unsaid. Chief Justice Marshall's opinion for the Court summarizes Maryland's arguments against the bank and offers responses drawn directly from the bank's lawyers' own arguments. But as Schwartz observes, to focus on the chief justice's words is to miss the most important part of his famous opinion—namely, the words he left unsaid, the arguments he left unnoted.

> These arguments [against the bank] are familiar to us because Marshall summarizes them as he proceeds to rebut them. Marshall's rebuttals are all adopted from arguments of the Bank's counsel, which in turn are thus familiar to us, even though Marshall understandably asserts them as the Court's opinion without attribution. . . . What makes the oral argument worth a close read is to identify arguments made but *not* addressed or adopted in the *McCulloch* opinion; these show the limits of what Marshall was willing to do to advance the cause of nationalism in *McCulloch*.[94]

In other words, Marshall's narrow grounds for decision—namely, that after decades of operation, the national bank's status as "a convenient, a useful, and essential instrument in the prosecution of its fiscal operations" can no longer be "a subject of controversy"[95]—delivered victory to the bank but withheld from proponents of national power a much broader and more consequential victory and thus withheld from *opponents* of national power a much more controversial and threatening edict. In affirming the bank, Marshall's opinion gave his fellow nationalists a victory in this particular debate and great reason for optimism in future debates over national power, but it withheld any express judicial endorsement of the broader national agenda.

First, by affirming the bank as an essential instrument of Congress' "fiscal operations" without more specific explanation, Marshall delivered an opinion sufficiently vague to let both sides in the larger federal power debate declare victory or at least maintain that the larger debate was not lost: "Nationalists could claim that fiscal operations related to multiple powers . . . and all Jeffersonians (even perhaps hard line strict constructionists) might have noted that Marshall did not endorse a general governmental power to regulate the currency."[96]

Second, even when he suggests that the power to charter a bank was not "the end for which other powers are exercised, but a *means* by which other objects are accomplished,"[97] (emphasis added) Marshall subtly stops short of expressly describing precisely *which* great "objects" of national power are being accomplished, and thus he leaves his fellow nationalists without a foothold for future assertions of national power. Marshall makes general reference to some of the federal government's "great powers," especially its military and fiscal powers, but he stops short of identifying either of them (or any other of Congress' enumerated legislative powers) as the crux of the Court's analysis, the starting point for the next advance by proponents of national power. His construction of the necessary and proper clause is famous: "Let the end be legitimate, let it be within the scope of the Constitution, and all means which are appropriate, which are plainly adapted to that end, which are not prohibited, but consist with the letter and spirit of the Constitution, are Constitutional."[98] But it assumes a "legitimate" end of government without precisely specifying it.

"Reading the opinion carefully," Schwartz observes, "one sees that Marshall never actually applies his own test of 'necessary and proper' laws to the Bank." But while prominent scholars have speculated that Marshall's opacity reflects his desire to reach a pro-nationalist result that could not actually be achieved on the merits under public scrutiny, Schwartz sees precisely the opposite explanation: Marshall had the bank's counsel's arguments at his disposal; he could "easily" have declared the bank to be a necessary and proper means for carrying out Congress' powers to tax, borrow, declare war, or regulate interstate commerce, but he chose another path instead, "avoid[ing] the analysis" to make the Court's decision "*less nationalistic, not more.*"[99]

Similarly, Chief Justice Marshall's opinion "steers entirely clear" of arguments advanced by Webster, Calhoun, Pinkney, and Hamilton with obvious ramifications for internal improvements: Pinkney's invocation of Congress' building of lighthouses and other internal improvements that, like the bank, were not expressly allowed under the Constitution; Webster's argument's invocation of the commerce clause; or Hamilton's and Calhoun's arguments that a national bank supports Congress' assumed power to impose a "uniform national currency."[100]

Finally, Schwartz highlights how even Marshall's embrace of the necessary and proper clause, in his discussion of Congress' need to have flexibility for meeting those "exigencies which, if foreseen at all, must have been seen dimly, and which can be best provided for as they occur,"[101] is less nationalistic than it appears at first glance. "While on the surface this language seems to support an aggressive nationalism interpretation of *McCulloch*, two ambiguities should be noted as an initial matter."[102]

The first ambiguity goes to Marshall's notion of necessity. His repeated references to Congress meeting "crises" and "exigencies" gives at least some weight to those who (like President Madison)[103] saw that Congress' power to charter banks was a national power contingent on temporary necessity, a necessity that would ebb and flow as emergencies themselves ebb and flow.[104] "This sort of caginess," Schwartz writes, "fails to endorse any significantly nationalist argument pressed on the Court at oral argument or readily found in the Bank's history and congressional debates. If anything, Marshall's references to crises and exigencies lean in a Madisonian direction."[105]

The second ambiguity is in his description of the Court's readiness to intervene in more difficult cases. Marshall eschewed the bank's lawyers' broad claims for judicial deference to Congress' judgment and instead couched his analysis with adverbs and other modifiers hinting that the Court retained power to scrutinize Congress' assertions of power in cases in which the need for the law was not so self-evident.[106] Again, "Let the end be legitimate, let it be within the scope of the Constitution, and all means which are appropriate, which are *plainly* adapted to that end, which are not prohibited, but consist with the *letter and spirit* of the Constitution, are Constitutional."[107] (Emphasis added.) Or, "But where the law is not prohibited, and is *really* calculated to effect any of the objects intrusted to the Government, to undertake here to inquire into the decree of its necessity would be to pass the line which circumscribes the judicial department and to tread on legislative ground."[108] (Emphasis added.) Congress would get great deference in its assessment of exigency or necessity—but not *unbounded* deference. As Marshall vaguely indicated, the Court would remain ready to undertake the "painful duty" of negating Congress' pre-textual or utterly unreasonable claims of necessity[109]—at least in theory.

Schwartz, parsing the terms of Chief Justice Marshall's opinions and the terms of counsel's oral arguments, keenly observes that Marshall quietly rejected the far more consequential formulations Webster and Pinkney urged.[110] Thus, Marshall's opinion for the Court "gives plenty of ammunition to both sides of a debate over the role of the Court and the standard which it will apply." For every occasion that Marshall's opinion suggests the Court *must* defer to Congress's legislative choices, another part of the opinion tempers such suggestions with a countervailing hint of the Court's power to second guess that choice.[111]

Having highlighted clearly the distance between the arguments of bank counsel and the reasoning of Marshall's opinion for the Court, Schwartz compellingly demonstrates that "Chief Justice John Marshall was far more concerned with avoiding controversy than with affirmatively endorsing expansive congressional power."[112] Schwartz keenly identifies Marshall's deft use of silence, self-restraint, and ambiguity. We can best understand them as Mansfield's Burkean statesmanship: a careful "vagueness" that is not "accidental, but intended and studied."[113] Thus, John Marshall's carefully framed argument serves not to stifle his and others' aspirations for a truly great nation, but rather to advance them—preserving the political viability of their national agenda by not making the already fractious debate over the First Bank of the United States into an even more factious debate over all other aspects of their national agenda.

For Marshall, "American Nationalism was [his] one and only great conception, and the fostering of it the purpose of his life."[114] Thus, the distance between Marshall's *McCulloch* opinion and the arguments his fellow nationalists advanced is best understood as a measure of Marshall's own judicial statesmanship: the Burkean statesmanship of a judge who (in R. Kent Newmyer's words) "understood that half a nationalist loaf was better than none, which is to say he was willing to let doctrinal inconsistencies stand unresolved as the price paid for winning majority support on the Court."[115] Adopting the much more aggressive arguments of Webster, Wirt, or Pinkney (to say nothing of the late Hamilton) may have risked unsettling the unanimity that the chief justice labored to maintain throughout his tenure on the bench and may also have risked public support—or even accelerated the nation's eventual fracture.

As William Nelson writes, Marshall "recognized better than his more extreme Federalist brethren that no American statesman could or should ignore the people's will." For him, the task at hand "was to reconcile the people's transcendent power with the law's immutable principles."[116] The *McCulloch* decision was controversial enough, as Marshall himself would experience firsthand after the Court issued its opinion.[117] ("Our opinion in the bank case has roused the sleeping spirit of Virginia," Marshall wrote to Joseph Story, two weeks after the Court issued its decision.[118]) His task was to minimize the controversy, at least as much as possible.

To that end, Chief Justice Marshall relied on judicial statesmanship—not a statesmanship of supplementing the Constitution's terms with values of his own choosing, but a statesmanship of knowing which constitutional principles *not* to advance at a given moment, no matter how genuinely he might have believed in them.

Brief Closing Thoughts on Judicial Statesmanship

McCulloch's most famous line is found in Marshall's approach to construing the constitutional text: "[The Constitution's] nature, therefore, requires that only its great outlines should be marked, its important objects designated, and the minor ingredients which compose those objects be deduced from the nature of the objects themselves. . . . We must never forget, that it is *a Constitution* we are expounding."[119] But Marshall—unlike Hamilton in his report on the bank or Pinkney at oral argument—never says that the Constitution should be construed "liberally."[120] Rather, Marshall says that constitutional adjudication requires "a *fair* construction of the whole instrument."[121]

Reading those words, it is hard not to hear echoes of Hamilton's earlier words in *Federalist* 78, in which Publius suggested that the courts should affirm a challenged statute's constitutionality so long as there is not an "irreconcilable variance" between the Constitution and the statute—which is to say, the Court should always take care to reconcile seeming variances whenever possible. "So far as they can, by any *fair* construction, be reconciled to each other, reason and law conspire to dictate that this should be done."[122] (Emphasis added.)

This seems to be the place where Publius' judiciary—one that must exercise "neither force nor will, but merely judgment"—affords space for a judicial statesmanship of at least the Burkean variety. Publius' judges are challenged not merely to declare the "best" meaning of constitutional or statutory phrases, but to respect that (as Madison, too, recognized) the law sometimes is susceptible to at least a small range of possible meanings and that in such cases the judge in our democratic republic should err on the side of allowing democratic enactments to stand.[123] In deciding whether a particular legal interpretation is "fair" or "unfair," "reconcilable" or "irreconcilable," the judge is left with at least some discretion and thus with a choice that may require an act of judicial statesmanship, rightly understood.

Finally, it is worth considering whether Chief Justice Marshall's capacity for judicial statesmanship reflected the fact that he was not merely a justice of the Supreme Court, but the "Chief Justice of the United States,"[124] an office vested by law and tradition with unique powers over the operation of the Court, including especially the management of the justices' deliberations and votes and the assignment of judicial opinions.[125] In these powers and duties, the chief justice has opportunities unlike any of his colleagues to shape the substance and tenor of the Court's opinions. Chief Justice Marshall used his office (albeit at a much earlier and informal stage) to shape the Court in a way that none of his colleagues, including Justice Story, ever could; so have Marshall's successors.

Perhaps judicial statesmanship is a matter reserved exclusively to the chief justice of the United States who, first among equals,[126] presides over a Court that history will remember by reference to his own name—the

Marshall Court then, the Roberts Court now. If so, then the chief justice exemplifies—or tests—Publius' maxim that "the interest of the man must be connected with the constitutional rights of the place."[127]

Acknowledgments

An earlier version of this essay was presented at the American Enterprise Institute's conference on *McCulloch v. Maryland*'s 200th anniversary on February 28, 2019. Many thanks to Abram Shulsky and Nelson Lund for helpful comments and to Alexander Khan for excellent research assistance.

Notes

1. William H. Rehnquist, *The Supreme Court* (New York: Vintage Books, 1987), 24.

2. Felix Frankfurter, "John Marshall and the Judicial Function," *Harvard Law Review* 69, no. 2 (December 1955): 217, 219.

3. For that reason, R. Kent Newmyer can write at length on John Marshall's statesmanlike personal qualities then abruptly stop short of concluding that statesmanship is exhibited in "Marshall's jurisprudence—the substance as well as the rhetoric of his opinions." On this point, Newmyer offers only that the question is "highly speculative," though there was "if not a causal connection, then at least an interesting parallel between Marshall's republican character and his law." R. Kent Newmyer, "John Marshall as an American Original: Some Thoughts on Personality and Judicial Statesmanship," *University of Colorado Law Review* 71 (2000): 1365, 1375. In this chapter, I attempt to focus on Marshall's republican law in *McCulloch*, rather than on his republican character. Others have looked for judicial statesmanship in other famous Marshall opinions. See Samuel R. Olken, "The Ironies of *Marbury v. Madison* and John Marshall's Judicial Statesmanship," *John Marshall Law Review* 37 (2004): 391.

4. Antonin Scalia, *A Matter of Interpretation: Federal Courts and the Law* (Princeton, NJ: Princeton University Press, 1997), 46.

5. John O. McGinnis, "Judicial Statesmanship Versus Judicial Fidelity," Law & Liberty, February 15, 2019, https://www.lawliberty.org/2019/02/15/judicial-statesmanship-versus-judicial-fidelity.

6. For example, Publius indicated in *Federalist* 78 that judges should declare a statute unconstitutional when it is at an "irreconcilable variance" with the Constitution, thus implying that some variances are actually "reconcilable" and should be preserved. As he further observed, "So far as they can, by any fair construction, be reconciled to each other, reason and law conspire to dictate that this should be done."

7. This was Justice Antonin Scalia's felicitous characterization of Tocqueville in his dissenting opinion in *Hein v. Freedom from Religion Foundation*, 551 US 587, 635 (2007).

8. Alexis de Tocqueville, *Democracy in America*, trans. and ed. Harvey C. Mansfield and Delba Winthrop (Chicago: University of Chicago Press, 2002), 142.

9. Congress added the eighth and ninth seats to the Court in 1837, soon after *Democracy in America*'s publication. Tocqueville, *Democracy in America*, 142.

10. Tocqueville, *Democracy in America*, 142.

11. Tocqueville, *Democracy in America*, 257.

12. Tocqueville, *Democracy in America*, 96–97.

13. Tocqueville, *Democracy in America*, 97.

14. Tocqueville, *Democracy in America*, 142.

15. Tocqueville, *Democracy in America*, 96.

16. Oliver Wendell Holmes and Felix Frankfurter, *Holmes and Frankfurter: Their Correspondence, 1912–1934*, ed. Robert M. Mennell and Christine L. Compston (Hanover, NH: University Press of New England, 1996); and Alexander M. Bickel, *The Supreme Court and the Idea of Progress* (New York: Harper & Row Publishers, 1970), 21–22.

17. Felix Frankfurter, "Twenty Years of Mr. Justice Holmes' Constitutional Opinions," *Harvard Law Review* 36 (1923): 909, 911.

18. "Assuredly Mr. Justice Holmes did not bring to the Court the gifts of a lawyer who had been immersed in great affairs, and yet his work is in the school of statesmanship. He is philosopher become king. Where others are guided through experience of life he is led by the humility of the philosopher and the imagination of the poet." Frankfurter, "Twenty Years of Mr. Justice Holmes' Constitutional Opinions," 919.

19. Frankfurter, "Twenty Years of Mr. Justice Holmes' Constitutional Opinions," 918.

20. Frankfurter is quoting Thomas Reed Powell, "Supreme Court Decisions on the Commerce Clause and the State Police Power, 1910–1914 II," *Columbia Law Review* 22 (1922): 28, 48. But, perhaps unsurprisingly, Frankfurter strikes a much different tone regarding the Constitution's provisions for due process of law and the equal protection of law, which "present very different problems of statecraft" because "they open the door to the widest differences of opinion" and thus counsel in favor of judicial restraint, lest "such power, affecting the intimate life of Nation and States, be entrusted, ultimately, to five men." Frankfurter, "Twenty Years of Mr. Justice Holmes' Constitutional Opinions," 914–15.

21. "His more general comments on the subject are sufficiently vague that they can be taken to apply to different judicial approaches to constitutional adjudication." See Gary J. Jacobsohn, "Felix Frankfurter and the Ambiguities of Judicial Statesmanship," *New York University Law Review* 49 (1974): 1, 5. See also Gary J. Jacobsohn, *Pragmatism, Statesmanship, and the Supreme Court* (Ithaca, NY: Cornell University Press, 1977).

22. Neil S. Siegel, "The Virtue of Judicial Statesmanship," *Texas Law Review* 86 (2008): 959, 979.

23. Siegel, "The Virtue of Judicial Statesmanship," 970–71.

24. Siegel, "The Virtue of Judicial Statesmanship," 974–76.

25. Siegel, "The Virtue of Judicial Statesmanship," 981. Siegel is quoting Roscoe Pound, "The Causes of Popular Dissatisfaction with the Administration of Justice," *American Law* 14 (1906): 445.

26. Siegel, "The Virtue of Judicial Statesmanship," 983. Siegel is quoting Alexander M. Bickel, *The Least Dangerous Branch: The Supreme Court at the Bar of Politics*

(Indianapolis, IN: Bobbs-Merrill Company, 1962), 26.

27. Bickel, *The Least Dangerous Branch*, 25.

28. Siegel, "The Virtue of Judicial Statesmanship," 983.

29. Siegel, "The Virtue of Judicial Statesmanship," 983–84.

30. Siegel, "The Virtue of Judicial Statesmanship," 994.

31. Siegel, "The Virtue of Judicial Statesmanship," 997.

32. Harry M. Clor, "Judicial Statesmanship and Constitutional Interpretation," *South Texas Law Journal* 26 (1985): 397.

33. Clor, "Judicial Statesmanship and Constitutional Interpretation," 399–400.

34. Clor, "Judicial Statesmanship and Constitutional Interpretation," 400.

35. Clor, "Judicial Statesmanship and Constitutional Interpretation," 400. Clor is citing Ralph Lerner, "The Supreme Court as Republican Schoolmaster," *Supreme Court Review* 127 (1967).

36. Clor, "Judicial Statesmanship and Constitutional Interpretation," 407.

37. *Federalist*, no. 78 (Alexander Hamilton).

38. Clor, "Judicial Statesmanship and Constitutional Interpretation," 407.

39. *Fletcher v. Peck*, 10 US 87 (1810).

40. Clor, "Judicial Statesmanship and Constitutional Interpretation," 409–10.

41. Clor, "Judicial Statesmanship and Constitutional Interpretation," 418; John Hart Ely, *Democracy and Distrust: A Theory of Judicial Review* (Cambridge, MA: Harvard University Press, 1980); and Ronald Dworkin, *Taking Rights Seriously* (Cambridge, MA: Harvard University Press, 1978).

42. Clor, "Judicial Statesmanship and Constitutional Interpretation," 417.

43. Clor, "Judicial Statesmanship and Constitutional Interpretation," 415–16. Clor is citing Raoul Berger, *Government by Judiciary: The Transformation of the Fourteenth Amendment* (Indianapolis, IN: Liberty Fund, 1977), 284.

44. Clor, "Judicial Statesmanship and Constitutional Interpretation," 423.

45. Matthew Franck, "Statesmanship and the Judiciary," *Review of Politics* 51 (1989): 510, 514.

46. Franck, "Statesmanship and the Judiciary," 515.

47. Franck, "Statesmanship and the Judiciary," 516–19

48. Franck, "Statesmanship and the Judiciary," 520.

49. Franck, "Statesmanship and the Judiciary," 520–21. Franck is quoting *Federalist*, no. 78.

50. Franck, "Statesmanship and the Judiciary," 528.

51. Siegel, "The Virtue of Judicial Statesmanship," 423.

52. Clor, "Judicial Statesmanship and Constitutional Interpretation."

53. Given the subject of this chapter, it should be noted that although Franck expressed skepticism of "judicial statesmanship," he also has written favorably regarding Chief Justice Marshall's opinion in *McCulloch*. See Matthew J. Franck, "Would That John Marshall's Great Opinion Were Cited Oftener Today," Law & Liberty, March 6, 2019, https://www.lawliberty.org/liberty-forum/would-that-john-marshalls-great-opinion-were-cited-oftener-today/.

54. Edmund Burke, *Thoughts on the Cause of the Present Discontents*, 1770.

55. Harvey Mansfield, *Statesmanship and Party Government: A Study of Burke and*

Bolinbroke (Chicago: University of Chicago Press, 1965), 20–21.

56. Mansfield, *Statesmanship and Party Government*, 21.

57. Mansfield, *Statesmanship and Party Government*, 17.

58. Mansfield, *Statesmanship and Party Government*, 17.

59. Mansfield, *Statesmanship and Party Government*, 17.

60. Burke, *Thoughts on the Cause of the Present Discontents*.

61. Mansfield, *Statesmanship and Party Government*, 163.

62. Mansfield, *Statesmanship and Party Government*, 163.

63. Mansfield, *Statesmanship and Party Government*, 229–30.

64. Mansfield, *Statesmanship and Party Government*, 245.

65. Harlow Giles Unger, *John Marshall: The Chief Justice Who Saved the Nation* (Cambridge, MA: Da Capo Press, 2014), 293.

66. Jean Edward Smith, *John Marshall: Definer of a Nation* (New York: Henry Holt & Company, 1996), 445.

67. Marshall not only "put a constitutional foundation under the second Bank of the United States" but "also permitted Congress to institute a system of federal internal improvements." R. Kent Newmyer, *John Marshall and the Heroic Age of the Supreme Court* (Baton Rouge, LA: LSU Press, 2001), 291, 301.

68. G. Edward White, *The Marshall Court and Cultural Change, 1815–35* (New York: Macmillan Publishing Company, 1988), 544.

69. David S. Schwartz, "Misreading *McCulloch v. Maryland*," *University of Pennsylvania Journal of Constitutional Law* 18, no. 1 (2015); and David S. Schwartz, *The Spirit of the Constitution: John Marshall and the 200-Year Odyssey of McCulloch v. Maryland* (Oxford, UK: Oxford University Press, 2019).

70. Schwartz, "Misreading *McCulloch v. Maryland*," 28–29. Schwartz is citing Alexander Hamilton, "Final Version of the Second Report on the Further Provision Necessary for Establishing Public Credit (Report on a National Bank), 13 December 1790," National Archives, Founders Online, https://founders.archives.gov/documents/Hamilton/01-07-02-0229-0003.

71. Max Farrand, ed., *The Records of the Federal Convention of 1787* (New Haven, CT: Yale University Press, 1911), 615–16.

72. Alexander Hamilton, "Final Version of an Opinion on the Constitutionality of an Act to Establish a Bank, [23 February 1791]," National Archives, Founders Online, https://founders.archives.gov/documents/Hamilton/01-08-02-0060-0003.

73. Hamilton, "Final Version of an Opinion on the Constitutionality of an Act to Establish a Bank."

74. Schwartz, "Misreading *McCulloch v. Maryland*," 42–46.

75. Schwartz, "Misreading *McCulloch v. Maryland*," 38. Schwartz is citing John Marshall, *The Life of George Washington* (Oxford, UK: Oxford University Press, 1805), 390–97.

76. Marshall, *The Life of Washington*, 395.

77. Marshall, *The Life of Washington*, 52–81.

78. *McCulloch v. Maryland*, 17 US 316, 400 (1819).

79. *McCulloch v. Maryland*, 17 US 316, 400 (1819).

80. *McCulloch v. Maryland*, 17 US 316, 400–01 (1819).

81. *McCulloch v. Maryland*, 17 US 316, 423 (1819).

82. *McCulloch v. Maryland*, 17 US 316 (1819).

83. Tocqueville, *Democracy in America*, 97.

84. *McCulloch v. Maryland*, 17 US 316, 401 (1819).

85. This message from President James Madison to the Senate of the United States on January 30, 1815, was reprinted in M. St. Clair Clarke and D. A. Hall, *Legislative and Documentary History of the Bank of the United States* (Washington, DC: Gales and Seaton, 1832), 594. Late in his life, President Madison reiterated these themes in an 1831 letter to Charles Ingersoll, defending his change of positions on the bank: "The charge of inconsistency between my objection to the constitutionality of such a bank, in 1791, and my assent in 1817, turns on the question, how far legislative precedents, expounding the constitution, ought to give succeeding legislatures, and to overrule individual opinions." That said, "Madison's justification of his *volte-face*," offered in that letter and elsewhere, "was not entirely convincing to his contemporaries." See Donald O. Dewey, "James Madison Helps Clio Interpret the Constitution," *American Journal of Legal History* 15 (1971): 38, 53.

86. *Federalist*, no. 37. For a description of Madison's theory of "liquidation," as exemplified by the bank debate, see William Baude, "Constitutional Liquidation," *Stanford Law Review* 71, no. 1 (2019).

87. *McCulloch v. Maryland*, 17 US 316, 407 (1819).

88. *McCulloch v. Maryland*, 17 US 316, 408 (1819).

89. *McCulloch v. Maryland*, 17 US 316, 407–11 (1819).

90. *McCulloch v. Maryland*, 17 US 316, 408 (1819).

91. *McCulloch v. Maryland*, 17 US 316, 415 (1819).

92. *McCulloch v. Maryland*, 17 US 316, 415–16 (1819).

93. *McCulloch v. Maryland*, 17 US 316, 418 (1819).

94. Schwartz, "Misreading *McCulloch v. Maryland*," 53–54. (Footnote omitted.) *McCulloch v. Maryland*, 17 US 316, 402–03 (1819).

95. *McCulloch v. Maryland*, 17 US 316, 422 (1819).

96. Schwartz, "Misreading *McCulloch v. Maryland*," 60–61. Schwartz also suggests that "moderate Jeffersonians could claim that the Bank was justified merely to facilitate tax collections until state banks resumed redemption of their notes in specie," but it is hard to square this suggestion with Chief Justice Marshall's own assertion that "the existence of State banks can have no possible influence on the question" of the bank's necessity. See *McCulloch v. Maryland*, 17 US 316, 424 (1819).

97. *McCulloch v. Maryland*, 17 US 316, 411 (1819).

98. *McCulloch v. Maryland*, 17 US 316, 421 (1819).

99. Schwartz, "Misreading *McCulloch v. Maryland*," 62.

100. Schwartz, "Misreading *McCulloch v. Maryland*," 63–64.

101. *McCulloch v. Maryland*, 17 US 316, 415 (1819).

102. Schwartz, "Misreading *McCulloch v. Maryland*," 73.

103. See James Madison, "Seventh Annual Message," University of Virginia, Miller Center, December 5, 1815, https://millercenter.org/the-presidency/presidential-speeches/december-5-1815-seventh-annual-message. "If the operation of the State banks can not produce this result, the probable operation of a national bank will merit consideration."

104. Schwartz, "Misreading *McCulloch v. Maryland*," 73.

105. Schwartz, "Misreading *McCulloch v. Maryland*," 61.

106. Schwartz, "Misreading *McCulloch v. Maryland*," 73–74.

107. *McCulloch v. Maryland*, 17 US 316, 421 (1819).

108. *McCulloch v. Maryland*, 17 US 316, 423 (1819).

109. *McCulloch v. Maryland*, 17 US 316, 423 (1819).

110. Schwartz, "Misreading *McCulloch v. Maryland*," 74–78.

111. Schwartz, "Misreading *McCulloch v. Maryland*," 78.

112. Schwartz, "Misreading *McCulloch v. Maryland*," 91.

113. Mansfield, *Statesmanship and Party Government*, 21.

114. Albert J. Beveridge, *The Life of John Marshall, Vol. 4* (Boston, MA: Houghton Mifflin, 1919), 1. This was quoted in Newmyer, *John Marshall and the Heroic Age of the Supreme Court*, 267.

115. Newmyer, *John Marshall and the Heroic Age of the Supreme Court*, 316.

116. William E. Nelson, "The Eighteenth-Century Background of John Marshall's Constitutional Jurisprudence," *Michigan Law Review* 76 (1978): 893, 933.

117. See, for example, Gerald Gunther, ed., *John Marshall's Defense of McCulloch v. Maryland* (Palo Alto, CA: Stanford University Press, 1969); and Mark R. Killenbeck, *M'Culloch v. Maryland: Securing a Nation* (Lawrence, KS: University Press of Kansas, 2006), 123–58.

118. Joel Richard Paul, *Without Precedent: Chief Justice John Marshall and His Times* (New York: Riverhead Books, 2018), 344.

119. *McCulloch v. Maryland*, 17 US 316, 407 (1819).

120. See Schwartz, "Misreading *McCulloch v. Maryland*," 79.

121. For the "fair and just interpretation," see *McCulloch v. Maryland*, 17 US 316, 404–07 (1819). For "fair construction," see *McCulloch v. Maryland*, 17 US 316, 406 (1819).

122. *Federalist*, no. 78.

123. *Federalist*, no. 37 (James Madison). "All new laws, though penned with the greatest technical skill, and passed on the fullest and most mature deliberation, are considered as more or less obscure and equivocal, until their meaning be liquidated and ascertained by a series of particular discussions and adjudications."

124. 28 USC § 1.

125. See, for example, Kenneth W. et al., *The Office of Chief Justice* (Charlottesville, VA: Miller Center, 1984).

126. Alpheus Thomas Mason, "The Chief Justice of the United States: Primus Inter Pares," *Journal of Public Law* 17 (1968), 20.

127. *Federalist*, no. 51 (James Madison).

Appendix A

United States Supreme Court: *McCulloch v. Maryland*, 17 US 316 (1819)

Chief Justice John Marshall delivered the opinion of the Court.[1]

In the case now to be determined, the defendant, a sovereign State, denies the obligation of a law enacted by the legislature of the Union, and the plaintiff, on his part, contests the validity of an act which has been passed by the legislature of that State. The Constitution of our country, in its most interesting and vital parts, is to be considered, the conflicting powers of the Government of the Union and of its members, as marked in that Constitution, are to be discussed, and an opinion given which may essentially influence the great operations of the Government. No tribunal can approach such a question without a deep sense of its importance, and of the awful responsibility involved in its decision. But it must be decided peacefully, or remain a source of hostile legislation, perhaps, of hostility of a still more serious nature; and if it is to be so decided, by this tribunal alone can the decision be made. On the Supreme Court of the United States has the Constitution of our country devolved this important duty.

The first question made in the cause is—has Congress power to incorporate a bank?

It has been truly said that this can scarcely be considered as an open question entirely unprejudiced by the former proceedings of the Nation respecting it. The principle now contested was introduced at a very early period of our history, has been recognised by many successive legislatures, and has been acted upon by the Judicial Department, in cases of peculiar delicacy, as a law of undoubted obligation.

It will not be denied that a bold and daring usurpation might be resisted after an acquiescence still longer and more complete than this. But it is conceived that a doubtful question, one on which human reason may pause and the human judgment be suspended, in the decision of which the great principles of liberty are not concerned, but the respective powers of those who are equally the representatives of the people, are to be adjusted, if not put at rest by the practice of the Government, ought to receive a considerable impression from that practice. An exposition of the Constitution, deliberately established by legislative acts, on the faith of which an immense property has been advanced, ought not to be lightly disregarded.

The power now contested was exercised by the first Congress elected under the present Constitution.

The bill for incorporating the Bank of the United States did not steal upon an unsuspecting legislature and pass unobserved. Its principle was completely understood, and was opposed with equal zeal and ability. After being resisted first in the fair and open field of debate, and afterwards in the executive cabinet, with as much persevering talent as any measure has ever experienced, and being supported by arguments which convinced minds as pure and as intelligent as this country can boast, it became a law. The original act was permitted to expire, but a short experience of the embarrassments to which the refusal to revive it exposed the Government convinced those who were most prejudiced against the measure of its necessity, and induced the passage of the present law. It would require no ordinary share of intrepidity to assert that a measure adopted under these circumstances was a bold and plain usurpation to which the Constitution gave no countenance. These observations belong to the cause; but they are not made under the impression that, were the question entirely new, the law would be found irreconcilable with the Constitution.

In discussing this question, the counsel for the State of Maryland have deemed it of some importance, in the construction of the Constitution, to consider that instrument not as emanating from the people, but as the act of sovereign and independent States. The powers of the General Government, it has been said, are delegated by the States, who alone are truly sovereign, and must be exercised in subordination to the States, who alone possess supreme dominion.

It would be difficult to sustain this proposition. The convention which framed the Constitution was indeed elected by the State legislatures. But the instrument, when it came from their hands, was a mere proposal, without obligation or pretensions to it. It was reported to the then existing

Congress of the United States with a request that it might "be submitted to a convention of delegates, chosen in each State by the people thereof, under the recommendation of its legislature, for their assent and ratification."

This mode of proceeding was adopted, and by the convention, by Congress, and by the State legislatures, the instrument was submitted to the people. They acted upon it in the only manner in which they can act safely, effectively and wisely, on such a subject—by assembling in convention. It is true, they assembled in their several States—and where else should they have assembled? No political dreamer was ever wild enough to think of breaking down the lines which separate the States, and of compounding the American people into one common mass. Of consequence, when they act, they act in their States. But the measures they adopt do not, on that account, cease to be the measures of the people themselves, or become the measures of the State governments.

From these conventions the Constitution derives its whole authority. The government proceeds directly from the people; is "ordained and established" in the name of the people, and is declared to be ordained, "in order to form a more perfect union, establish justice, insure domestic tranquillity, and secure the blessings of liberty to themselves and to their posterity."

The assent of the States in their sovereign capacity is implied in calling a convention, and thus submitting that instrument to the people. But the people were at perfect liberty to accept or reject it, and their act was final. It required not the affirmance, and could not be negatived, by the State Governments. The Constitution, when thus adopted, was of complete obligation, and bound the State sovereignties.

It has been said that the people had already surrendered all their powers to the State sovereignties, and had nothing more to give. But surely the question whether they may resume and modify the powers granted to Government does not remain to be settled in this country. Much more might the legitimacy of the General Government be doubted had it been created by the States. The powers delegated to the State sovereignties were to be exercised by themselves, not by a distinct and independent sovereignty created by themselves. To the formation of a league such as was the Confederation, the State sovereignties were certainly competent. But when, "in order to form a more perfect union," it was deemed necessary to change this alliance into an effective Government, possessing great and sovereign powers and acting directly on the people, the necessity of referring it to the people, and of deriving its powers directly from them, was felt and acknowledged by all. The Government of the Union then (whatever may be the influence of this fact on the case) is, emphatically and truly, a Government of the people. In form and in substance, it emanates from them. Its powers are granted by them, and are to be exercised directly on them, and for their benefit.

This Government is acknowledged by all to be one of enumerated powers. The principle that it can exercise only the powers granted to it would seem too apparent to have required to be enforced by all those arguments which its enlightened friends, while it was depending before the people, found it necessary to urge; that principle is now universally admitted. But the question respecting the extent of the powers actually granted is perpetually arising, and will probably continue to arise so long as our system shall exist. In discussing these questions, the conflicting powers of the General and State Governments must be brought into view, and the supremacy of their respective laws, when they are in opposition, must be settled.

If any one proposition could command the universal assent of mankind, we might expect it would be this—that the Government of the Union, though limited in its powers, is supreme within its sphere of action. This would seem to result necessarily from its nature. It is the Government of all; its powers are delegated by all; it represents all, and acts for all. Though any one State may be willing to control its operations, no State is willing to allow others to control them. The nation, on those subjects on which it can act, must necessarily bind its component parts. But this question is not left to mere reason; the people have, in express terms, decided it by saying, "this Constitution, and the laws of the United States, which shall be made in pursuance thereof," "shall be the supreme law of the land," and by requiring that the members of the State legislatures and the officers of the executive and judicial departments of the States shall take the oath of fidelity to it. The Government of the United States, then, though limited in its powers, is supreme, and its laws, when made in pursuance of the Constitution, form the supreme law of the land, "anything in the Constitution or laws of any State to the contrary notwithstanding."

Among the enumerated powers, we do not find that of establishing a bank or creating a corporation. But there is no phrase in the instrument which, like the Articles of Confederation, excludes incidental or implied powers and which requires that everything granted shall be expressly and minutely described. Even the 10th Amendment, which was framed for the purpose of quieting the excessive jealousies which had been excited, omits the word "expressly," and declares only that the powers "not delegated to the United States, nor prohibited to the States, are reserved to the States or to the people," thus leaving the question whether the particular power which may become the subject of contest has been delegated to the one Government, or prohibited to the other, to depend on a fair construction of the whole instrument. The men who drew and adopted this amendment had experienced the embarrassments resulting from the insertion of this word in the Articles of Confederation, and probably omitted it to avoid those embarrassments. A Constitution, to contain an accurate detail of all the subdivisions of which its great powers will admit, and of all the means by which they may be carried into execution, would partake of the prolixity of a legal code, and could scarcely be embraced by the human mind. It would probably never be understood by the public. Its nature, therefore, requires that only its great outlines should be marked, its important objects designated, and the minor ingredients which compose those objects be deduced from the nature of the objects themselves. That this idea was entertained by the framers of the American Constitution is not only to be inferred from the nature of the instrument, but from the language. Why else were some of the limitations found in the 9th section of the 1st article introduced? It is also in some degree warranted by their having omitted to use any restrictive term which might prevent its receiving a fair and just interpretation. In considering this question, then, we must never forget that it is *a Constitution* we are expounding.

Although, among the enumerated powers of Government, we do not find the word "bank" or "incorporation," we find the great powers, to lay and collect taxes; to borrow money; to regulate commerce; to declare and conduct a war; and to raise and support armies and navies. The sword and the purse, all the external relations, and no inconsiderable portion of the industry of the nation are intrusted to its Government. It can never be pretended that these vast powers draw after them others of inferior importance merely because they are inferior. Such an idea can never be advanced. But it may with great reason be contended that a Government intrusted with such ample powers, on the due execution of which the happiness and prosperity of the Nation so vitally depends, must also be intrusted with ample means for their execution. The power being given, it is the interest of the Nation to facilitate its execution. It can never be their interest, and cannot be presumed to have been their intention, to clog and embarrass its execution by withholding the most appropriate means. Throughout this vast republic, from the St. Croix to the Gulf of Mexico, from the Atlantic to the Pacific, revenue is to be collected and expended, armies are to be marched and supported. The exigencies of the Nation may require that the treasure raised in the north should be transported to the south that raised in the east, conveyed to the west, or that this order should be reversed. Is that construction of the Constitution to be preferred which would render these operations difficult, hazardous and expensive? Can we adopt that construction (unless the words imperiously require it) which would impute to the framers of that instrument, when granting these powers for the public good, the intention of impeding their exercise, by withholding a choice of means? If, indeed, such be the mandate of the Constitution, we have only to obey; but that instrument does not profess to enumerate the means by which the powers it confers may be executed; nor does it prohibit the creation of a corporation, if the existence of such a being be essential, to the beneficial exercise of those powers. It is, then, the subject of fair inquiry how far such means may be employed.

It is not denied that the powers given to the Government imply the ordinary means of execution. That, for example, of raising revenue and applying it to national purposes is admitted to imply the power of conveying money from place to place as the exigencies of the Nation may require, and of employing the usual means of conveyance. But it is denied that the Government has its choice of means, or that it may employ the most convenient means if, to employ them, it be necessary to erect a corporation. On what foundation does this argument rest? On this alone: the power of creating a corporation is one appertaining to sovereignty, and is not expressly conferred on Congress. This is true. But all legislative powers appertain to sovereignty. The original power of giving the law on any subject whatever is a sovereign power, and if the Government of the Union is restrained from creating a corporation as a means for performing its functions, on the single reason that the creation of a corporation is an act of sovereignty, if the sufficiency of this reason be acknowledged, there would be some difficulty in sustaining the authority of Congress to pass other laws for the accomplishment of the same objects. The Government which has a right to do an act and has imposed on it the duty of performing that act must, according to the dictates of reason, be allowed to select the means, and those who contend that it may not select any appropriate means that one particular mode of effecting the object is excepted take upon themselves the burden of establishing that exception.

The creation of a corporation, it is said, appertains to sovereignty. This is admitted. But to what portion of sovereignty does it appertain? Does it belong to one more than to another? In America, the powers of sovereignty are divided between the Government of the Union and those of the States. They are each sovereign with respect to the objects committed to it, and neither sovereign with respect to the objects committed to the other. We cannot comprehend that train of reasoning, which would maintain that the extent of power granted by the people is to be ascertained not by the nature and terms of the grant, but by its date. Some State Constitutions were formed before, some since, that of the United States. We cannot believe that their relation to each other is in any degree dependent upon this circumstance. Their respective powers must, we think, be precisely the same as if they had been formed at the same time. Had they been formed at the same time, and had the people conferred on the General Government the power contained in the Constitution, and on the States the whole residuum of power, would it have been asserted that the Government of the Union was not sovereign, with respect to those objects which were intrusted to it, in relation to which its laws were declared to be supreme? If this could not have been asserted, we cannot well comprehend the process of reasoning which maintains that a power appertaining to sovereignty cannot be connected with that vast portion of it which is granted to the General Government, so far as it is calculated to subserve the legitimate objects of that Government. The power of creating a corporation, though appertaining to sovereignty, is not, like the power of making war or levying taxes or of regulating commerce, a great substantive and independent power which cannot be implied as incidental to other powers or used as a means of executing them. It is never the end for which other powers are exercised, but a means by which other objects are accomplished. No contributions are made to charity for the sake of an incorporation, but a corporation is created to administer the charity; no seminary of learning is instituted in order to be incorporated, but the corporate character is conferred to subserve the purposes of education. No city was ever built with the sole object of being incorporated, but is incorporated as affording the best means of being well governed. The power of creating a corporation is never used for its own sake, but for the purpose of effecting something else. No sufficient reason is therefore perceived why it may not pass as incidental to those powers which are expressly given if it be a direct mode of executing them.

But the Constitution of the United States has not left the right of Congress to employ the necessary means for the execution of the powers conferred on the Government to general reasoning. To its enumeration of powers is added that of making "all laws which shall be necessary and proper for carrying into execution the foregoing powers, and all other powers vested by this Constitution in the Government of the United States or in any department thereof."

The counsel for the State of Maryland have urged various arguments to prove that this clause, though in terms a grant of power, is not so in effect, but is really restrictive of the general right which might otherwise be implied of selecting means for executing the enumerated powers. In support of this proposition, they have found it necessary to contend that this clause was inserted for the purpose of conferring on Congress the power of making laws. That, without it, doubts might be entertained whether Congress could exercise its powers in the form of legislation.

But could this be the object for which it was inserted? A Government is created by the people having legislative, executive and judicial powers. Its legislative powers are vested in a Congress, which is to consist of a senate and house of representatives. Each house may determine the rule of its proceedings, and it is declared that every bill which shall have passed both houses shall, before it becomes a law, be presented to the President of the United States. The 7th section describes the course of proceedings by which a bill shall become a law, and then the 8th section enumerates the powers of Congress. Could it be necessary to say that a legislature should exercise legislative powers, in the shape of legislation? After allowing each house to prescribe its own course of proceeding, after describing the manner in which a bill should become a law, would it have entered into the mind of a single member of the convention that an express power to make laws was necessary to enable the legislature to make them? That a legislature, endowed with legislative powers, can legislate is a proposition too self-evident to have been questioned.

But the argument on which most reliance is placed is drawn from that peculiar language of this clause. Congress is not empowered by it to make all laws which may have relation to the powers conferred on the Government, but such only as may be "necessary and proper" for carrying them into execution. The word "necessary" is considered as controlling the whole sentence, and as limiting the right to pass laws for the execution of the granted powers to such as are indispensable, and without which the power would be nugatory. That it excludes the choice of means, and leaves to Congress in each case that only which is most direct and simple.

Is it true that this is the sense in which the word "necessary" is always used? Does it always import an absolute physical necessity so strong that one thing to which another may be termed necessary cannot exist without that other? We think it does not. If reference be had to its use in the common affairs of the world or in approved authors, we find that it frequently imports no more than that one thing is convenient, or useful, or essential to another. To employ the means necessary to an end is generally understood as employing any means calculated to produce the end, and not as being confined to those single means without which the end would be entirely unattainable. Such is the character of human language that no word conveys to the mind in all situations one single definite idea, and nothing is more common than to use words in a figurative sense. Almost all compositions contain words which, taken in their rigorous sense, would convey a meaning different from that which is obviously intended. It is essential to just construction that many words which import something excessive should be understood in a more mitigated sense—in that sense which common usage justifies. The word "necessary" is of this description. It has not a fixed character peculiar to itself. It admits of all degrees of comparison, and is often connected with other words which increase or diminish the impression the mind receives of the urgency it imports. A thing may be necessary, very necessary, absolutely or indispensably necessary. To no mind would the same idea be conveyed by these several phrases. The comment on the word is well illustrated by the passage cited at the bar from the 10th section of the 1st article of the Constitution. It is, we think, impossible to compare the sentence which prohibits a State from laying "imposts, or duties on imports or exports, except what may be absolutely necessary for executing its inspection laws," with that which authorizes Congress "to make all laws which shall be necessary and proper for carrying into execution" the powers of the General Government without feeling a conviction that the convention understood itself to change materially the meaning of the word "necessary," by prefixing the word "absolutely." This word, then, like others, is used in various senses, and, in its construction, the subject, the context, the intention of the person using them are all to be taken into view.

Let this be done in the case under consideration. The subject is the execution of those great powers on which the welfare of a Nation essentially depends. It must have been the intention of those who gave these powers to insure, so far as human prudence could insure, their beneficial execution. This could not be done by confiding the choice of means to such narrow limits as not to leave it in the power of Congress to adopt any which might be appropriate, and which were conducive to the end. This provision is made in a Constitution intended to endure for ages to come, and consequently to be adapted to the various crises of human affairs. To have prescribed the means by which Government should, in all future time, execute its powers would have been to change entirely the character of the instrument and give it the properties of a legal code. It would have been an unwise attempt to provide by immutable rules for exigencies which, if foreseen at all, must have been seen dimly, and which can be best provided for as they occur. To have declared that the best means shall not be used, but those alone without which the power given would be nugatory, would have been to deprive the legislature of the capacity to avail itself of experience, to exercise its reason, and to accommodate its legislation to circumstances.

If we apply this principle of construction to any of the powers of the Government, we shall find it so pernicious in its operation that we shall be compelled to discard it. The powers vested in Congress may certainly be carried into execution, without prescribing an oath of office. The power to exact this security for the faithful performance of duty is not given, nor is it indispensably necessary. The different departments may be established; taxes may be imposed and collected; armies and navies may be raised and maintained; and money may be borrowed, without requiring an oath of office. It might be argued with as much plausibility as other incidental powers have been assailed that the convention was not unmindful of this subject. The oath which might be exacted—that of fidelity to the Constitution—is prescribed, and no other can be required. Yet he would be charged with insanity who should contend that the legislature might not superadd to the oath directed by the Constitution such other oath of office as its wisdom might suggest.

So, with respect to the whole penal code of the United States, whence arises the power to punish in cases not prescribed by the Constitution? All admit that the Government may legitimately punish any violation of its laws, and yet this is not among the enumerated powers of Congress. The right to enforce the observance of law by punishing its infraction might be denied with the more plausibility because it is expressly given in some cases.

Congress is empowered "to provide for the punishment of counterfeiting the securities and current coin of the United States," and "to define and punish piracies and felonies committed on the high seas, and offences against the law of nations." The several powers of Congress may exist in a very imperfect State, to be sure, but they may exist and be carried into execution, although no punishment should be inflicted, in cases where the right to punish is not expressly given.

Take, for example, the power "to establish post-offices and post-roads." This power is executed by the single act of making the establishment. But from this has been inferred the power and duty of carrying the mail along the post road from one post office to another. And from this implied power has again been inferred the right to punish those who steal letters from the post office, or rob the mail. It may be said with some plausibility that the right to carry the mail, and to punish those who rob it, is not indispensably necessary to the establishment of a post office and post road. This right is indeed essential to the beneficial exercise of the power, but not indispensably necessary to its existence. So, of the punishment of the crimes of stealing or falsifying a record or process of a Court of the United States, or of perjury in such Court. To punish these offences is certainly conducive to the due administration of justice. But Courts may exist, and may decide the causes brought before them, though such crimes escape punishment.

The baneful influence of this narrow construction on all the operations of the Government, and the absolute impracticability of maintaining it without rendering the Government incompetent to its great objects, might be illustrated by numerous examples drawn from the Constitution and from our laws. The good sense of the public has pronounced without hesitation that the power of punishment appertains to sovereignty, and may be exercised, whenever the sovereign has a right to act, as incidental to his Constitutional powers. It is a means for carrying into execution all sovereign powers, and may be used although not indispensably necessary. It is a right incidental to the power, and conducive to its beneficial exercise.

If this limited construction of the word "necessary" must be abandoned in order to punish, whence is derived the rule which would reinstate it when the Government would carry its powers into execution by means not vindictive in their nature? If the word "necessary" means "needful," "requisite," "essential," "conducive to," in order to let in the power of punishment for the infraction of law, why is it not equally comprehensive when required to authorize the use of means which facilitate the execution of the powers of Government, without the infliction of punishment?

In ascertaining the sense in which the word "necessary" is used in this clause of the Constitution, we may derive some aid from that with which it is associated. Congress shall have power "to make all laws which shall be necessary and proper to carry into execution" the powers of the Government. If the word "necessary" was used in that strict and rigorous sense for which the counsel for the State of Maryland contend, it would be an extraordinary departure from the usual course of the human mind, as exhibited in composition, to add a word the only possible effect of which is to qualify that strict and rigorous meaning, to present to the mind the idea of some choice of means of legislation not strained and compressed within the narrow limits for which gentlemen contend.

But the argument which most conclusively demonstrates the error of the construction contended for by the counsel for the State of Maryland is founded on the intention of the convention as manifested in the whole clause. To waste time and argument in proving that, without it, Congress might carry its powers into execution would be not much less idle than to hold a lighted taper to the sun. As little can it be required to prove that, in the absence of this clause, Congress would have some choice of means. That it might employ those which, in its judgment, would most advantageously effect the object to be accomplished. That any means adapted to the end, any means which tended directly to the execution of the Constitutional powers of the Government, were in themselves Constitutional. This clause, as construed by the State of Maryland, would abridge, and almost annihilate, this useful and necessary right of the legislature to select its means. That this could not be intended is, we should think, had it not been already controverted, too apparent for controversy.

We think so for the following reasons:

1st. The clause is placed among the powers of Congress, not among the limitations on those powers.

2d. Its terms purport to enlarge, not to diminish, the powers vested in the Government. It purports to be an additional power, not a restriction on those already granted. No reason has been or can be assigned for thus concealing an intention to narrow the discretion of the National Legislature under words which purport to enlarge it. The framers of the Constitution wished its adoption, and well knew that it would be endangered by its strength, not by its weakness. Had they been capable of using language which would convey to the eye one idea and, after deep reflection, impress on the mind another, they would rather have disguised the grant of power than its limitation. If, then, their intention had been, by this clause, to restrain the free use of means which might otherwise have been implied, that intention would have been inserted in another place, and would have been expressed in terms resembling these. "In carrying into execution the foregoing powers, and all others," &c., "no laws shall be passed but such as are necessary and proper." Had the intention been to make this clause restrictive, it would unquestionably have been so in form, as well as in effect.

The result of the most careful and attentive consideration bestowed upon this clause is that, if it does not enlarge, it cannot be construed to restrain, the powers of Congress, or to impair the right of the legislature to exercise its best judgment in the selection of measures to carry into execution the Constitutional powers of the Government. If no other motive for its insertion can be suggested, a sufficient one is found in the desire to remove all doubts respecting the right to legislate on that vast mass of incidental powers which must be involved in the Constitution if that instrument be not a splendid bauble.

We admit, as all must admit, that the powers of the Government are limited, and that its limits are not to be transcended. But we think the sound construction of the Constitution must allow to the national legislature that discretion with respect to the means by which the powers it confers are to be carried into execution which will enable that body to perform the high duties assigned to it in the manner most beneficial to the people. Let the end be legitimate, let it be within the scope of the Constitution, and all means which are appropriate, which are plainly adapted to that end, which are not prohibited, but consist with the letter and spirit of the Constitution, are Constitutional.[2]

That a corporation must be considered as a means not less usual, not of higher dignity, not more requiring a particular specification than other means has been sufficiently proved. If we look to the origin of corporations, to the manner in which they have been framed in that Government from which we have derived most of our legal principles and ideas, or to the uses to which they have been applied, we find no reason to suppose that a Constitution, omitting, and wisely omitting, to enumerate all the means for carrying into execution the great powers vested in Government, ought to have specified this. Had it been intended to grant this power as one which should be distinct and independent, to be exercised in any case whatever, it would have found a place among the enumerated powers of the Government. But being considered merely as a means, to be employed only for the purpose of carrying into execution the given powers, there could be no motive for particularly mentioning it.

The propriety of this remark would seem to be generally acknowledged by the universal acquiescence in the construction which has been uniformly put on the 3d section of the 4th article of the Constitution. The power to "make all needful rules and regulations respecting the territory or other property belonging to the United States" is not more comprehensive than the power "to make all laws which shall be necessary and proper for carrying into execution" the powers of the Government.

Yet all admit the constitutionality of a Territorial Government, which is a corporate body.

If a corporation may be employed, indiscriminately with other means, to carry into execution the powers of the Government, no particular reason can be assigned for excluding the use of a bank, if required for its fiscal operations. To use one must be within the discretion of Congress if it be an appropriate mode of executing the powers of Government. That it is a convenient, a useful, and essential instrument in the prosecution of its fiscal operations is not now a subject of controversy. All those who have been concerned in the administration of our finances have concurred in representing its importance and necessity, and so strongly have they been felt that Statesmen of the first class, whose previous opinions against it had been confirmed by every circumstance which can fix the human judgment, have yielded those opinions to the exigencies of the nation. Under the Confederation, Congress, justifying the measure by its necessity, transcended, perhaps, its powers to obtain the advantage of a bank; and our own legislation attests the universal conviction of the utility of this measure. The time has passed away when it can be necessary to enter into any discussion in order to prove the importance of this instrument as a means to effect the legitimate objects of the Government.

But were its necessity less apparent, none can deny its being an appropriate measure; and if it is, the decree of its necessity, as has been very justly observed, is to be discussed in another place. Should Congress, in the execution of its powers, adopt measures which are prohibited by the Constitution, or should Congress, under the pretext of executing its powers, pass laws for the accomplishment of objects not intrusted to the Government, it would become the painful duty of this tribunal, should a case requiring such a decision come before it, to say that such an act was not the law of the land. But where the law is not prohibited, and is really calculated to effect any of the objects intrusted to the Government, to undertake here to inquire into the decree of its necessity would be to pass the line which circumscribes the judicial department and to tread on legislative ground. This Court disclaims all pretensions to such a power.

After this declaration, it can scarcely be necessary to say that the existence of State banks can have no possible influence on the question. No trace is to be found in the Constitution of an intention to create a dependence of the Government of the Union on those of the States, for the execution of the great powers assigned to it. Its means are adequate to its ends, and on those means alone was it expected to rely for the accomplishment of its ends. To impose on it the necessity of resorting to means which it cannot control, which another Government may furnish or withhold, would render its course precarious, the result of its measures uncertain, and create a dependence on other Governments which might disappoint its most important designs, and is incompatible with the language of the Constitution. But were it otherwise, the choice of means implies a right to choose a national bank in preference to State banks, and Congress alone can make the election.

After the most deliberate consideration, it is the unanimous and decided opinion of this Court that the act to incorporate the Bank of the United States is a law made in pursuance of the Constitution, and is a part of the supreme law of the land.

The branches, proceeding from the same stock and being conducive to the complete accomplishment of the object, are equally constitutional. It would have been unwise to locate them in the charter, and it would be unnecessarily inconvenient to employ the legislative power in making those subordinate arrangements. The great duties of the bank are prescribed; those duties require branches; and the bank itself may, we think, be safely trusted with the selection of places where those branches shall be fixed, reserving always to the Government the right to require that a branch shall be located where it may be deemed necessary.

It being the opinion of the Court that the act incorporating the bank is constitutional, and that the power of establishing a branch in the State of Maryland might be properly exercised by the bank itself, we proceed to inquire:

2. Whether the State of Maryland may, without violating the Constitution, tax that branch?

That the power of taxation is one of vital importance; that it is retained by the States; that it is not abridged by the grant of a similar power to the Government of the Union; that it is to be concurrently exercised by the two Governments—are truths which have never been denied. But such is the paramount character of the Constitution that its capacity to withdraw any subject from the action of even this power is admitted. The States are expressly forbidden to lay any duties on imports or exports except what may be absolutely necessary for executing their inspection laws. If the obligation of this prohibition must be conceded—if it may restrain a State from the exercise of its taxing power on imports and exports—the same paramount character would seem to restrain, as it certainly may restrain, a State from such other exercise of this power as is in its nature incompatible with, and repugnant to, the constitutional laws of the Union. A law absolutely repugnant to another as entirely repeals that other as if express terms of repeal were used.

On this ground, the counsel for the bank place its claim to be exempted from the power of a State to tax its operations. There is no express provision for the case, but the claim has been sustained on a principle which so entirely pervades the Constitution, is so intermixed with the materials which compose it, so interwoven with its web, so blended with its texture, as to be incapable of being separated from it without rending it into shreds.

This great principle is that the Constitution and the laws made in pursuance thereof are supreme; that they control the Constitution and laws of the respective States, and cannot be controlled by them. From this, which may be almost termed an axiom, other propositions are deduced as corollaries, on the truth or error of which, and on their application to this case, the cause has been supposed to depend. These are, 1st. That a power to create implies a power to preserve; 2d. That a power to destroy, if wielded by a different hand, is hostile to, and incompatible with these powers to create and to preserve; 3d. That, where this repugnancy exists, that authority which is supreme must control, not yield to that over which it is supreme.

These propositions, as abstract truths, would perhaps never be controverted. Their application to this case, however, has been denied, and both in maintaining the affirmative and the negative, a splendor of eloquence, and strength of argument seldom if ever surpassed have been displayed.

The power of Congress to create and, of course, to continue the bank was the subject of the preceding part of this opinion, and is no longer to be considered as questionable.

That the power of taxing it by the States may be exercised so as to destroy it is too obvious to be denied. But taxation is said to be an absolute power which acknowledges no other limits than those expressly prescribed in the Constitution, and, like sovereign power of every other description, is intrusted to the discretion of those who use it. But the very terms of this argument admit that the sovereignty of the State, in the article of taxation itself, is subordinate to, and may be controlled by, the Constitution of the United States. How far it has been controlled by that instrument must be a question of construction. In making this construction, no principle, not declared, can be admissible which would defeat the legitimate operations of a supreme Government. It is of the very essence of supremacy to remove all obstacles to its action within its own sphere, and so to modify every power vested in subordinate governments as to exempt its own operations from their own influence. This effect need not be stated in terms. It is so involved in the declaration of supremacy, so necessarily implied in it, that the expression of it could not make it more certain. We must, therefore, keep it in view while construing the Constitution.

The argument on the part of the State of Maryland is not that the States may directly resist a law of Congress, but that they may exercise their acknowledged powers upon it, and that the Constitution leaves them this right, in the confidence that they will not abuse it. Before we proceed to examine this argument and to subject it to test of the Constitution, we must be permitted to bestow a few considerations on the nature and extent of this original right of taxation, which is acknowledged to remain with the States. It is admitted that the power of taxing the people and their property is essential to the very existence of Government, and may be legitimately exercised on the objects to which it is applicable, to the utmost extent to which the Government may choose to carry it. The only security against the abuse of this power is found in the structure of the Government itself. In imposing a tax, the legislature acts upon its constituents. This is, in general, a sufficient security against erroneous and oppressive taxation.

The people of a State, therefore, give to their Government a right of taxing themselves and their property, and as the exigencies of Government cannot be limited, they prescribe no limits to the exercise of this right, resting confidently on the interest of the legislator and on the influence of the constituent over their representative to guard them against its abuse. But the means employed by the Government of the Union have no such security, nor is the right of a State to tax them sustained by the same theory. Those means are not given by the people of a particular State, not given by the constituents of the legislature which claim the right to tax them, but by the people of all the States. They are given by all, for the benefit of all—and, upon theory, should be subjected to that Government only which belongs to all.

It may be objected to this definition that the power of taxation is not confined to the people and property of a State. It may be exercised upon every object brought within its jurisdiction.

This is true. But to what source do we trace this right? It is obvious that it is an incident of sovereignty, and is coextensive with that to which it is an incident. All subjects over which the sovereign power of a State extends are objects of taxation, but those over which it does not extend are, upon the soundest principles, exempt from taxation. This proposition may almost be pronounced self-evident.

The sovereignty of a State extends to everything which exists by its own authority or is introduced by its permission, but does it extend to those means which are employed by Congress to carry into execution powers conferred on that body by the people of the United States? We think it demonstrable that it does not. Those powers are not given by the people of a single State. They are given by the people of the United States, to a Government whose laws, made in pursuance of the Constitution, are declared to be supreme. Consequently, the people of a single State cannot confer a sovereignty which will extend over them.

If we measure the power of taxation residing in a State by the extent of sovereignty which the people of a single State possess and can confer on its Government, we have an intelligible standard, applicable to every case to which the power may be applied. We have a principle which leaves the power of taxing the people and property of a State unimpaired; which leaves to a State the command of all its resources, and which places beyond its reach all those powers which are conferred by the people of the United States on the Government of the Union, and all those means which are given for the purpose of carrying those powers into execution. We have a principle which is safe for the States and safe for the Union. We are relieved, as we ought to be, from clashing sovereignty; from interfering powers; from a repugnancy between a right in one Government to pull down what there is an acknowledged right in another to build up; from the incompatibility of a right in one Government to destroy what there is a right in another to preserve. We are not driven to the perplexing inquiry, so unfit for the judicial department, what degree of taxation is the legitimate use and what degree may amount to the abuse of the power. The attempt to use it on the means employed by the Government of the Union, in pursuance of the Constitution, is itself an abuse because it is the usurpation of a power which the people of a single State cannot give.

We find, then, on just theory, a total failure of this original right to tax the means employed by the Government of the Union, for the execution of its powers. The right never existed, and the question whether it has been surrendered cannot arise.

But, waiving this theory for the present, let us resume the inquiry, whether this power can be exercised by the respective States, consistently with a fair construction of the Constitution?

That the power to tax involves the power to destroy; that the power to destroy may defeat and render useless the power to create; that there is a plain repugnance in conferring on one Government a power to control the constitutional measures of another, which other, with respect to those very measures, is declared to be supreme over that which exerts the control, are propositions not to be denied. But all inconsistencies are to be reconciled by the magic of the word CONFIDENCE. Taxation, it is said, does not necessarily and unavoidably destroy. To carry it to the excess of destruction would be an abuse, to presume which would banish that confidence which is essential to all Government.

But is this a case of confidence? Would the people of any one State trust those of another with a power to control the most insignificant operations of their State Government? We know they would not. Why, then, should we suppose that the people of any one State should be willing to trust those of another with a power to control the operations of a Government to which they have confided their most important and most valuable interests? In the Legislature of the Union alone are all represented. The Legislature of the Union alone, therefore, can be trusted by the people with the power of controlling measures which concern all, in the confidence that it will not be abused. This, then, is not a case of confidence, and we must consider it is as it really is.

If we apply the principle for which the State of Maryland contends, to the Constitution generally, we shall find it capable of changing totally the character of that instrument. We shall find it capable of arresting all the measures of the Government, and of prostrating it at the foot of the States. The American people have declared their Constitution and the laws made in pursuance thereof to be supreme, but this principle would transfer the supremacy, in fact, to the States.

If the States may tax one instrument, employed by the Government in the execution of its powers, they may tax any and every other instrument. They may tax the mail; they may tax the mint; they may tax patent rights; they may tax the papers of the custom house; they may tax judicial process; they may tax all the means employed by the Government to an excess which would defeat all the ends of Government. This was not intended by the American people. They did not design to make their Government dependent on the States.

Gentlemen say they do not claim the right to extend State taxation to these objects. They limit their pretensions to property. But on what principle is this distinction made? Those who make it have furnished no reason for it, and the principle for which they contend denies it. They contend that the power of taxation has no other limit than is found in the 10th section of the 1st article of the Constitution; that, with respect to everything else, the power of the States is supreme, and admits of no control. If this be true, the distinction between property and other subjects to which the power of taxation is applicable is merely arbitrary, and can never be sustained. This is not all. If the controlling power of the States be established, if their supremacy as to taxation be acknowledged, what is to restrain their exercising control in any shape they may please to give it? Their sovereignty is not confined to taxation; that is not the only mode in which it might be displayed. The question is, in truth, a question of supremacy, and if the right of the States to tax the means employed by the General Government be conceded, the declaration that the Constitution and the laws made in pursuance thereof shall be the supreme law of the land is empty and unmeaning declamation.

In the course of the argument, the Federalist has been quoted, and the opinions expressed by the authors of that work have been justly supposed to be entitled to great respect in expounding the Constitution. No tribute can be paid to them which exceeds their merit; but in applying their opinions to the cases which may arise in the progress of our Government, a right to judge of their correctness must be retained; and to understand the argument, we must examine the proposition it maintains and the objections against which it is directed. The subject of those numbers from which passages have been cited is the unlimited power of taxation which is vested in the General Government. The objection to this unlimited power, which the argument seeks to remove, is stated with fulness and clearness. It is "that an indefinite power of taxation in the latter (the Government of the Union) might, and probably would, in time, deprive the former (the Government of the States) of the means of providing for their own necessities, and would subject them entirely to the mercy of the National Legislature. As the laws of the Union are to become the supreme law of the land; as it is to have power to pass all laws that may be necessary for carrying into execution the authorities with which it is proposed to vest it; the National Government might, at any time, abolish the taxes imposed for State objects upon the pretence of an interference with its own. It might allege a necessity for doing this, in order to give efficacy to the national revenues; and thus, all the resources of taxation might, by degrees, become the subjects of federal monopoly, to the entire exclusion and destruction of the State Governments."

The objections to the Constitution which are noticed in these numbers were to the undefined power of the Government to tax, not to the incidental privilege of exempting its own measures from State taxation. The consequences apprehended from this undefined power were that it would absorb all the objects of taxation, "to the exclusion and destruction of the State Governments." The arguments of the Federalist are intended to prove the fallacy of these apprehensions, not to prove that the Government was incapable of executing any of its powers without exposing the means it employed to the embarrassments of State taxation. Arguments urged against these objections and these apprehensions are to be understood as relating to the points they mean to prove. Had the authors of those excellent essays been asked whether they contended for that construction of the Constitution which would place within the reach of the States those measures which the Government might adopt for the execution of its powers, no man who has read their instructive pages will hesitate to admit that their answer must have been in the negative.

It has also been insisted that, as the power of taxation in the General and State Governments is acknowledged to be concurrent, every argument which would sustain the right of the General Government to tax banks chartered by the States, will equally sustain the right of the States to tax banks chartered by the General Government.

But the two cases are not on the same reason. The people of all the States have created the General Government, and have conferred upon it the general power of taxation. The people of all the States, and the States themselves, are represented in Congress, and, by their representatives, exercise this power. When they tax the chartered institutions of the States, they tax their constituents, and these taxes must be uniform. But when a State taxes the operations of the Government of the United States, it acts upon institutions created not by their own constituents, but by people over whom they claim no control. It acts upon the measures of a Government created by others as well as themselves, for the benefit of others in common with themselves. The difference is that which always exists, and always must exist, between the action of the whole on a part, and the action of a part on the whole—between the laws of a Government declared to be supreme, and those of a Government which, when in opposition to those laws, is not supreme.

But if the full application of this argument could be admitted, it might bring into question the right of Congress to tax the State banks, and could not prove the rights of the States to tax the Bank of the United States.

The Court has bestowed on this subject its most deliberate consideration. The result is a conviction that the States have no power, by taxation or otherwise, to retard, impede, burden, or in any manner control the operations of the constitutional laws enacted by Congress to carry into execution the powers vested in the General Government. This is, we think, the unavoidable consequence of that supremacy which the Constitution has declared.

We are unanimously of opinion that the law passed by the Legislature of Maryland, imposing a tax on the Bank of the United States is unconstitutional and void.

This opinion does not deprive the States of any resources which they originally possessed. It does not extend to a tax paid by the real property of the bank, in common with the other real property within the State, nor to a tax imposed on the interest which the citizens of Maryland may hold in this institution, in common with other property of the same description throughout the State. But this is a tax on the operations of the bank, and is, consequently, a tax on the operation of an instrument employed by the Government of the Union to carry its powers into execution. Such a tax must be unconstitutional.

JUDGMENT. This cause came on to be heard, on the transcript of the record of the Court of Appeals of the State of Maryland, and was argued by counsel; on consideration whereof, it is the opinion of this Court that the act of the Legislature of Maryland is contrary to the Constitution of the United States, and void, and therefore that the said Court of Appeals of the State of Maryland erred, in affirming the judgment of the Baltimore County Court, in which judgment was rendered against James W. McCulloch; but that the said Court of Appeals of Maryland ought to have reversed the said judgment of the said Baltimore County Court, and ought to have given judgment for the said appellant, McCulloch. It is, therefore, adjudged and ordered that the said judgment of the said Court of Appeals of the State of Maryland in this case be, and the same hereby is, reversed and annulled. And this Court, proceeding to render such judgment as the said Court of Appeals should have rendered, it is further adjudged and ordered that the judgment of the said Baltimore County Court be reversed and annulled, and that judgment be entered in the said Baltimore County Court for the said James W. McCulloch.

Notes

1. Official Supreme Court case law is found only in the print version of the United States Reports. For an online version of the text, see Cornell Law School, Legal Information Institute, "McCulloch v. Maryland," https://www.law.cornell.edu/supremecourt/text/17/316.

2. See *Montague v. Richardson*, 24 Conn. 348.

About the Authors

Rebecca Burgess is a research fellow at the American Enterprise Institute (AEI), where her work focuses on veterans, the public policies that affect them and their families, and their role in civil society and politics. She is concurrently the manager of AEI's Program on American Citizenship, a program that fosters original research on civic education, the health of America's public institutions, and the principles of American democracy.

Nelson Lund is a university professor at the Antonin Scalia Law School at George Mason University.

Gary J. Schmitt is a resident scholar in strategic studies and American institutions at the American Enterprise Institute (AEI). Previously, he was director of AEI's Program on American Citizenship. He is the coeditor and a contributing author of two recent volumes, *The Imperial Presidency and the Constitution* and *Is Congress Broken? The Virtues and Defects of Partisanship and Gridlock*.

Abram N. Shulsky is a senior fellow at the Hudson Institute. He has served in various positions in the Office of the Secretary of Defense and on the staff of the Senate Select Committee on Intelligence. Shulsky is the coauthor, with Gary J. Schmitt, of a college textbook on intelligence, *Silent Warfare: Understanding the World of Intelligence*.

Robert Webking is professor emeritus in the Department of Political Science at the University of Texas at El Paso. He joined the faculty there in 1978.

Adam J. White is a resident scholar at the American Enterprise Institute, where he focuses on American constitutionalism, the Supreme Court, and the administrative state. Concurrently, he is assistant professor of law and the director of the C. Boyden Gray Center for the Study of the

Administrative State at the Antonin Scalia Law School at George Mason University.

Christopher Wolfe is an affiliate professor of politics at the University of Dallas, emeritus professor political science at Marquette University, and president of the American Public Philosophy Institute. His main areas of research and teaching for two decades have been constitutional law and American political thought. He is the author of *The Rise of Modern Judicial Review: From Constitutional Interpretation to Judge-Made Law*.

Michael Zuckert is Nancy R. Dreux Professor of Political Science Emeritus at the University of Notre Dame. He has written extensively about constitutional history and political philosophy.

www.ingramcontent.com/pod-product-compliance
Lightning Source LLC
Chambersburg PA
CBHW021558210326
41599CB00010B/503